For the Lion

A History of the Scottish Wars of Independence

RAYMOND CAMPBELL PATERSON

JOHN DONALD PUBLISHERS LTD
EDINBURGH

The publisher acknowledges subsidy from
the Scottish Arts Council towards the
publication of this volume.

ISBN 0 85976 435 4

A catalogue record for this book is available from the British Library

Typeset by WestKey Ltd, Falmouth, Cornwall
Printed and bound in Great Britain by
Bell & Bain Ltd., Glasgow

For the Lion
A History of the Scottish Wars of
Independence

Contents

Preface

In the early summer of 1328 Scotland was at peace after over thirty years of intermittent warfare with its powerful southern neighbour. Robert Bruce, the greatest king ever to occupy the throne of Scotland, was nearing the end of his life, exhausted by the long and bitter path he had taken to reach this goal. He had led a small and poor nation to the height of military glory on the field of Bannockburn in the hot mid-summer of 1314, where the English suffered their worst defeat since the loss of Normandy to the French over a century before. A humiliation on the scale of Bannockburn could not be easily forgotten, and it took a further fourteen years before England agreed to recognise that Scotland was a free country within the borders that King Edward I had crossed in wrath in 1296.

The Scottish peace was not popular in England. Her young king, Edward III, who had obtained an uncomfortably close acquaintance with Scottish military skill at Stanhope Park in County Durham the previous year, was known to be unhappy. Edward was still a minor, and the peace treaty, ratified by the English Parliament at North-ampton in May 1328, had been the work of his guardians—his mother Queen Isabella and her lover Roger Mortimer, Lord of Wigmore. He made his personal feelings known when he failed to attend the marriage of his sister Joan to King Robert's infant son David, celebrated at Berwick in July 1328 in fulfilment of one of the conditions of the peace treaty. English chroniclers condemned the Treaty of Northampton as a *turpis pax*—a cowardly peace—brought about by a tyrannical and unpopular government; and the people of London, according to legend, physically prevented the return of the Stone of Destiny, the ancient coronation stone of Scotland's kings, looted by Edward I in 1296.

Apart from the slight to English national pride the treaty of 1328 contained some serious defects. Bruce was well aware of the con-tinuing threat of English power, and reserved Scotland's right to adhere to the treaty of mutual assistance concluded with France in 1326. England's fear of encirclement therefore remained exactly as it had been in 1295, when the Scottish king John Balliol had agreed to the first formal Franco-Scottish alliance. Edward I's attempt to eliminate this danger, one of his own creation, and to impose his implacable will on a client kingdom began the great struggle we now call the Wars of Independence. What started as a war between two nations also became, after 1306, a civil war between the supporters of Robert Bruce on the one hand, and the Balliol and Comyn families on the other. The losers in this parallel conflict were deprived of all they owned in Scotland, and as the *exheredati*—the disinherited— living in English exile, and ignored by the Treaty of Northampton, became the bitterest opponents of the peace.

The treaty of 1328 simply left too many issues unresolved to be the basis for a lasting peace. The King of England still believed he had the right to be the overlord of Scotland; Scotland's links with France forced England to look to its back in any future entanglements on the continent; and the disinherited lords continued to challenge the legitimacy of the Bruce dynasty. All three undermined the stability of the peace; but it was the question of legitimacy that opened the way in 1332 to the Second War of Independence.

This book is intended as an examination of the origins, course and effects of the Anglo-Scottish struggles of the thirteenth and fourteenth centuries. It embraces the whole course of the conflict from the invasion of 1296 to the Treaty of Berwick in 1357, when the release of King David II from English captivity served to symbolise Scotland's survival as an independent nation. Although the embers of the war continued to burn for many years after 1357 never again was Scotland to face the systematic challenge to its right to exist that it had during the reigns of the first three Edwards. The First and Second Wars of Independence were part of a great national crisis for Scotland and became arguably the most formative phase of the whole national experience. Modern Scotland cannot be properly understood without some reference to this period. While it is true that nationalism in the modern sense was largely a creation of the eighteenth and nineteenth centuries, and that loyalties in the middle ages were focused on kings and chieftains rather than on abstract concepts of race and nation, the sentiments and ideals contained in the 1320 Declaration of Arbroath stand comparison with all of the great statements of national self determination.

The conflict in Scotland was important for other reasons, chief amongst which was the revolution it brought to the art of war itself. It ended forever the domination of feudal cavalry, introduced into England by William the Conqueror in 1066. The repeated failures of English horse when faced with Scots infantry led to the development of new tactics in battle. By the early 1330's England had come to appreciate the power of the longbow—the machine gun of the middle ages—a weapon that enabled her to command the battlefields of Britain and western Europe for over a century and to build an Empire in France. The Scots learned to their cost that Bannockburn was a glorious exception to the rule, and that they could rarely expect to gain the better of the English in open battle. The essence of Robert Bruce's political and military genius was his recognition that Scotland could not hope to match England in men and materials, and could only prevail against so mighty a foe by the steady application of guerrilla warfare—or 'secret war' as it was known at the time. This enabled the Scots to make the best use of their country's natural defences and their enemy's inability to keep armies in the field for longer than a short campaigning season. Most important of all, guerrilla warfare wore down England's resolve; and it was this, not battlefield success, that finally gained Scotland's freedom.

The task before me is to bring history alive, and to make as real as possible the struggles of those long dead; to introduce a whole range of people—some forgotten and others only half remembered—whose importance will become clear as the story unfolds. I am indebted to all those who have gone before me in the field of Scottish history, and in particular to the authors whose names appear in the bibliography. I owe a particular debt of love and gratitude to my wife, Fiona Spencer Paterson, for her help and encouragement. It is to her and to the memory of my mother, Margaret Miller Campbell, that this book is dedicated.

Edinburgh, 1996   R.C.P.

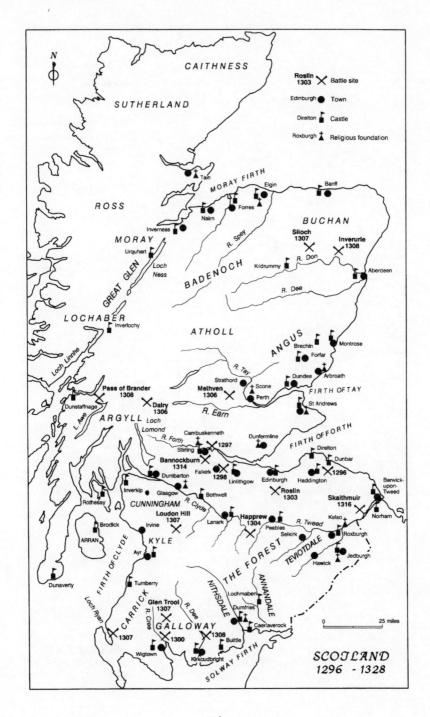

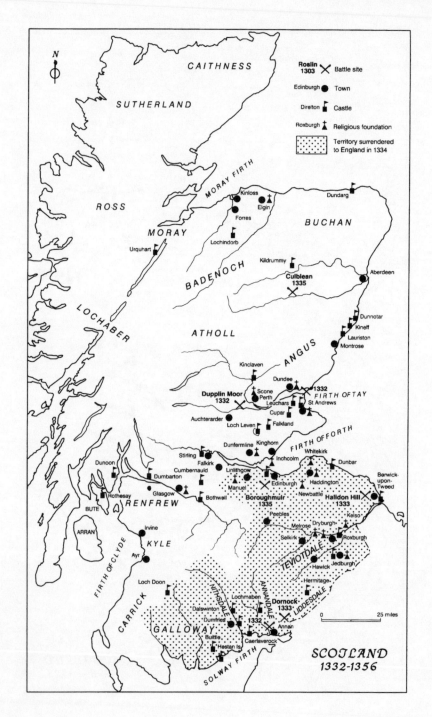

Key:
Roslin 1303 ✕ Battle site
Edinburgh ● Town
Dirleton ■ Castle
Roxburgh ⛪ Religious foundation
⬚ Territory surrendered to England in 1334

CAITHNESS

SUTHERLAND

ROSS

MORAY FIRTH

MORAY

Kinloss
Elgin
Forres
Lochindorb

BADENOCH

BUCHAN

Dundarg

Urquhart

LOCHABER

ATHOLL

Kildrummy

Culblean
1335 ✕

Aberdeen

Dunnotar
Kineff
Lauriston
Montrose

ANGUS

Kinclaven

Dupplin Moor
1332 ✕

Scone
Perth
Leuchars

Dundee

✕ 1332
St Andrews

FIRTH OF TAY

Auchterarder

Loch Leven
Cupar
Falkland

Dunfermline
Kinghorn

Stirling
Falkirk

FIRTH OF FORTH

Whitekirk

Inchcolm

Dunoon

Cumbernauld
Dumbarton

Manuel
Linlithgow
Bothwell

Haddington

Dunbar

Berwick-
upon-
Tweed

Rothesay

Glasgow

RENFREW

✕ Edinburgh

Boroughmuir
1335

Newbattle

Halidon Hill
1333 ✕

BUTE

ARRAN

FIRTH OF CLYDE

Irvine

KYLE

Ayr

Peebles

Melrose
Dryburgh

Kelso

Selkirk

Roxburgh

TEVIOTDALE

Hawick

Jedburgh

Loch Doon

CARRICK

NITHSDALE

ANNANDALE

Hermitage

LIDDESDALE

0   25 miles

Lochmaben

Dornock
1333 ✕

Dalswinton
Dumfries

✕ 1332

Annan

Buittle
Hestan Is.

Caerlaverock

GALLOWAY

SOLWAY FIRTH

SCOTLAND
1332-1356

N

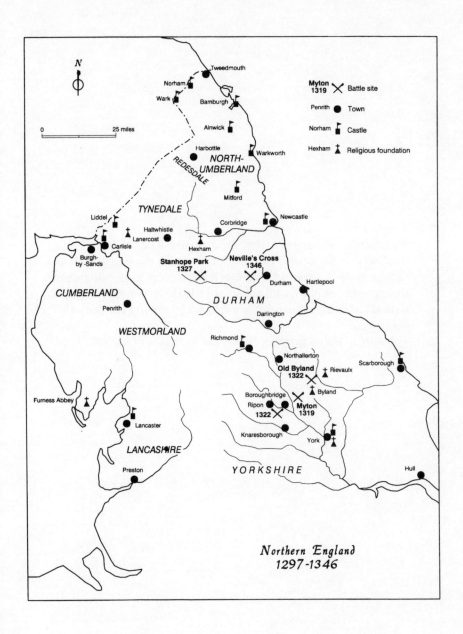

Northern England
1297-1346

Admonish and exhort the King of the English for whom that which he possesses ought to suffice, seeing that of old England used to be enough for seven kings or more, to leave us Scots dwelling in this little Scotland, beyond which there is no human abode, and desiring nothing but our own.

—*Letter of the barons of Scotland to Pope John XXII, 1320*

CHAPTER 1
A Nation in Crisis, 1290–1296

In the autumn of 1290 Scotland stood on the verge of a dynastic war. Her infant queen, Margaret, granddaughter of the late King Alexander III, and the last direct descendant of the royal line established by Malcolm Canmore after the death of MacBeth, had died on her way to Scotland from Norway. Since 1286, when Alexander died, the country had been ruled by a group of six Guardians, chosen from the leading figures in the church and state. The Guardians had managed to preserve the peace of the kingdom in the years between the death of the king and the expected arrival of his heir, the little Maid of Norway. Her death now threatened to destroy the delicate balance they had maintained and reduce the land to anarchy.

The two strongest claimants to the vacant throne both held lands in the south-west of Scotland: John Balliol, Lord of Galloway, and Robert Bruce, Lord of Annandale, grandfather of the future king. Both were descended from David, Earl of Huntingdon, the youngest of the three grandsons of King David I: Balliol was the grandson of Earl David's eldest daughter, Margaret, and Bruce was the son of his second daughter, Isabella. In terms of the law of primogeniture John Balliol had the stronger claim. But Robert Bruce of Annandale, known to history as 'The Competitor', was a far more forceful man than his rival, and was prepared to take up arms to defend his claim if necessary. He had already demonstrated this shortly after Alexander's death in 1286 when, together with his son Robert, Earl of Carrick, he had raised a force and seized the royal castles of Dumfries and Wigtoun, as well as the Balliol castle at Buittle. Although this first Bruce rising had been settled peaceably, he once again took up arms on hearing of the death of the Maid of Norway, and arrived with his army at Perth, where the chief men of the realm were gathered. It was rumoured that he was to be joined there by his allies, the earls of Mar and Atholl. John Balliol, now styling himself *heres regni Scotiae*—heir of Scotland—appears to have been in England at this time engaged in unspecified secret negotiations with Anthony Bek, the Bishop of Durham, who was Edward I's chief representative in the north.

1

King Edward had for some time been taking a close interest in affairs in Scotland. He had completed the subjugation of Wales and was now considering his position within the British Isles as a whole. While it was politically independent, Scotland had long had a subordinate status in relation to its southern neighbour. From time to time English kings had forced their Scottish counterparts to recognise them as feudal superiors. The Popes in Rome refused to approve the anointing of Scottish kings, a sacred part of the coronation ceremony which implied that the kingdom was held only of God, because of the objections raised by the kings of England, who maintained that Scotland was a fief of the English crown.

Edward's father, King Henry III, tried unsuccessfully to obtain a recognition of his rights as feudal superior from the young Alexander III in 1251. Edward himself pressed the same claim without any more success in 1278. The untimely death of Alexander and the succession to the throne of a female infant offered Edward a new way to enforce his authority. He obtained the agreement of the Scottish Guardians to a marriage between Margaret and his own son and heir, Edward of Caenarvon. While agreeing to the marriage the Guardians were anxious to preserve the liberty of Scotland when the terms were settled at Birgham-on-Tweed in July 1290. This was to be a mere personal union of the crowns, and Scotland was to remain 'separate, apart and free in itself without subjugation to the English kingdom'. But Edward insisted on inserting his favourite caveat into the Treaty of Birgham—'Saving always the rights of the King of England which belonged, or ought to belong to him', which must have caused the Guardians some concern. As if to demonstrate his true intentions Edward took possession of the Isle of Man, then a Scottish territory, in the summer of 1290 without reference to the Guardians or Queen Margaret.

The death of the Maid ended Edward's plan to absorb Scotland by a dynastic union. However, he was quick to take advantage of the political uncertainty in the north. Fearful of the outcome of Bruce's sabre rattling, William Fraser, the Bishop of St Andrews and one of the Guardians, wrote to Edward in October 1290 advising him of the rumoured death of Margaret and the armed rising of Robert of Annandale. The Bishop proceeded to ask Edward to intervene to prevent bloodshed and recommended that he reach an understanding with John Balliol, whose supporter he was. Edward was delighted to agree to the Bishop's plea for help.

History has not been kind to Bishop Fraser. He stands condemned by the tendency to read the past backwards from consequences to causes. Some judgements have been particularly harsh: '. . . by this letter he opened the door to half a century of savage bloodshed.' (John Prebble *The Lion in the North*, p.71). Yet the fact remains that in 1290 Scotland could not settle the dynastic question by any acceptable internal process. There is surely no one who seriously believes that Edward would have stood aside while Scotland descended into chaos. If Edward intended to subjugate Scotland this would have been far easier in 1290, when there was no king, than in 1296. Edward was generally respected as an arbiter in international affairs, who had taken pains on the continent to prevent political quarrels ending in warfare. His intervention in Scotland was widely accepted by the national community, offering the only way out of a potentially lethal deadlock. Even Bruce, had he been so minded, could not have defied Edward, to whom he owed allegiance for the various lands he held in England. Bishop Fraser's chief fault, perhaps, was not his invitation to Edward but his recommendation of John Balliol, one of history's great losers.

Edward arrived at the Bishop of Durham's castle at Norham on the Anglo-Scottish border on 10 May 1291. He was met there by the leading magnates and prelates of Scotland who expected an arbiter; but Edward came determined to be an overlord and judge. The Scots were promptly presented with the demand that they recognise the King as their feudal superior and Lord Paramount of Scotland. To back up this demand Edward summoned the armed forces of the northern counties to meet him at Norham on 3 June; a summons which ironically included Robert Bruce and John Balliol, both of whom held lands in the region. Although the Scots made a spirited attempt to resist, arguing that they could not make a decision of such gravity in the absence of a lawfully appointed king, Edward would not be deflected from his purpose. He was, after all, in a uniquely powerful position, and was able to counter the reluctance of the Guardians to agree to his demands by exploiting the ambitions and desires of the various competitors, of whom there were to be thirteen in all. In the face of such pressure there was little to be done. Edward made it plain that he would not judge the claims until he was first recognised as Scotland's feudal overlord and given possession of her principal castles. Continuing resistance would surely have been met by military force which Scotland, lacking the leadership provided by the crown, would not have been able to match. Edward had his way. In early June most of the competitors, Bruce and Balliol amongst them, agreed to recognise him as overlord and abide by his decision in the matter of the succession; and on the 13 June at Uppsettlingham on the banks of the Tweed the Guardians, the competitors and all the chief men of the realm swore fealty to Edward I. The tenancy of the Scottish throne could now be settled.

Bruce and Balliol were joined at Norham by eleven other claimants. Many of these bids were frivolous: claims from relatively obscure men, illegitimate offshoots of the royal tree, who clearly hoped for a slice if there was any share out of the national cake. There were, however, two other serious contenders: John Hastings of Abergavenny, an Englishman, who was the grandson of Earl David's third daughter, Ada; and Florence V, Count of Holland, who was descended from David's sister, also called Ada.

In terms of hereditary right the Count's claim was a weak one; but he made the remarkable assertion that Earl David had set aside his claim to the throne in favour of his sister during the reign of their brother King William the Lion. This was a major upset to the plans of both Bruce and Balliol. Edward adjourned his court for almost a year while a search was mounted for documentary proof of Florence's claim. None was found.

John Hastings' bid is an interesting one. As grandson of the youngest of David of Huntingdon's three daughters his position was weak: he could neither claim seniority of line (Balliol's bid) nor nearness of degree (Bruce's bid). He recognised this himself and argued that Scotland was not a true kingdom but a feudal estate like any other, and as such should be divided between the three heirs of Earl David. It might be supposed that Edward would favour such a solution, which would have done much to weaken Scotland and advance his own imperial ambitions; but he recognised it as legally unsound and politically dangerous. Once a precedent like this was established it might, after all, be applied one day to England itself. Hastings' argument was quickly dismissed. The two serious competitors were each allowed to appoint 40 auditors to a great feudal court, to which Edward added a further 24, drawn from his own council. The court assembled at Berwick for the final deliberations in the summer of 1292.

By November 1292 the matter was decided. Scotland had her King—John Balliol. The panel of 104 auditors, presided over by King Edward, had rejected Bruce's claim of nearness of degree as David of Huntingdon's grandson, in favour of Balliol's seniority as the descendent of the eldest daughter. In terms of feudal law the judgement was a fair one, notwithstanding the circumstances in which it came about. Only time declared Balliol to be the creature of Edward's ambition. The strength of his claim is supported by the fact that 29 of Bruce's own auditors, including some of his closest associates, voted for Balliol. He was crowned King of Scots on Saint Andrew's day, 30 November 1292; and on the 26 of December he met Edward at Newcastle and did homage for his kingdom.

For Bruce the Competitor it was a bitter outcome. According to the chronicle of Sir Thomas Gray he made his feelings plain to all: '. . . all the magnates of Scotland yielded allegiance to John de Balliol with oath and homage, except Robert de Bruce the elder, who persisted in his claim, and declared in the hearing of King Edward that he would never do homage.' It's certainly true that rather than submit to King John he resigned his lordship of Annandale and his claim to the throne to his son the Earl of Carrick, retaining only his English estates. Shortly after this the younger Bruce resigned his own earldom of Carrick, which he held in right of his wife, to his son, the future king, now 18 years old. Robert of Annandale left Scotland in early 1293, thus avoiding paying homage to Balliol like his father, and keeping alive the Bruce claim to be the rightful King of Scotland.

History is rightly concerned with what actually happened and not with what might have been; but it is surely fortunate for the reputation of the Bruce family that they lost the contest of 1292; for a claim to the throne was, in the circumstances of the time, far better than the reality. John Balliol, surely Scotland's most unfortunate king, was soon to learn the price of his subject crown. Soon after his 'appointment' Edward exhorted him in the hearing of all to be '. . . careful in doing justice to his new subjects least by giving cause for complaint he should render necessary the interference of his lord paramount.' In other words, Edward made it widely known that he was prepared to hear appeals from Balliol's courts, thus seriously undermining the authority and dignity of the crown. When Balliol protested in January 1293 that this was contrary to the promises made in the Treaty of Birgham, he was brusquely told that these no longer applied. Word soon spread that the King's courts were no longer supreme.

Balliol was mercilessly bullied by Edward I, a sergeant-major draped in the vestments of royalty, to the point where he gave the appearance of holding Scotland as a bailiff rather than a king. While it is true that the appeals coming from Scotland were not numerous Edward used them to crush Balliol under the burden of his feudal inferiority. Not only did Edward insist on hearing appeals outside Scotland, but he also demanded that John should be present on these occasions, and liable for any damages that might occur. Balliol made some attempt to resist Edward's demands; but when he appeared before the English Parliament in late 1293 he was treated with such brutal discourtesy that his efforts to withstand the pressure being placed upon him collapsed in ignominy. It appeared increasingly obvious that Edward, who used law like a weapon, was determined to provoke the hapless Balliol into rebellion, which would allow him to annex Scotland outright as a forfeited fief.

The final crisis in John's short reign came in June 1294 when Edward summoned him together with ten of his earls and sixteen of his barons, including the elderly Bruce the Competitor, to serve in a war against France. This 'invitation' came wrapped in a telling irony. Since the time of Henry II England had held Gascony in south-west France and, as Duke of Aquitaine Edward owed feudal homage to the French crown. A brutal but unofficial naval war between England and France in the Channel caused the French King, Philip IV, also known as Philip the Fair, to summon Edward to appear before him at his feudal court in Paris. Edward refused to attend, resisting the demands of his own feudal superior at a time when he was placing the most onerous burdens on Scotland. The irony was not lost on the leading men of the realm, who by 1295 had lost all confidence in their deeply compromised king. The time had come to stand up to Edward even if this meant war. But it was clear to everyone by now that John lacked the courage and strength of character required. In July 1295 the direction of affairs was taken out of John's hands at a Parliament held at Stirling and given to a council of twelve—in practice a new panel of Guardians—made up equally of bishops, earls and barons. The time was right for Scotland to assert its independence: not only was Edward at war with France but he was still busy putting down a rebellion in Wales. The new council had two tasks before it: the preparation of the nation's defences, and the conclusion of an alliance with France.

Although there had been links between Scotland and France going back to the twelfth century, the treaty concluded on the 23 October 1295 was the first formal agreement and the beginning of the 'auld alliance'. The alliance provided for mutual assistance in the event of war with England, and was to be cemented by a marriage between King John's son and heir Edward and Jeanne de Valois, niece to King Philip. The infant Prince Edward Balliol, destined one day to be the scourge of the Bruce dynasty, was described as the 'future King of Scotland', and guaranteed to be John's heir by the Scots envoys in Paris. By this marriage the French were to be given a direct interest in the fate of Scotland and the survival of the Balliol monarchy. King John renounced his allegiance to Edward and prepared for war. By the time the treaty was ratified by the Scots Parliament in February 1296 the English army was already making progress towards the border.

So, Edward Plantagenet, by a combination of pride, arrogance and high-handedness, all seasoned with a liberal helping of political blindness, transformed Scotland from a peaceful northern neighbour into an ever present threat to English security. He became the single most important architect of Scotland's alliance with France. Although he was soon to succeed in destroying his puppet king, he began what was to become a 'war of the seasons', in which the fruits of summer victories vanished with the onset of winter. England was about to start the first of its two great and ruinous conflicts of the middle ages.

CHAPTER 2
The Darkest Hour, 1296–1299

The war opened for Edward with great promise. The Scots host which gathered at Cadonlee near Selkirk in March 1296 was an ill-prepared, badly disciplined and inexperienced force. It had last seen action in 1263 at the Battle of Largs, where only a small proportion of the Scottish army had been engaged against the Norwegian enemy; and the last significant victory over the English had been at the Battle of Carham in 1018. The English army of 1296 was superior in both cavalry and infantry, and included many veterans of the Welsh wars. The Scots were also weakened by the absence of a number of important magnates who remained loyal to Edward—Patrick de Dunbar, Earl of March, Gilbert de Umfraville, Earl of Angus and the Bruces of Carrick and Annandale.

The absence of the Bruces was no surprise, for they had been consistently hostile to the Balliol monarchy. Robert the Competitor had died in 1295, defiant to the last. His son, the Lord of Annandale and his grandson, the Earl of Carrick, refused to answer John's summons to join the Scottish host. Their lands in Annandale were then seized and placed under the control of John Comyn, the Earl of Buchan, who proceeded to use the area as a base for raids on England. On Easter Monday 1296 seven of Scotland's earls together with John Comyn the younger of Badenoch, known as the 'Red Comyn', cousin of the Earl of Buchan and nephew of King John, advanced on Carlisle with a large infantry force and attempted to storm the city. The garrison commanded by Robert Bruce of Annandale repulsed the attempt with little difficulty. Buchan had no siege equipment and was obliged to withdraw after two days. Meanwhile, the real war had begun in the east.

Edward's preparations for the invasion of Scotland had been thorough. The feudal host was summoned to meet at Newcastle on the 1 March. On the 19 February writs were issued for the assembly of a naval force in the east coast ports, to include '. . . ships, galleys, barges and other suitable vessels to number a hundred or more.' Edward's formidable war machine then lumbered into action, moving with slow determination by land and sea towards Berwick, arriving before its defences on the 30 March 1296.

At that time Berwick was Scotland's chief port and the centre of the wool trade. It was, the *Lanercost Chronicle* reports, '. . . a city so populous, and of such trade that it might be called another Alexandria, whose riches were the sea and the water its walls.' Despite this the town was poorly fortified. Led by the King on his favourite horse, Bayard, the English swept over the flimsy ditch and timber palisade on their first assault, overwhelming the defenders, who had been augmented by a party of soldiers from Fife. Once in the town the only serious resistance they faced was from a small group of Flemish merchants in their base at the Red Hall, who killed Richard of Cornwall, Edward's cousin. The brave Flemings continued to fight until they perished in the flames that consumed the Red Hall. Berwick was then given over to the passions of Edward's soldiery.

It is impossible to say with any accuracy just how many people were butchered in the sack of Berwick. Chroniclers vary in their estimates from a low of seven thousand (Hector Boece) to a high of sixty thousand (Matthew of Westminster). There is little doubt that the carnage was great. In 1301, five years after the event, in the instructions given by the Scottish government to their procurators in Rome it was said that after taking Berwick the King of England and his army committed the most barbarous cruelties on its inhabitants, who were slain without distinction of rank, sex or age; and that churches offered no sanctuary to those who fled to them. The slaughter continued until Edward was finally persuaded to call a halt by the pleas of the clergy or, according to the rhyming chronicle of Andrew Wyntoun, until he witnessed the following:

Thus they slayed ware sa fast
All the day qwhill [until] at the last
This Kyng Edward saw in that tyde
A woman slayne and of her syde
A barne [child] he saw fall out, sprewled [sprawling]
Besyd that woman slayne lyand
'Lasses, lasses' that cryd he;
'Leave off, leave of' that word should be.

The corpses of the dead were piled up in the streets until the stench became so overpowering that they had to be buried in pits or thrown into the sea. The castle's garrison, commanded by Sir William Douglas 'The Hardy', surrendered without a fight, chastened, perhaps, by the spectacle they impotently witnessed from the battlements. Berwick ceased to be the chief town and port of Scotland. It was systematically rebuilt as the headquarters of the English occupation.

Edward was in no hurry to complete the conquest of Scotland and remained at Berwick for a month, supervising the strengthening of its defences, which consisted principally of the digging of a huge fosse or ditch. On 5 April he received a message from King John renouncing his homage, to which Edward remarked, more in contempt than anger: 'O foolish knave! What folly he commits. If he will not come to us we will go to him.' Three days later a large Scottish force crossed the border to the east of Edward and laid waste to Redesdale, Cockerdale and Tyndale. Harbottle Castle resisted attack, but the monastery at Hexham and the nunnery at Lambley were destroyed by fire. At Corbridge the raiders are said to have set fire to a school, burning alive two hundred schoolboys. Other than providing fuel for English propaganda the raid achieved nothing. Edward and his army remained firmly entrenched at Berwick.

The next objective in the campaign was the Earl of March's castle at Dunbar, a few miles up the coast from Berwick. March was with the English but his wife, Marjory Comyn, sister of the Earl of Buchan, did not share her husband's political loyalties and allowed the Scots to occupy the castle. Edward sent one of his chief lieutenants, John de Warenne, the Earl of Surrey and Balliol's own father-in-law, northwards with a strong force of knights to invest the stronghold. The defenders sent messages to King John, bivouacked with the main body of his army at nearby Haddington, asking for urgent assistance. In response the army, or a large part of it, advanced to the rescue of Dunbar. John, who was showing even less skill as a commander than he had as a king, did not accompany it. The war was now about to enter its final phase.

The two armies came in sight of each other on 27 April 1296. Leaving a small force to cover the castle, Warenne turned to face the enemy. The Scots occupied a strong position on some high ground to the east. To reach them Warenne's cavalry had to cross a gully intersected by the Spot Burn. As they did so their ranks broke up, and the Scots, deluded into thinking the English were leaving the field, abandoned their position in a disorderly downhill charge, only to find that Warenne's ranks had reformed and were advancing in perfect order. The English routed the disorganised Scots in a single charge, the leaders fleeing the field along with the common soldiers. Only Sir Patrick Graham stood and fought to the death. According to the English sources over ten thousand Scots died at the Battle of Dunbar, hardly a credible figure, given the speed with which the whole affair was concluded. The survivors fled westwards some forty miles to the safety of Selkirk Forest. The following day King Edward appeared in person and the castle surrendered. Some important prisoners were taken, amongst them three earls—Atholl, Ross and Mentieth—together with 130 knights and esquires. All were sent into captivity in England.

The Battle of Dunbar effectively ended the war of 1296. The remainder of the campaign was little more than a grand mopping up operation. James, the hereditary Stewart of Scotland, surrendered the important border fortress of Roxburgh without attempting a defence, and others were quick to follow his example. Only Edinburgh held out for a week against Edward's siege engines. The garrison sent for help to John, who had fled north to Forfar, but were told to provide for their own safety. In the south-west young Robert Bruce of Carrick crossed the Solway and recaptured his father's lands in Annandale, dominated by Lochmaben Castle. Edward's advance into central and northern Scotland in pursuit of the fugitive King John, abandoned by all apart from his Comyn kinsmen, resembled a leisurely royal progress rather than a serious military operation. Stirling Castle, which guarded the vital passage across the River Forth, was deserted save for a porter who stayed behind to hand the keys to the English. Edward reached Perth on the 21 June, where he received messages from King John begging for peace. Peace was granted and Edward prepared a bitter cup for the king he had made, and was now about to break.

John Balliol, having lost all honour and dignity, submitted himself to a protracted abasement. At Kincardine Castle on 2 July he confessed his rebellion and prayed for forgiveness. Five days later in the kirkyard of Stracathro he abandoned the treaty with the French. The final humiliation came at Montrose on the 8 July, where he formally surrendered the kingdom of Scotland. Dressed for the occasion Balliol was ceremoniously stripped of the vestments of royalty. Anthony Bek, the Bishop of Durham, Balliol's former friend and ally, ripped the red and gold arms of Scotland from his surcoat, thus bequeathing to history the nickname of Toom Tabard—empty coat—by which John has been known to generations of Scottish schoolchildren. As far as those who were present were concerned, Scots as well as English, this spectacle brought to an end the ancient Scottish monarchy whose roots extended deeper into history than those of the Plantagenet conqueror.

From Montrose John and his infant son Edward were sent south to the Tower of London. They were joined in captivity by the Red Comyn and the Earl of Buchan, as well as many other prominent Scots, including Sir Andrew Murray of Petty and Avoch, and his son, also called Andrew, who was destined shortly to be one of the leaders of the Scots resistance. In the meantime King Edward continued on his northern progress, reaching the shores of the Moray Firth in July. From there he turned back towards Berwick. To mark his triumph he took with him as booty the regalia of Scotland, the Black Rood of Saint Margaret, a holy relic containing the canonised Queen's fragment of the true cross, and the Stone of Destiny, the ancient coronation stone of the Scottish kings and a symbol of the nation's freedom. Shortly after his arrival at Berwick in late August he held a Parliament of both realms and the formal submission of the principal Scots landowners was set down in the 'Ragman Roll', so called because of the great number of ribbons hanging from the various seals.

Edward had good reason to be satisfied with his conquest. The Scots had shown themselves to be vastly inferior to the English in battle and most of the country's natural leaders were now in prison. A large part of those who remained, like the Bruces, were Edward's allies. Before leaving for England Edward set up an occupation regime, sparing little thought for the feelings of the conquered. The new administration was headed by the Earl of Surrey as Lieutenant; Hugh de Cressingham (soon to be one of the most despised figures in Scottish history) was to be the Treasurer; and Walter of Amersham became Chancellor. A number of justices and sheriffs were appointed, chief amongst whom was William Ormsby. Those clergy who had been expelled from their benefices for supporting the English were restored. Scotland was firmly under an English heel, centuries of political independence counting for nothing. Bruce of Annandale's plea after Dunbar, that Edward consider his claim to the throne, was dismissed with contempt: 'Have we nothing to do but win kingdoms for you.' Edward was pleased: he had crushed the Welsh rebellion of 1294/5 and had captured Scotland with consummate ease. He was now master of the whole of the British Isles and was free to turn his full attention to France, his last remaining enemy. Before taking leave of de Warenne in September Edward expressed his contempt for Scotland by remarking 'A man does well who rids himself of a turd.'

Scotland had reached the lowest point in its history. It had been overrun with considerably less effort than it had taken to conquer Wales. Its king was a broken man and the country, devoid of its natural leaders, was ruled by an alien regime personified, above all, in the corpulent Cressingham, dubbed 'the treacherer' by the Scots. All of the chief strongholds were occupied by English garrisons. And yet, even in these dark days, there was reason for hope. The conquest had been too swift; the occupation too superficial. The country had been stunned, not crushed.

Even before the close of the year there were reports of trouble from various places, especially in the north. Some attempt seems to have been made, moreover, to re-establish links with France. In January 1297 Edward instructed John de Warenne to allow no one to leave Scotland without the King's express permission, and to arrest anyone caught in the possession of letters. Ordinances were also issued to prevent correspondence with the continent, and a close watch was maintained on all ports. Edward's instructions were precise: 'And the King wishes that messengers be closely searched and examined, so that nothing may pass whereby harm and damage may come to the King or the realm.'

The disturbances continued throughout the winter and blossomed into a full scale uprising in the spring of 1297, when the free men of the realm took up arms under William Wallace of Elderslie in the south, and in the north under Andrew Murray the younger of Avoch, who sometime over the winter had managed to escape from his prison in Chester Castle. These popular risings received valuable support from the surviving leaders of the Scottish community: most notably from James Stewart, who was Wallace's feudal superior, and Robert Wishart, the Bishop of Glasgow.

The support of the Scottish church was to be of crucial import-ance to the patriots in the First War of Independence. It had long jealously guarded its own independent traditions within the univer-sal church, resisting all attempts to subordinate it to the archdio-cese of York, owing direct obedience to the Pope alone. All attempts at dilution were resisted, causing Pope Nicholas IV to censure the clergy in 1289 for objecting to the promotion of foreigners to ecclesiastical dignities in Scotland. Now Edward's conquest brought with it once again the prospect of submission to York or Canterbury and the appointment of English clergy to vacant Scottish benefices.

Amongst the many distinguished churchmen who gave their support to the national struggle, first place must surely go to Robert Wishart, Bishop of Glasgow and a former Guardian. In his mind the independence of Scotland and the independence of the Scottish church could not be separated; and when the occasion demanded he was even prepared to defy the Pope in pursuit of this central aim. The hostile *Lanercost Chronicle* says of him and others who took his lead:

> In like manner, as we know, that it is truly written, that evil priests are the cause of people's ruin, so the ruin of the realm of Scotland had its source within the bosom of her church; . . . for with one consent both those who discharged the office of prelate and those who were preachers, corrupted the ears and minds of the nobles and commons, by advice and exhortation, both publicly and secretly, stirring them to enmity against the king and nation . . . declaring falsely that it was far more justifiable to attack them than the Saracen.

In May 1297 William Wallace, the second son of a minor Renfrewshire knight, stepped dramatically on to the stage of history, when he killed William Heselrig, the English sheriff of Lanark. After the death of Heselrig much of southern and central Scotland rose in revolt. Wallace, a man who was clearly possessed of natural leadership qualities, gathered sufficient force to be able to advance openly on Scone, where Edward's Justiciar, William de Ormesby, was holding court. At Perth he was joined by William Douglas, the former commander of Berwick Castle, and both fell upon the Justiciar. Ormesby only narrowly escaped capture, fleeing to Edinburgh to alert Cressingham to the growing crisis. While at Scone Wallace and Douglas learned of a new rising in the west by a section of the Scottish aristocracy led by James Stewart and Robert Wishart.

In June the Stewart and Wishart, who had given secret encouragement to Wallace, provoked beyond endurance by Edward's demands for men and money for his war with Philip the Fair, raised their own standard and summoned their supporters to join them at Irvine in Ayrshire, declaring that '. . . the King (Edward) would have seized all the middle people of Scotland to send them overseas in his war, to their great damage and destruction.' The Irvine rising was not destined to be a great success, but it is notable for one thing—the rebels were joined by Robert Bruce, Earl of Carrick.

It's difficult to know exactly why Bruce joined the rising. Hitherto he had been a loyal supporter of Edward, to whom his own father continued to adhere. He would appear to have had everything to lose and little to gain. It may be that he was angry at Edward's contemptuous dismissal of his father's reminder that the Bruces still nurtured a claim to the throne of Scotland. It may be that with Balliol gone and the Comyns out of the way the time was right to revive this claim amongst the leaders of the 'community of the realm'; after all, both the Stewart and Wishart had been friends and supporters of his family in the past; both now had full measure of the qualities of John Balliol, and both would detect in Robert of Carrick, a far more forceful man than his father, something of the energy and drive that motivated the old Competitor. It may also be that the Bruces, father and son, were playing a double game, having a foot in both camps. There was a precedent for this in family history in 1138 when Bruces had both supported and opposed David I's invasion of England, and fought on opposite sides at the Battle of the Standard. Or he may simply have joined the Scots, as Walter of Guisborough says, because he was a Scotsman, the grandson on his mother's side of the last Celtic Earl of Carrick.

Whatever the circumstances of his defection the facts are as follows: when Edward learned of William Douglas's actions he ordered Bruce's father, as Governor of Carlisle, to send his son with the knights of Annandale to attack the rebel's castle in Douglasdale. Carrick's motives seem to have been under suspicion at this time, and just before he left England he was made to take a special oath of loyalty by the Bishop of Carlisle. Scarcely was he over the border than he told the men of Annandale that he had taken this oath under duress, and that he now intended to join the patriots. His father's knights declined to follow him; but with the men of Douglasdale and his own earldom of Carrick he rode north to the Stewart and Wishart at Irvine. There he was met by Wallace and Douglas, fresh from their success in central Scotland.

Things did not go well at Irvine. Disputes broke out amongst the leaders, caused, it is said, by the distrust of Robert Bruce amongst the Balliol loyalists, of whom Wallace was the chief. Divided amongst themselves the Scots were ill-prepared to meet the strong English cavalry force under Henry Percy, grandson of John de Warenne, and Robert Clifford advancing rapidly through Annandale and Nithsdale. Quite apart from their political differences most of the Scots leaders at this time still thought in conventional military terms: their army was made up chiefly of foot soldiers, long considered inferior to heavy cavalry. Percy and Clifford advancing north from Ayr, a few miles south of Irvine, were met by envoys from the Stewart and Douglas asking for surrender terms. One of the Scots knights, Sir Richard Lundie, was so disgusted by this that he promptly changed sides. Wallace also left the camp, but with an entirely different aim in mind: he was soon to be firmly at the head of a 'popular revolution', basing himself in the safety of Selkirk Forest at the head of a large force.

The aristocratic rising ended when the remaining Scots leaders capitulated at Irvine on 7 July. Although Wishart was kept in temporary imprisonment, the others were allowed to go free after giving assurances of their good behaviour and promising to produce hostages as guarantees of their future loyalty. Douglas failed to produce his hostages on time, and was sent in chains to Berwick Castle, where he was said by his captors to be 'savage and abusive'. He was later taken to the Tower of London, where he died sometime in 1299, a bitter enemy of the English King. He was succeeded by his eldest son James de Douglas—the Black Douglas—destined to avenge his father as one of Robert Bruce's greatest commanders.

Robert Bruce's own capitulation at Irvine was clearly insincere, for he never produced his own hostages, one of whom was to be his infant daughter Marjory. He continued as one of the leading figures amongst the patriots until 1302, when he finally agreed to surrender some two years before the other leaders of the resistance, at a time when the restoration of King John seemed to be a strong possibility.

With the capitulation at Irvine the initiative passed to the 'common folk of the realm' led by Wallace and Murray: the middle people—freeholders and burgesses—whom Edward would have taken to die in a foreign war. While Wallace was active in the south Andrew Murray raised the standard of King John and Scottish independence at his father's castle of Avoch in the Black Isle, where he was joined by the townsmen of Inverness led by Alexander Pilchie. Murray attacked the various English garrisons in the north-east, beginning with Urquhart Castle on the shores of Loch Ness. By the end of August he had seized the castles of Inverness, Elgin and Banff. The sheriff of Aberdeenshire, Henry of Latholm, an Englishman, joined the rebellion and opened the gates of Aberdeen Castle. The efforts and resources of the English supporters in the area led by Henry Cheyne, Bishop of Aberdeen—the only prominent Scots churchman to take Edward's side—and Countess Effie of

Ross—whose husband was a prisoner of the English—were wholly inadequate to the task of resisting Murray. From Selkirk Forest Wallace came north. He was joined by Macduff, son of the Earl of Fife, and crossed the Tay, laying siege to Dundee Castle before meeting up with Murray sometime before the end of August 1297. The two leaders were acknowledged by their followers as 'commanders of the army of the kingdom of Scotland and the community of the realm'. Together they would fight for King John, worthy subjects of a worthless king.

For much of the summer of 1297 the English seem to have seriously underestimated the scope of the crisis in central and northern Scotland, in the mistaken belief that they had settled matters at Irvine. The Lieutenant, the Earl of Surrey, took little interest in his Scottish bailiwick, retiring the previous year to his estates in England after he claimed that the climate was bad for his health. Hugh de Cressingham, the man on the spot, was becoming increasingly alarmed. In late July he wrote to King Edward, preparing for an expedition to Flanders, telling him of the difficulties of raising revenue following from the steady collapse of English administration and complaining of Surrey's inactivity:

> Not a penny can be raised until my lord de Warenne shall enter into your land and compel the people by sentence and force of law. By far the greater part of your counties in the realm of Scotland are still unprovided by keepers because they have been killed, besieged or imprisoned; and some have abandoned their bailiwicks and dare not go back; and in some counties the Scots have established and placed bailiffs and officials. Thus no county is in proper order, excepting Berwickshire and Roxburghshire, and they only recently.

An alien administration was disappearing like snow on a summer's day, to be replaced by that which had been set aside in 1296.

Edward appears not to have been unduly concerned by the reports from the north, seemingly content that the main rising was over with the capitulation at Irvine. Apart from persuading the Earl of Buchan and John Comyn of Badenoch to change their allegiance and sending them north to help restore the peace, where their dubious conduct soon attracted the adverse comment of Cressingham, he was confident enough to leave the settlement of his affairs in Scotland to the Treasurer and the elderly Surrey. He then left for the continent in August 1297 to begin his war against France.

   With most of northern Scotland now under the control of Wallace and Murray, de Warenne at last took to the field. He joined Cressingham at Berwick and advanced into central Scotland with a large force of infantry and cavalry, arriving at Stirling in early September. Wallace and Murray came south to meet him, and took up position on the slope of the Abbey Craig, about a mile north of the narrow wooden bridge across the River Forth. The river crossing here, dominated by nearby Stirling Castle, was the most strategically vital in Scotland. Below Stirling the river was too deep and wide to cross, and to the west lay the impassable marsh known as Flanders Moss. Stirling Bridge served as a belt, tying the north and south of Scotland together. In view of what happened at Dunbar the previous year there were clearly great risks to the Scots in facing English cavalry in open battle; but Wallace and Murray had to deny de Warenne this crossing or lose all they had gained in the north. The troops at their disposal were infantrymen, armed principally with twelve foot long spears. In all respects their army was inferior to the grand feudal host which gathered in the plain below them to the south of the river.
   Before the battle there was some attempt at mediation. James the Stewart and Malcolm, Earl of Lennox, now at peace with the English, made some attempt to persuade the rebels to surrender, but their labours were fruitless. Surrey made one final effort to resolve the issue without bloodshed. Two Dominican friars were sent to the enemy commanders asking them to yield. Wallace is said to have replied: 'Tell your commander that we are not here to make peace but to do battle to defend ourselves and liberate our kingdom. Let them come on and we shall prove this in their very beards.'
   De Warenne had won a comfortable victory over the aristocracy of Scotland at Dunbar, and his belief that he was now dealing with a rabble seems to have affected his judgement. The bridge at Stirling was only broad enough to allow two horsemen to cross abreast. With the Scots placed in a commanding position dominating the soft, flat ground to the north of the river the dangers were obvious. Sir Richard Lundie, the Scots knight who joined the English at Irvine, offered to outflank the enemy by leading a cavalry force over a nearby ford, where sixty horsemen could cross at the same time. Cressingham, anxious to avoid any unnecessary expense in prolonging the war, persuaded the Earl to reject this sound advice and order a direct attack across the bridge.
   The Scots waited in tense silence as the English knights and

infantry made their slow progress across the bridge on the morning of 11 September. The arrogant and disorderly force of 1296 was gone: Wallace and Murray's hold over their men was firm. They had held back earlier in the day when many of the English and Welsh archers and infantry crossed, only to be recalled because Warenne had overslept. The two commanders now waited, according to the *Chronicle of Hemingburgh*, until 'as many of the enemy had come over as they believed they could overcome.' Then they ordered the attack. The Scots spearmen came down from the high ground in rapid advance towards Stirling Bridge, quickly seizing the English bridgehead. Warenne's vanguard was now cut off from the rest of the army. The heavy cavalry to the north of the bridge was trapped and cut to pieces. Their comrades to the south were powerless to help them. Only one knight, the Yorkshireman, Sir Marmaduke Tweng, showed great presence of mind and managed to fight his way through the thicket of spears back across the bridge; but over a hundred of his fellow knights were slain, including the portly Cressingham, whose body was subsequently flayed and the skin cut into small pieces as tokens of the victory. Losses amongst the infantry, many of them Welsh, were also high. Those who could threw off their armour and swam across the river. The Battle of Stirling Bridge is an important landmark in the history of war: it showed that in certain circumstances, where the conditions were right, infantry could be superior to cavalry. But it was to be some time before this lesson was absorbed.

Warenne, who had remained on the south bank of the river, was still in a powerful position. The bulk of his army remained intact and he could have held the line of the Forth, denying the triumphant Scots a passage to the south. But his confidence was gone. After Tweng's escape he ordered the bridge destroyed and retreated with his army towards Berwick, leaving the garrison at Stirling Castle isolated and abandoning the lowlands to the rebels. The Stewart and Lennox, observing the carnage to the north of the bridge, had withdrawn their men from Warenne's camp, afterwards launching an attack on his baggage train, killing many of the fleeing English.

Scots casualties at the battle appear to have been light, but Andrew Murray was severely wounded. He continued to exercise joint leadership with Wallace for a number of weeks after the battle, perhaps in name only, finally dying some time in November. His son, also called Andrew, born posthumously, was destined in manhood also to be one of the great champions of Scottish independence, but in the name of Bruce rather than Balliol.

After Stirling Bridge Edward lost almost all the gains of Dunbar. The English garrisons at Stirling, Dundee and Dumbarton all surrendered. Only Edinburgh, Dunbar, Roxburgh and Berwick remained. Scotland proudly declared its freedom to Europe. From Haddington Wallace and Murray wrote to the country's old trading partners in the Hanseatic League, informing them that Scotland had 'recovered by war from the power of the English.' Shortly afterwards Wallace crossed the border and took the conflict into northern England. The Scots raided deep into Northumberland and as far south as County Durham in October and November, carrying off much booty and, according to the sources, committing many gruesome atrocities along the way. The cry 'The Scots are coming' spread panic throughout the north east, causing those who could to flee to the safety of the south. While Wallace's raid was destructive it did little to advance the Scots cause in the war. Lacking siege equipment he was unable to take any of the strongholds he attacked and was forced by deteriorating weather conditions to return north towards the end of November. In retaliation Sir Robert Clifford led a raid into Annandale in December, destroying ten settlements. Warenne recovered enough of his own composure to lead a force early in the new year to the relief of Berwick and Roxburgh Castles. After this no further military action was attempted until King Edward returned.

The death of Murray in November 1297 left Wallace as the supreme leader of the Scottish resistance. From this time until July 1298 he ruled Scotland as a plenipotentiary for the absent King John and by the consent of the *communiitas regni Scotie*—the community of the realm of Scotland. Sometime before the end of March 1298 he was knighted by one of the leading magnates—Robert Bruce according to legend—and appointed sole Guardian of the kingdom. This was a remarkable achievement: Wallace, the son of a minor landowner, enjoyed powers that had previously been held collectively by earls, bishops and barons. He was at the height of his prestige; but his position was far from easy. In normal circumstances he would never have been called to a leading role in a highly conservative feudal society. Although he enjoyed a measure of support from the bulk of Scotland's magnates, this was anything but wholehearted. His power was based on the army and ultimately on the prestige of Stirling Bridge. He would only remain Guardian for as long as he enjoyed success in battle.

20

One of Wallace's most important acts as Guardian was to secure the appointment of William Lamberton, chancellor of Wishart's Glasgow diocese, as Bishop of St Andrews. The see had lain vacant since the death of Bishop Fraser in France in August 1297. Lamberton was to be as tenacious as Wishart in his defence of the national cause. When he was consecrated in Rome in June 1298 he used the occasion to bring Scotland's plight to the attention of Pope Boniface VIII. His efforts were rewarded when Boniface wrote to Edward urging him to end his aggression and release John Balliol. But by the time the letter arrived Edward had once again triumphed over his enemies and was in no mood for compromise.

Edward was in Flanders when he learned of Warenne's defeat. After concluding a truce with King Philip the Fair, always ready to leave his Scottish allies in the lurch, he returned to England in March and immediately began organising an army for his second invasion of Scotland. He brought with him from the Continent a young knight, Henry de Beaumont, son of Louis de Brienne, Viscount of Beaumont in Maine, who had taken up service under the king. Beaumont was destined to become one of the most experienced soldiers in the Anglo-Scots war and in time to come one of the principal architects of a new style of warfare. He was soon to experience his first taste of combat in the British Isles.

Edward moved the centre of English government to York, where it remained for the next six years. His commanders in the north, de Warenne and Clifford, had already been told to stop all further action and wait for his arrival. A council was held at York in April to finalise the details of the invasion. The Scots magnates were summoned to attend and when none came they were all declared to be traitors. Edward ordered his army to assemble at Roxburgh on 25 June. The force he gathered was impressive: over 2,000 horse and 12,000 infantry, including many Welshmen armed with the longbow, a weapon originating in south Wales and unique to the British Isles.

While Edward held his council at York John Balliol issued a statement from the house of Anthony Bek near London, condemning his former subjects, saying that 'when he possessed and ruled the realm of Scotland . . . he found in the men of that realm such malice, deceit, treason and treachery . . . that it is not his intention to enter or go into the realm of Scotland at any time to come . . . or have anything to do with the Scots who . . . had tried to poison him.' This was an obvious and clumsy attempt to undermine the political basis for the uprising in Scotland. One assumes that John would have been pressurised into making it; but, there again, he was not the kind of man to allow principle or honour to stand in the way of abject surrender.

In early July the march northwards began. Things did not go well. Wallace had ordered a scorched earth policy, denying the invaders fresh supplies. The Scots gave ground, drawing the English ever deeper into barren and hostile territory. Edward's own supply fleet was delayed by bad weather; and when the army reached central Scotland it was close to starvation. The capture of Dirleton and two other East Lothian castles by the warlike Anthony Bek did little to raise morale. The Welsh infantry in particular were badly demoralised and close to mutiny. Edward injudiciously ordered his available supplies of wine to be distributed amongst the troops in an attempt to raise their spirits. The Welsh got drunk and began a brawl with their English comrades, killing several priests. They were promptly attacked by the English knights, who killed eighty of them and drove off the remainder to the margins of the camp. With his army falling apart and no sign of the enemy Edward faced the prospect of the kind of ignominious withdrawals that were to become a regular feature of his son's campaigns in the succeeding reign. Just as he was on the point of falling back on Edinburgh Patrick de Dunbar, Earl of March and Gilbert de Umfraville, Earl of Angus, Scots who had remained loyal to Edward, brought a scout who told him that Wallace had taken up position in the wood of Callender near Falkirk, only thirteen miles away, ready to pursue the retreating English. Edward was delighted to receive this news: 'As God lives . . . they need not pursue me, for I will go and meet them this day.' Wallace had made his greatest mistake.

The Scots army, again made up chiefly of spearmen as at Stirling Bridge, was arranged in four great armoured hedgehogs known as schiltrons. The long spears pointed outwards at various heights gave these formations a formidable and impenetrable appearance. The gaps between the schiltrons was filled with archers, armed with the Scottish short bow; and to the rear there was a small force of light cavalry, provided by the Comyns and other magnates. The ground was considerably inferior to that chosen at Stirling Bridge, indicating, perhaps, the crucial role that Murray had played in that battle.

On Tuesday 22 July the English cavalry, divided into three battalions, finally caught sight of their elusive enemy. The left was commanded by Roger Bigod, Earl of Norfolk, and the Earls of Hereford and Lincoln. The right was under the command of Anthony Bek, while the King commanded the centre, still a little distance to the rear of the vanguard. Once in sight of the enemy Norfolk and his colleagues began an immediate attack, but on encountering a marsh to the front of the Scots position made a long detour to the west before being able to make contact with the right of Wallace's army. In doing so they exposed their flank to the Scots bowmen, whose weapons appear to have lacked the power and range to take advantage of this opportunity. Bek tried to hold back his own battalion to give the King time to get into position, but he was overruled by his impatient knights anxious to join their comrades on the left in an immediate attack. In a disorganised pell-mell the cavalry finally closed on the Scots on the right and left. The ground thundered as the schiltrons braced themselves for the onslaught. The sight of the lowered lances and the large war-horses was too much for the Scottish cavalry, who turned and fled the field. The bowmen, commanded by Sir John Stewart, the younger brother of the High Stewart, stood their ground and were quickly destroyed. But the schiltrons held firm, absorbing the shock of the impact. The knights made no impression on the dense forest of long spears and were soon threatened with impalement. A large number of horses were killed under their riders, including Henry Beaumont's. The King arrived in time to witness the discomfiture of his cavalry and quickly restored discipline. The knights were ordered to withdraw and Edward prepared to employ the tactics that had been used to defeat the Welsh spearmen at the Battle of Maes Moydog in 1295.

Despite their success against the English cavalry the schiltrons were isolated and locked into a static defensive position. Edward's archers were brought into place and went to work with their deadly longbows. Their fire was supplemented by crossbow and slingshot. The schiltrons were an easy target: they had no defence and nowhere to hide. Unable to retreat or attack the battle was lost for the Scots almost as soon as the first arrows began to fall. The cavalry waited, this time observing the King's command, until the Scots ranks were thin enough to allow them to enter and finish the job. A great many were killed, among them Macduff of Fife. The survivors, Wallace included, escaped as best they could. In his classic study *The Welsh Wars of Edward I* the historian J.E. Morris argued that the Battle of Falkirk was the first great victory of the longbow.

It was some time, though, before the aristocratic horseman agreed to give first place to the plebeian archer.

For England Falkirk was a curious battle: a victory that contained the seeds of future defeat. The arrogance and indiscipline of the knights had been potentially disastrous. Warfare was becoming a grimly professional business, and the day of the wild charge which carried all before it was over. Dunbar had, in retrospect, been the last significant victory of medieval cavalry unsupported by archers and infantry. Bravery was no substitute for organisation and discipline. Above all, the ability to exercise effective command in battle was decisive. Edward I succeeded at Falkirk; but Edward II, faced with similar circumstances, was to fail, and disastrously so, at Bannockburn.

While Falkirk was a far bloodier battle than Dunbar, it was considerably less decisive. Although Wallace's credibility had been destroyed the kingdom was not conquered, thanks in large measure to the Guardian's scorched earth tactics. Edward's army, weakened by hunger and disease, was in no condition to carry on with a prolonged campaign. The King had little choice but to order a withdrawal through the south west of Scotland towards Carlisle, once again leaving an isolated garrison at Stirling Castle, which was starved into surrender at the end of 1299. On his way back to the border he attacked Robert Bruce's base at Ayr and captured his castle at Lochmaben, along with Stirling, the only prize of an expensive and fruitless campaign. He tried to hold the army together at Carlisle for a fresh offensive, but many deserted, including a large part of Bek's contingent from Durham. The Earls of Norfolk and Hereford, who had been prominent in a major constitutional dispute with Edward in the previous year, refused to serve further, arguing that they had lost too many horses. The King tried to prevent further desertions by holding out the prospect of gaining Scots lands to those who remained, which only led to even more disputes. Edward had no option but to dismiss the greater part of his army, although he himself remained on the border until the end of the year, after which he returned to the south convinced that the disloyalty of his barons had robbed him of the fruits of Falkirk. He ordered the army to reassemble for a new invasion in the summer of 1299; but it was to be two years before he reappeared.

CHAPTER 3
A War to the Finish, 1299–1305

Even before Edward crossed back into England the Scots began to reorganise. Wallace's failure at Falkirk ended the 'popular' phase of the national revolution. The great hero, who had no independent power base in Scotland, sank into relative obscurity, flitting in and out of history over the next seven years. He was replaced as Guardian by an aristocratic duumvirate, comprising Robert Bruce of Carrick and John Comyn of Badenoch. This was at best an uneasy alliance. Comyn was the son of Eleanor Balliol, the sister of King John, and the senior representative of the powerful Balliol/Comyn faction. Bruce was known to harbour designs on the throne, even though he was, at least for the time being, prepared to act with Comyn in 'the name of the illustrious King John'. But this was a 'marriage of convenience' that was not destined to last. It came close to breaking down in August 1299, following a bitter and potentially murderous quarrel between the two in the Selkirk Forest near Peebles after an abortive raid on Roxburgh. An English spy in the Scots camp reported these events:

> At the council Sir David Graham demanded the lands and goods of Sir William Wallace because he was leaving the kingdom without the leave or approval of the Guardians. And Sir Malcolm Wallace, Sir William's brother, answered that neither his lands nor his goods should be given away, for they were protected by the peace in which Wallace had left the kingdom. At this, the two knights gave the lie to each other and drew their daggers. And since Sir David Graham was of Sir John Comyn's following and Sir Malcolm Wallace of the Earl of Carrick's following, it was reported to the Earl of Buchan and John Comyn that a fight had broken out without their knowing it; and John Comyn leaped at the Earl of Carrick and seized him by the throat, and the Earl of Buchan turned on the Bishop of St Andrews, declaring that treason and lesemajestie were being plotted. Eventually the Stewart and others came between them and quietened them.

At this time William Lamberton of St Andrews joined Bruce and Comyn as the third Guardian, clearly with the task of keeping peace between the other two. Lamberton was given custody of all the castles in Scottish hands, because, it appears, of the lack of trust between the two magnates. Bruce stepped down as Guardian some time before May 1300, to be replaced by Ingram de Umfraville. Prior to this the Guardianship threatened to break down altogether after Comyn declared that he no longer wished to serve with Lamberton. The appointment of Umfraville, a kinsman of John Balliol's and an ally of the Comyns, appears to have been an acceptable compromise.

The year 1299 was not a happy one for Edward. The national unity caused by the disaster at Stirling Bridge was gone. He faced a growing constitutional dispute with his magnates centring on the arbitrary nature of royal power, and money, always a problem, was in very short supply. Moreover, their was little enthusiasm beyond the royal household for the war in Scotland. An attempt to gather an army for a winter campaign, always unpopular in the Middle Ages, had been a fiasco, and the King was obliged to spend a gloomy Christmas at Berwick with insufficient forces at his disposal to prevent the fall of Stirling Castle.

He had, however, been able to bring his inconclusive French war to a close by a marriage treaty concluded at Montreuil in June, and was confident enough in his relations with the devious Philip the Fair to allow John Balliol to be released into the custody of the papal nuncio, the Bishop of Vicenza. Edward Balliol was held in captivity in the keeping of his grandfather, John de Warrene, Earl of Surrey, as a guarantee for his father's good behaviour. The wretched King received his final humiliation from the English at Dover, just as he was about embark for the continent. His luggage was opened and searched: the seal of Scotland and a golden crown which he managed to retain, in hiding one assumes, throughout the three years of his captivity, were confiscated. It is unlikely that he ever saw his young son again.

Edward's next campaign in Scotland was launched in the spring of 1300. The army he gathered was far weaker than the impressive host of 1298, and its objectives were much more limited. The main thrust this time was in the south-west, across the Solway and into Galloway. Caerlaverock Castle was captured after a brief siege, celebrated in a colourful French poem which exaggerates the event far beyond its military importance. The King continued his advance in a westerly direction, along the coastal plain of Galloway. At Kirkcudbright he agreed to hold peace talks with John Comyn and the Earl of Buchan. If Edward expected surrender or even some political concessions from the Scots he was to be disappointed. The terms laid before him were those of a victor rather than a nation on the defensive: King John was to be restored and his son Edward was to be recognised as heir to the throne. Scots magnates, more-over, were to be given the opportunity to redeem their confiscated English estates. Edward was 'warned' that if these terms were refused the war would continue. Not surprisingly, the King rejected these demands in one of his famous high rages, and the talks were abandoned after two days. His temper was not improved by the arrival in Galloway of Robert Winchelsey, the Archbishop of Can-terbury, bearing a letter from Pope Boniface VIII criticising his conduct in Scotland, claiming that the country was a fief of Rome and therefore only the Pope had the right to dispose of her crown. As the Archbishop read the letter the King interrupted in fury 'By God's blood! For Zion's sake I will not be silent, and for Jerusalem's sake I will not be at rest, but with all my strength I will defend my right which is known to all the world'. Edward and his barons later replied to the Pope in more measured terms, justifying his actions and drawing on the usual bogus historical antecedents popular at the time.

Edward's political frustrations were compounded by disappoint-ments in the field. Although his army got the better of the Scots in some skirmishing on the banks of the River Cree, his enemies managed to escape and the issue was no nearer settlement. Beyond the capture of Caerlaverock the campaign had achieved nothing of significance. Edward soon returned to England, leaving most of the country still under the control of the Guardians. A truce was granted to last from October 1300 to May 1301. But the King was in no mood to entertain further proposals of peace from the Scots.

Some time during this truce the triumvirate of Comyn, Lamberton and Umfraville broke down, to be replaced by Sir John Soules, brother of William Soules, the Lord of Liddesdale, as sole Guardian. Soules was closely associated with the deposed King John, and may have been appointed to the post with his express approval. During the new Guardian's tenure of office government documents, pre-viously issued on behalf of the absent King, now appeared in the name of John himself 'to be valid at our will or that of our dearest son Edward or of John de Soules Guardian of our Kingdom.' Most important of all, Soules' time as Guardian coincides with the strongest diplomatic efforts ever made to secure John's restoration. These attempts were headed by the Scots representatives in Rome and Paris, whose labours had already been rewarded by Boniface's letter to Edward.

The Scots presence in the papal court was particularly strong at the turn of the century. In June 1299 David Murray, kinsman of the late Andrew Murray, was consecrated in Rome as the Bishop of Moray, becoming the third of the great patriot bishops. William Wallace, who left Scotland in 1299 on a diplomatic mission, may have visited the Pope on his travels; but the greatest Scottish spokesman in Rome was undoubtedly Master Baldred Bisset—'a wise and cunning clerk'—a graduate of Bologna University, the great centre of law in the Middle Ages, who became an active and persuasive advocate of the national cause. Bisset was appointed by Soules as the chief of three Scots envoys to the Holy See. Together with Master William of Eaglesham and Master William Frere, Archdeacon of Lothian, he presented Boniface with a *Processus*—a legal argument—attacking Edward's response to the Pope's letter. Bisset attempted to undercut Edward's spurious historical justifications for his conduct in Scotland with his own equally fantastic mythology; but concluded by saying that the past need not act as a model for the present, and that one kingdom had no right in law to subjugate another.

The efforts of the Scots in Rome were soon to have important effects. Balliol, technically on his release from England a 'prisoner' of the church, was referred to in increasingly respectful terms in papal documents—rising from 'called King of Scotland' in July 1299 to 'illustrious King of Scots' by September 1300. Finally, in the summer of 1301 he was released from papal custody and allowed to settle in the ancient home of the Balliols at Bailleul-en-Vimeu in Picardy. King Edward was campaigning, once again, in the southwest of Scotland when he received this unwelcome news, and it came laced with a dangerous rumour; 'the King of France's people have taken Sir John Balliol from the place where he was to reside by the Pope to his castle of Bailleul in Picardy, and some people believe that the King of France will send him with a great force to Scotland as soon as possible'. Edward had released Balliol believing he would sink into obscurity; this was proving to be a serious political miscalculation.

Edward intended the new campaign he planned for 1301 to be decisive. He planned to destroy the remaining pockets of resistance in the south west, and to this end would keep his army in the field for as long as possible. For the first time he divided his available forces in two, with the intention of advancing into the western lowlands in a pincer movement. The King's son, Edward of Caernarvon, recently named Prince of Wales, entered Scotland from Carlisle in the west, while Edward himself, with the largest part of the army, crossed the border at Coldstream in the east, moving in a westerly direction towards Peebles. From there he marched up Clydesdale towards the castle at Bothwell near Glasgow. But after Falkirk the Scots were wary about meeting the English in battle and continued to elude Edward's embrace, concentrating their hit-and-run tactics on the flank and rear of the enemy's force. The Prince of Wales's march along the shores of Galloway was no more successful than his father's had been in the previous year. Although the King managed to capture the great stronghold of Bothwell in September, the two arms of the pincer never met. Prince Edward was only able to advance as far as Loch Ryan, before returning to Carlisle. Edward's grand design was frustrated by the skill and mobility of the Scots, who, under Soules' guidance, made the first sustained use of guerrilla warfare.

The King's plans were also hampered by continuing financial problems. He brought his master builder, Master James of St George, who had been responsible for the construction of the great Welsh strongholds, to Scotland with instructions to build a new castle at Linlithgow, which would provide an important link between Edinburgh and Stirling. He was originally authorised to build in stone, but lack of cash forced him to construct a considerably inferior wooden structure instead, completed by early 1302. Edward's worries about money and the frustrations this caused him are clearly expressed in a letter he wrote to his exchequer at this time:

> And you can be certain that if it had not been for lack of money we would have finished the bridge which was started to cross the Scottish Sea (the Firth of Forth), and you must understand for sure that if we had been able to cross this season, we would have achieved such an exploit against our enemies that our business in these parts would have been brought to a good and honourable conclusion in a short time.

Problems of finance and desertions from the army, unwilling to face the rigours of a Scottish winter, forced Edward to abandon his campaign early in the new year. When the Abbot of Compiègne, acting on behalf of King Philip, arrived in Scotland urging a truce, the King was happy to agree. A truce was granted from January to November 1302, and Edward returned to England in February, no doubt preoccupied by the threat from France and the growing possibility of a Balliol restoration. He was not alone.

For Robert of Carrick the rapidly changing political situation was alarming. He was clearly alienated from the Comyn leadership of the national cause, and seems to have played little part in the war since he was replaced as Guardian in 1300, retiring to his tent in the fashion of Achilles, only defending his own territories. The return of King John and his son Edward would obviously deprive him of any prospect of ruling Scotland; but in view of his own ambiguous conduct, and the continuing loyalty of his father to the English, he might be in danger of losing his parental inheritance in Annandale, or perhaps even the earldom of Carrick itself. With these fears at the front of his mind the time had come for him to make his peace with Edward. The document which lays out the terms of his submission specifically mentions the possibility that Edward might lose control of Scotland—'which God forbid'—and that the kingdom would be handed back to the Balliols. By February 1302 Robert Bruce was once again Edward's loyal subject; but always, in his own mind, reserving those rights he believed to be his.

Edward had now led four invasions of Scotland, only one of which could be described as an unqualified success. It's worth pausing here from the main thrust of our narrative to consider the reasons for these repeated strategic failures. The position is well summarised by J.E. Morris in his history of the Welsh wars:

> Each year up to 1303 the same facts are seen: there may be a summer campaign, more or less successful in appearance, but the English army cannot keep the field in the autumn and winter . . . Scotland would never be conquered until the same policy could be followed as in Wales. The war must be fought without intermission.

But this is only part of the explanation. It should also be remembered that it had taken the English close on two hundred years to absorb Wales, a country that lacked a unified leadership for much of its history. Even the conquest of the last independent fragment, the Principality of Llewelyn ap Gruffud in the north of Wales had been accomplished with some difficulty. It had taken fifteen months of sustained campaigning to overcome Llewelyn's stronghold in 1282-3, and a further eight months to break the Madog rebellion of 1294-5. Even then the country could only be held down by the construction of a mighty ring of castles and fortified towns at Caernarvon, Conway, Harlech, Beaumaris and other places. Yet in logistical terms the conquest of the principality had been comparatively easy. It was less than a third the size of Scotland and, as Sir Charles Oman pointed out in *The Art of War in the Middle Ages*, at no point was it very far removed from the main English supply bases at Hereford, Chester and Shrewsbury. In an emergency fresh men and materials could quickly be brought into battle. Similarly, north Wales was easy to sail round, and the new strongholds could be kept supplied by ships from Chester, Bristol and Dublin. Resistance was soon confined to the mountains of Snowdonia and then destroyed. But the whole process had been enormously expensive: in the period up to 1301 Edward spent well over £67,000 on his various Welsh bastions on building costs alone, a vast sum in those days. Indeed, the last of the Welsh castles, Beaumaris in Anglesey, was never completed because the money simply ran out. It's difficult to escape the conclusion that this kind of war could only be fought once in a generation.

Scotland, in contrast, presented an entirely different set of problems. The country was politically unified, with a similar social and military system to feudal England. The logistical problems in invading the country from England were immense, for the distances involved were far greater and naval support less easy. The nearest major supply base was at York, which meant that men and materials had to be transported over long distances in difficult country on poor or non-existent roads. Unlike Wales fresh forces could not be brought quickly to trouble spots. Besieged garrisons were often cut off for months, and starved into surrender, like Stirling in 1299. Long supply columns were always vulnerable to attack; and the ability of the defenders to deny the invaders the prospect of living off the land by means of a scorched earth policy reduced more than one English army to the verge of desperation, and beyond.

The English war in Scotland was, in essence, a war against geography. The mountains of north Wales are formidable, but cover a relatively small area. Scotland appears to invite invasion, with a series of broad valleys running from north to south all the way along the English border. But once inside the country the difficulties begin. The Scottish terrain of rolling hills, deep valleys, dense forests, impenetrable marshes and high mountains favoured the defenders, and did not allow the English to bottle their enemy in by the construction of a few well placed strongpoints. Edward could hardly afford to repair and maintain the existing castles, let alone build the huge number that would have been required to hold down the country in the Welsh fashion. For, in the final analysis these logistical and geographical problems were all compounded by simple lack of cash.

Edward began his war in Scotland when his exchequer was already strained to the limit. His political problems with his magnates made him reluctant to call Parliaments to ask for grants of money after 1298, forcing him to borrow heavily from foreign bankers. His open-ended war in Scotland placed an intolerable burden on the English economy, which ultimately denied him the means to bring the struggle to a successful conclusion. The problem, in other words, was not one of conquest but of consolidation. Even when the King recognised the limitations of his previous campaigns, as he assuredly did in 1303, which after 1296 failed to penetrate the heart of the old Celtic kingdom beyond the Tay, and carry out a 'war without intermission', it was probably too late to make good past mistakes. England could not hope to absorb Scotland without the continuing support of the native aristocracy, which does much to explain Edward's repeated indulgence towards former rebels like Robert Bruce. But these hopes were built on the shifting sands of Scottish politics.

In the same year that Bruce made his peace with Edward the always distant prospect of a Balliol restoration ended forever on the fields of Flanders. On 11 July 1302 Flemish infantry destroyed the proud knights of France at the Battle of Courtrai, confirming to all Europe that Stirling Bridge had been the harbinger of a new kind of warfare. Any hope that France would intervene in the Scottish war disappeared. Philip fell over himself in his hurry to conclude a definitive peace with Edward. Even the Pope could no longer be relied upon; for Boniface had quarrelled with France and was looking to England for support. He wrote to the Scots bishops blaming them for the war, expressing his particular disapproval of Robert Wishart. To try to prevent Scotland being overlooked in the coming Anglo-French peace treaty Sir John Soules led a strong delegation to Paris, leaving the Red Comyn as sole Guardian, a position he had probably always aspired to. The Soules mission was doomed to failure; for John Balliol, styling himself 'King of Scotland', had written to Philip the Fair authorising him to act on his behalf and settle matters 'either by peace or truce', thus betraying all those who had fought so hard for him over the past five years.

On Edward's insistence Scotland was excluded from the Treaty of Paris, signed on 20 May 1303, and left to its inevitable fate. The Scots ambassadors wrote to John Comyn with the news, urging him to continue the struggle: 'For God's sake do not despair. If you have done brave deeds, do braver ones now. The swiftest runner who falls before the winning post has run in vain'. But it was already too late: Edward had come to Scotland; this time, he hoped, to settle matters for good. Toom Tabard's light now faded forever and he dropped out of history, dying sometime in 1313 or 1314, still calling himself King of Scotland to the end of his life, a title he had done nothing to earn. The loyal John Soules never returned to Scotland, preferring to remain in France, where he died in 1310. The failure of his Paris mission gave him the full measure of his royal master, and before his death he was the most prominent of the old Balliol loyalists to give their support to Robert Bruce.

The year 1303 opened reasonably well for Scotland when John Comyn and Sir Simon Fraser of Oliver Castle, a former supporter of Edward but now one of the staunchest patriots, defeated an English reconnaissance force commanded by Sir John Seagrave on 23 February at the Battle of Roslin near Edinburgh; but this was a twilight victory overtaken by the ensuing darkness.

Edward came well prepared. For once Parliament was with him, and he obtained the necessary funds without too much difficulty. This time he would fight a war to the finish throughout the summer and on into the autumn and winter. He looked for victory, not in the south as he had in 1300 and 1301, but in Scotland north of the Forth—the ancient kingdom of Alba. He left Roxburgh on 25 May with a powerful field army and all the latest siege equipment. The support fleet sailing up the east coast carried three huge prefabricated bridges to allow the army to by-pass Stirling Castle, the toughest nut to be left to last, and cross into Fife on the lower reaches of the Forth. For the first time since 1296 the English moved into northern Scotland in strength. The main thrust was supported by supplementary actions in the west. The Prince of Wales and Amyer de Valence were active in Galloway. Robert Bruce's father-in-law, Richard de Burgh, the Red Earl of Ulster, led a large Irish expeditionary force up the Firth of Clyde, capturing Rothesay Castle on the Isle of Bute, and landing on the mainland near Inverkip, eventually joining up with Edward for the opening stages of the siege of Stirling Castle.

Edward occupied Perth in June and from there continued northwards, all resistance evaporating before him. Only at Brechin Castle was his progress halted at the end of July by a courageous defence, which continued until the death of its commander, Sir Thomas Maule, on 9 August. The advance continued through Aberdeen, Banff and Elgin, finally coming to a halt at Kinloss on the Moray Firth before returning south. At Lochindorb he was pleased to receive the submission of most of the northern magnates, who surrendered their castles into his hands. By early November the King was in Dunfermline, where he made his winter quarters in the Abbey.

There appears to have been little military action over the winter season, although William Wallace, back in Scotland, but no longer a figure of any great importance, and Sir Simon Fraser, were defeated at a small engagement at Happrew near Peebles in early 1304. Wallace remained in the field with a few followers, only to be defeated again in his final action near the River Earn in September, after which he took to hiding as an outlaw.

For the Scots the military situation was hopeless, and Comyn's leadership seems to have been far from inspired. There was no attempt at any point to use scorched earth or the kind of nascent guerrilla tactics employed by Soules in 1301. Edward was well aware that the advantage was his and offered terms to all those who agreed to surrender; apart, that is, from William Wallace, who had acquired the status of a demon in English eyes, and was to be pursued with implacable hostility. The official capitulation came when John Comyn agreed to accept Edward's offer of peace at Strathord near Perth on 9 February 1304. The surrender was certainly more honourable than Balliol's in 1296, and Edward dignified it by promising to protect the law of the realm, and only to change it with the consent of the responsible men of the land; but as far as Wallace was concerned Edward made the position absolutely plain:

> No words of peace are to be held out to William Wallace in any circumstances whatever unless he places himself utterly and absolutely in our will. The Stewart, Sir John de Soules and Sir Ingram de Umfraville are not to have safe conducts nor come within the King's power until Sir William Wallace is given up. Sir John Comyn, Sir Alexander Lindsay, Sir David Graham and Sir Simon Fraser shall exert themselves until twenty days after Christmas to capture Sir William Wallace and hand him over to the King, who will watch to see how each of them conducts himself so that he can do most favour to whoever shall capture Wallace.

Rather than accept these terms Sir John Soules remained in France. It is also unlikely that Simon Fraser, declared to be an outlaw after Comyn's submission, accepted the part of Judas allotted to him by Edward. When he eventually did submit he was only permitted to do so on terms far more severe than most of his fellow landowners. By the spring of 1304, apart from a few irreconcilables like Wallace, only Stirling Castle held out for Scotland.

Although Edward now believed himself to be close to final victory he had learned enough of Scots resilience, and the limits of his own resources, to try to avoid repeating the mistakes of 1296. Much more thought would have to be given to the way the country was to be governed after the conquest. With this at the front of his mind he summoned a Parliament to meet at St Andrews in early March 1304 to begin the reorganisation of the government of Scotland. The discussions continued at a Parliament held at Westminster a year later when Robert Bruce, Robert Wishart and John Mowbray were appointed to advise the King on the final settlement of the Scottish question. Acting on their recommendations Edward summoned ten Scots representatives to join twenty-one English councillors at Westminster in September 1305 to draft a constitution for Scotland. The result was the 'Ordinances for the Establishment of the Land of Scotland'. As far as possible the Ordinances involved the leading Scots magnates and prelates in the government of the country; but the principal posts were placed in the hands of Englishmen, headed by John of Brittany, Earl of Richmond, the King's lieutenant in Scotland. Scotland, moreover, was no longer referred to as a kingdom but merely as a 'land', and its leading magnates were to serve as props of an occupation regime.

While he was at St Andrews in March Edward wrote to Patrick de Dunbar, who was conducting operations in the vicinity of Stirling Castle, criticising his lack of success. Finally, at the beginning of May 1304 the King decided to come to Stirling himself to take personal charge of the reduction of the great stronghold. It was destined to be his last combat.

The epic siege of Stirling Castle began in earnest in early May and lasted until late July. It was to be the last act of the moribund Balliol cause in Scotland; but it was also the beginning of a new kind of struggle. Throughout the siege the royal standard, the Lion Rampant, fluttered above the castle's battlements. Few of the hardiest Balliol loyalists could now have believed in the restoration of that distant and hopeless figure Toom Tabard. The defenders of Stirling, commanded by Sir William Oliphant—'a very gallant knight'—held out against overwhelming odds, and without any hope of relief, on behalf 'of the Lion'. By their action the flag became more than a royal standard: in a deeper sense it had become a symbol of Scotland herself. This was a new theme in Scottish history, and it was to appear again.

The battle for Stirling Castle was one of the great dramas of the Wars of Independence. Edward's conduct towards the defenders was singularly unattractive. The young crusader who had saved Acre from the Saracens was now a vindictive old warrior, who displayed little of the chivalry that the Scots had shown to the English garrison in 1299. When Sir William Oliphant requested permission to send a messenger to Sir John Soules, who had entrusted him with the defence of the Castle when he was Guardian, Edward refused, remarking 'If he thinks it will be better for him to defend the castle than yield it, he will see.' All the power of Edward's many siege engines was brought to bear: great stone balls, some as heavy as 3 cwt apiece, fell on the walls of the castle; the defenders were fired upon from wooden towers, drawn up close to the battlements; battering rams thundered relentlessly against the defences. The garrison fought back as best they could, on one occasion grazing King Edward with a crossbow bolt, but there was little they could do to deflect the onslaught. When one of the engines finally made a breach in the walls Oliphant offered to surrender on terms. Edward initially refused to allow this, threatening the whole garrison—some fifty men—with the hideous butchery to which traitors were subject at the time. He was persuaded to allow them to live only after they had abased themselves before him, following which the survivors, Oliphant included, were sent to English prisons. The surrender had only been accepted after the castle had been subjected to bombardment by one of the King's latest 'toys'—a siege engine known as the 'Warwolf'.

With the fall of Stirling Castle on 20 July Edward's control of Scotland was complete. Unbeknown to him, however, an even greater threat to English security in Scotland was taking shape in his own camp. Robert Bruce was present with Edward during the siege, and would have recognised Oliphant's hopeless defiance as the final chapter of the Balliol cause. His father had died earlier in the year, bequeathing to his son the lordship of Annandale and the Bruce claim to the crown of Scotland, long submerged but never forgotten. On 11 June, as Edward's engines were raining missiles down on the nearby castle, Bruce met William Lamberton, Bishop of St Andrews, a long-time supporter and friend of William Wallace, at Cambuskenneth Abbey, and there they concluded a bond of friendship, promising to assist each other against unspecified 'rivals' and 'dangers'. No mention was made of their duty to Edward. Bruce—the 'king in waiting'—and Lamberton—the bishop of the Scots—had in effect concluded an alliance that was to be the basis of the revolution of 1306.

When Edward recrossed the border on 25 August 1304 he left behind a country that had been to all outward appearances completely subdued. But the elderly King had led his last campaign and England had made its greatest effort to crush Scotland by military force. Although the war was destined to run for another fifty years the campaign of 1303–4 was the last of its kind. Even Edward III's great offensive of 1335 was only a summer invasion, on much the same basis as that of 1298. Only once more, in 1336, did the English penetrate Scotland north of the Tay, and with only a fraction of the force of 1303. All that could be achieved by naked military effort had now been done; it only remained to see how well Scotland settled down to the conquest.

For William Wallace there was no rest or ease. He was finally hunted down near Glasgow in August 1305 by men acting for Sir John Mentieth, the warden of Dumbarton Castle, and taken to London. On 23 August, after a summary 'trial' at Westminster Hall, he was condemned as a traitor, although of all the Scots patriots he had never at any time sworn homage to Edward. From Westminster he was taken to Smithfield. Let the historian Matthew of Westminster describe the spectacle:

> First of all, he was led through the streets of London, dragged at the tail of a horse, and dragged to a very high gallows, made on purpose for him, where he was hanged with a halter, then taken down half dead, after which his genitals were cut off, and his bowels taken out and burnt in the fire, then his head was cut off, and his body divided into four quarters, and his head fixed on a stake and set in London. But his four quarters thus divided, were sent to the four quarters of Scotland.

Edward had killed an enemy and created a martyr. At the time of his death Wallace was of no military importance, and was little more than an irritant to the English. But more than this he was a symbol amongst the ordinary people of the realm of a spirit of national freedom, which had to be eliminated if the conquest was to be made safe. His achievements were soon to be overtaken by the greater triumphs of Robert Bruce; but Wallace deserves to be remembered as the first and greatest of Scotland's patriots who fought for no other cause but honour and freedom. And as such he will live in the hearts and minds of Scots forever.

CHAPTER 4
A New Birth of Freedom, 1306–1307

On that fateful day, 10 February 1306, when Robert Bruce met John Comyn before the high altar of Greyfriars Church in Dumfries, Scotland had been firmly under English control for eighteen months. Wallace was dead. The Ordinances of September 1305 seemed to have established the government of Scotland on a basis acceptable to the chief men of the realm, although they did little to disguise her subject status.

The exact purpose of Bruce's meeting with Comyn is unknown. It's reasonably safe to assume, though, that they went to Dumfries to discuss the future of Scotland. Bruce's ambitions were known, and despite his service in the English cause since 1302 by the close of 1305 Edward was beginning to have doubts about his loyalty. Any plans he had to revive Scottish kingship without the support of the Red Comyn, the head of Scotland's most powerful family, would have been extremely difficult. Given the conservative nature of political thought and personal loyalty at this time few people would have been prepared to support an outright seizure of power by Bruce. There was clearly no further point in fighting for John Balliol, who showed absolutely no desire to return to his lost kingdom. Even so, his son Edward was generally considered to have a stronger claim than Bruce. In the absence of Edward, a minor and a state prisoner of the English, John Comyn, the son of John's sister Eleanor, was the chief representative of the Balliol interest in Scotland. Indeed, in terms of the judgement of 1292 he had a better claim in his own right than his great rival, and may very well have entertained his own royal ambitions.

The venue for the meeting, the church of the minorite friars, confirms the deep mistrust with which the two men regarded each other. Theirs was a long standing and potentially violent rivalry. A church obviously offered the best prospect of mutual safety. It seems likely that Bruce offered Comyn some kind of pact, allowing one or the other to take the throne. Comyn refused to listen. Their discussions became violent, weapons were drawn and Comyn wounded. In the confusion that followed Comyn and his uncle, Sir

Robert Comyn, were killed by Bruce's followers, his brother-in-law, Christopher Seton, and James Kirkpatrick.

The murder of John Comyn was one of the most decisive acts in Scottish political history. But in no sense was it premeditated. While Bruce may very well have considered removing such a dangerous rival, he would certainly not have chosen a church in which to do so. It is difficult in our secular age to appreciate fully the power of the medieval church. Emperors and kings—Henry II and John of England amongst them—had been forced to bend before its authority. Bruce's act was one of supreme sacrilege. He faced the future as an enemy of both the church and state, an excommunicate and an outlaw. It was to be many years before the Pope was prepared to forgive him; but his pact with Lamberton and the support of the native Scottish church, prepared to take his side in defiance of Rome itself, was of inestimable importance to him in this moment of supreme crisis.

Without the support and encouragement of Bruce's clerical allies his cause would surely have been lost. He could never return to Edward's peace. The balance of power in Scotland was firmly in England's favour; for the powerful Balliol/Comyn clan, long in the forefront of the national struggle, were now guaranteed to fight on Edward's side. Bruce's Scottish enemies controlled large and strategically important territories throughout the realm, in Galloway, Argyll, Lochaber, Buchan and Ross. English garrisons controlled all the chief strongholds of the land, and Edward continued to enjoy the support of the Earls of Angus and March. The Scottish war of liberation was also to be at one and the same time a civil war.

Bruce's dramatic action came like a flash of lightning in the sultry night of the English occupation. There was only one way to go, and that was forward. It would take some time for Edward and his allies to learn the facts of Comyn's death, and Bruce took advantage of the confusion to raise the standard of rebellion, with the intention of having himself crowned as King of Scotland. From all over the country men rallied to his cause. A number of castles were seized, including that at Dumfries, captured by the Competitor in the first Bruce rising twenty years before.

Bruce went to Glasgow, where he met with Robert Wishart, in whose diocese the murder of Comyn had been committed. Rather than excommunicate the miscreant, as church law demanded, Wishart absolved him and urged his flock to rise in his support. He then accompanied Bruce to Scone, where he was joined by his brother bishops, William Lamberton and David Murray, together with two other prominent churchmen, Abbot Henry of Scone and Abbot Maurice of Inchaffray. Three of Scotland's earls were there— John of Atholl, Malcolm of Lennox and Alan of Mentieth; and Donald of Mar, Bruce's ward, may also have been present. Bruce's family came with him, his four brothers—Alexander, Thomas, Neil and Edward—his nephew, Thomas Randolph, and his brother-in-law, Christopher Seton. Other prominent supporters included young James de Douglas, the son of William the Hardy; Gilbert de la Haye of Errol and his brother Hugh; David Barclay of Cairns; Alexander Fraser, the brother of Sir Simon; Walter Sommerville of Carnwath; David de Inchmartin; Robert Boyd of Kilmarnock; and Robert Fleming. At Scone, on 25 March 1306, in an improvised ceremony, they all witnessed the crowning of King Robert I. A number of important elements of a traditional Scottish coronation were missing: the Stone of Destiny was in English hands, as was the Earl of Fife, whose family, the MacDuffs, according to the ancient custom, placed all new kings on the throne as the foremost Scottish earls. Bruce and his small party were astonished when his sister Isabel, wife of Bruce's principal Comyn enemy, the Earl of Buchan, arrived late and claimed the traditional right of the MacDuffs of Fife. Accordingly, a second coronation was duly held on 27 March. The Countess of Buchan's patriotism was soon to cost her dear.

Both ceremonies had been carried out in the Augustinian Abbey. Edward was later to signal his intense displeasure with the Scottish church and people when he unsuccessfully petitioned the Pope to have the Abbey removed stone by stone from 'the midst of a perverse nation', presumably to follow the Stone of Destiny into permanent English captivity. The feelings of those who attended the coronations are not recorded; but they were likely to have been wary rather than joyous; for they were surrounded by many enemies. Bruce's Queen, Elizabeth de Burgh, daughter of Edward's supporter, the Earl of Ulster, is reported to have said: 'It seems to me that we are but a summer king and queen whom children crown in their sport.' For Bruce winter was rapidly approaching.

The murder of John Comyn took Edward by complete surprise. News travelled slowly: it was some thirteen days after the event before it reached the King in Winchester, and even then the full circumstances were unclear. The murder was described as the work of 'some people who are doing their utmost to trouble the peace and quiet of the realm of Scotland'. When he learned the true facts he reacted with great fury. On 5 April he appointed Aymer de Valence, Comyn's brother-in-law, as his plenipotentiary in Scotland, with powers to raise the dragon banner, signifying that no quarter would be given to Bruce and his adherents. At Westminster on the 20 May the King knighted the Prince of Wales and a further 250 young noblemen in preparation for the coming war. A banquet was held after the ceremony during which two decorated swans were presented to the King. Edward then vowed 'by the God of Heaven and these swans', to avenge the death of John Comyn and the treachery of the Scots. On the King's demand all of the newly created knights took a similar oath. Finally, on 5 June at St Paul's Cathedral formal sentence of excommunication, recently passed by Pope Clement V, was pronounced on Bruce and some of his followers. This was to be a hunt to the death.

After his coronation Bruce and his adherents set about increasing the new King's grip on Scotland. Attacks were launched on the MacDoualls of Galloway and other prominent Balliol and Comyn supporters. The Earl of Strathern, Buchan's brother-in-law, was captured and forced to submit to King Robert. The elderly Robert Wishart attacked the castle of Kirkintilloch, where he used timber he had been given by the English to repair the bell tower of Glasgow Cathedral to build siege engines, and captured Cupar Castle in Fife. In the north the Bishop of Moray preached holy war against the English. The whole country was in turmoil.

With the approach of Amyer de Valence Bruce broke off all operations in Galloway and retired into central Scotland to wait for an opportunity to strike. De Valence moved quickly, taking both Wishart and Lamberton prisoner. Both were sent into captivity in England, where they only escaped execution because they were in holy orders. Edward was delighted by the capture of these 'traitors and rebels', and wrote to the Pope in September advising him that they were being held in close confinement and that custody of the See of St Andrews had been granted to Master William Comyn, brother of the Earl of Buchan, and that of Glasgow to Geoffrey de Mowbray. Only the Bishop of Moray remained at liberty, and de Valence was repeatedly ordered to capture this most dangerous churchman. Edward's anger at Moray is vividly reflected in his complaint to the Pope:

> The Bishop of Moray, by preaching so much against him, and by exhorting the flock of his bishopric to rebel with Sir Robert Bruce,

had incited them, nor does he yet cease to incite them daily as much as he is able, so that the flock of his bishopric of Moray who assembled to the help of the said Robert, and still hold themselves with him, have done this owing to the incitement, preaching, and exhorting of the said Bishop, because he told them that they were not less deserving of merit who rebelled with Sir Robert to help him against the King of England and his men, and took the part of the said Robert, than if they should fight in the Holy Land against pagans and Saracens.

As a former crusader this must have been particularly galling to Edward, no doubt making him even more anxious to capture the errant bishop. But Murray evaded all of de Valence's attempts to seize him, finally taking temporary refuge in the Orkney Isles, then a possession of Norway. Edward requested his extradition in early 1307, but without success.

By the middle of summer de Valence had made his base at Perth, where his army was joined by many Scots, kinsmen and allies of the Comyns. Robert came from the west ready to meet his enemies in battle. For once Bruce, not yet the great guerrilla commander, prepared to observe the gentlemanly conventions of feudal warfare, while the English adopted less orthodox tactics. De Valence was invited to leave the defences of Perth and join Bruce in battle, but he declined to do so. Bruce, perhaps believing that de Valence's refusal to accept his challenge was a sign of weakness, retired to nearby Methven where he prepared to camp for the night. There before dawn on 19 June his little army was taken by surprise and almost destroyed. Methven wasn't a battle; it was a disaster. The Scots had almost no time to rally and many prominent men were captured, including Thomas Randolph, David de Inchmartin, Alexander Fraser, David Berkeley, Hugh de la Haye and John de Sommerville. Bruce himself almost fell into the hands of the English, but he managed to fight his way free with the Earl of Atholl, James Douglas, Sir Neil Campbell of Lochawe, Edward Bruce, Gilbert de la Haye and a few hundred other followers, fleeing westwards into the hostile territory of Comyn's kinsman Alexander MacDougall, Lord of Argyll, and his son John of Lorne. The MacDougalls fell upon Bruce's remaining force and all but destroyed it at the Battle of Dalry, fought some time in July or August near Tyndrum. The army of Scotland now ceased to exist as an organised force, and King Robert, now styled 'King Hob' in English propaganda, was little better than a fugitive, facing the same kind of ignominious end as

William Wallace. But Methven had taught him a valuable lesson, and during the coming months in hiding he conceived plans for an entirely new form of warfare.

After Dalry Bruce and his small party took refuge in the mountains of Atholl. From here he sent Queen Elizabeth, his daughter Marjory by his first marriage, his sister Mary and the Countess of Buchan under the escort of his brother Neil and the Earl of Atholl to the relative safety of Kildrummy Castle, near the River Don in Aberdeenshire. With James Douglas and a few others he then escaped southwards into the territory of his friend the Earl of Lennox. Lennox helped Bruce and his company cross by way of Bute over to the Kintyre peninsula, the home of Neil Campbell, where he was aided by a new convert to his cause—Angus Og, a leading chief of the MacDonalds, and a bitter enemy of the MacDougalls; for in the complex politics of the highlands the old maxim always applied: 'my enemy's enemy is my friend.' Bruce now found a temporary haven in Dunaverty Castle near the Mull of Kintyre.

In October 1306 the ailing Plantagenet lion reached Lanercost Priory near Carlisle. Here he rested, too ill to proceed further, but close enough to be ready for the final capture of his prey. Those who fell into his claws could expect little mercy, and Scotland was subject to a brief and gruesome reign of terror. Neil Bruce, captured after Kildrummy Castle fell to Amyer de Valence and the Prince of Wales in September, was hanged and beheaded at Berwick; a fate to which Sir Simon Fraser of Oliver Castle, who had fought with Bruce at Methven, was also subject in London, where his head joined that of his old comrade William Wallace impaled above London Bridge. The Earl of Atholl left Kildrummy with the Bruce women at the approach of the English, only to be captured by the Balliol Earl of Ross at the sanctuary of St Duthac in Tain. Atholl was subsequently hanged in Westminster, the first earl to be executed in England for 230 years. Christopher Seton, the husband of Christian Bruce, was executed in Dumfries, where he had been party to the killing of John and Robert Comyn. His brother John was executed at Newcastle, on the same day as fifteen other adherents of Robert Bruce, most notably David de Inchmartin, taken prisoner at Methven, and Alexander Scrymgeour, the hereditary standard bearer of Scotland. Many others also died.

Edward's vengeance was not confined to the men. Mary Bruce was imprisoned in a cage in a tower of Roxburgh Castle; a similar fate to that of the Countess of Buchan, who 'was placed in a little house of timber in a tower of the castle of Berwick, the sides latticed so that all there could gaze on her as a spectacle'. Mary remained at Roxburgh until 1310, before being transferred to Newcastle. Isabel of Buchan was also kept in her cage until the same year, when she was finally released into the keeping of the Carmelite nuns in Berwick. In 1313 she became the ward of Henry Beaumont, by this time claimant by marriage to the earldom of Buchan, and recognised as earl by the English government when his wife Alice Comyn came of age in 1312. A similar cage was decreed for the twelve-year-old Marjory Bruce in the Tower of London, but she somehow managed to escape this fate, perhaps by a rare piece of royal compassion, and was placed in a Yorkshire nunnery instead. Queen Elizabeth, allegedly an unwilling participant in her husband's adventure, and the daughter of Edward's powerful friend, the Earl of Ulster, was also imprisoned in a less rigorous fashion, as was Bruce's other sister Christian, the widow of Christopher Seton. Bruce's young nephew and ward, Donald, Earl of Mar, was also captured at some time during the year and taken to England, where he grew up in the household of the Prince of Wales.

With his enemies closing in King Robert had no choice but to leave Scotland. From Dunnaverty Castle he took ship, and for several months disappeared out of the light of history into the mists of legend, seeking refuge in Rathlin Island near the coast of Ulster, according to some, or the Orkney Islands, according to others; into a twilight inhabited by the most famous spider of all time.

When he reappeared in February 1307 Bruce was set to take his greatest gamble. From the island of Arran in the Firth of Clyde he crossed to his own earldom of Carrick, which Edward had awarded to Henry Percy, landing near Turnberry where he knew the local people would be sympathetic, but where all the strongholds were occupied by the English. A similar landing in Galloway by his brothers Thomas and Alexander, accompanied by Sir Reginald Crawford, Malcolm MacQuillan of Kintyre, and an unnamed Irish chieftain, met with disaster on the shores of Loch Ryan at the hands of Dungal MacDouall, the principal Balliol adherent in the region, at the head of a mixed force of his own clansmen and their allies the MacCanns. Thomas and Alexander's little army of Irish and Islemen was destroyed and they were sent captive with Crawford to Carlisle, where all three were executed on the orders of King Edward. But against all the odds Robert survived, and with remarkable tenacity soon established himself in the hill country of Carrick and

Galloway. From feudal warlord Bruce was in the process of trans-
forming himself into one of history's great guerrilla leaders.

Bruce had learned well the sharp lesson delivered to him at
Methven: never again would he allow himself to be trapped by a
stronger enemy. His greatest weapon was an intimate knowledge of
the Scottish countryside, which he used to his advantage time and
again. Even at Bannockburn, where he temporarily abandoned his
guerrilla war, he chose his ground with genius, allowing his small
army to operate at maximum advantage. As well as making good
use of the country's natural defences, he made sure that his force
was as mobile as possible. Bruce was now fully aware that he could
rarely expect to get the better of the English in open battle. His army
was often weak in numbers and ill-equipped. It would be best used
in small scale hit-and-run tactics, allowing him to make best use
of his limited resources, keep the initiative and prevent the enemy
bringing his superior strength to bear. Whenever possible crops
would be destroyed and livestock removed from the path of the
enemy's advance, denying him fresh supplies and fodder for the
heavy war-horses. Most important of all, Bruce recognised the
seasonal nature of English invasions, which swept across the
country like summer tides, only to withdraw before the onset of
winter. Warfare of this kind demanded the use of strongpoints to
hold down the country between campaigns. The destruction of all
captured castles therefore became one of the central elements of
Bruce's guerrilla war.

Consider the perilous position of the King in the early spring of
1307: to his north was a strong force of knights under Amyer de
Valence; Sir Henry Percy controlled the sea ports and castles to the
west; Doungal MacDouall was based to the south in Wigtownshire
with a large force of Galloway clansmen; to the east Sir John de
Botetourt guarded Nithsdale with 70 horse and over 200 archers;
Sir Robert de Clifford and Sir John de Wigtoun stood guard on the
fords of the River Cree; and a special force of 300 Tynedale bowmen
under Sir Geoffrey de Mowbray was sent to search Glentrool. To
support these operations John of Lorne, son of the Lord of Argyll,
came south with a large body of Highlanders. Other Balliol supporters also joined the hunt, including Ingram de Umfraville, the former
Guardian, John Mentieth, the betrayer of Wallace, John Mowbray
and, surprisingly, David de Strathbogie, son of the executed Earl of
Atholl. Strathbogie's wife was Joan Comyn, eldest daughter of the
Red Comyn, and his respect for the feelings of his wife and her family

was clearly greater than any regrets he may have had over the death of his father.

But Bruce eluded them all and won his first success at Glentrool, where he ambushed an English cavalry force led by John Mowbray, sweeping down from the steep hillsides and driving them off with heavy losses. He then slipped through the gap in the enemy ring, passing along the moors by Dalwellington to Muirkirk, appearing in the north of Ayrshire in early May, where he was strengthened by fresh recruits. Here he met Amyer de Valence, the victor of Methven, at Loudon Hill near Kilmarnock on 10 May 1307. Bruce chose his position well: de Valence was forced to advance along a narrow roadway bounded on either side by a deep moss. To reduce the enemy's room for manœuvre still further Bruce ordered a series of ditches to be dug, running in parallel lines from the moss to the road. These preparations effectively neutralised the English superiority in numbers, and de Valence attacked along a dangerously constricted front on to the waiting Scottish spears, in a battle reminiscent in some respects of Stirling Bridge. As Bruce's spearmen pressed downhill on the disorganised English knights they fought with such vigour that the rear ranks began to flee in panic. Amyer de Valence managed to escape the carnage and fled to the safety of Bothwell Castle. Three days after the Battle of Loudon Hill Bruce attacked and defeated another English squadron led by Ralph de Monthermer, Earl of Gloucester, forcing him to take refuge in Ayr Castle.

For the now gravely ill King in impotent confinement at Lanercost the situation was highly frustrating. He had written to de Valence in February expressing his displeasure at the failure to capture Bruce and accusing his commander of timidity. A few days after the defeat at Loudon Hill he received an alarming report from one of his supporters in Scotland:

> I hear that Bruce never had the good will of his own followers or of the people generally so much with him as now. It appears that God is with him, for he has destroyed King Edward's power both among the English and Scots. The people believe that Bruce will carry all before him, exhorted by false preachers from Bruce's army, men who have previously been charged before the justices for advocating war and have been released on bail, but are now behaving worse than ever. . . For these preachers have told the people that they have found a prophecy of Merlin, that after the death of 'le Roy Coveytous' [the covetous king] the people of Scotland and the Welsh shall band

together and shall have full lordship and live in peace together until the end of the world.'

The campaign of terror designed to eliminate the Bruce threat was, as so often in these cases, having the opposite effect. Too late the King ordered his officials in Scotland to adopt a less harsh approach. Despite his condition Edward now tried to retrieve the deteriorating situation by taking to the field himself. He advanced a mere seven miles to Burgh-on-Sands, where he died on 7 July 1307, in sight of Scotland, but with his life's work incomplete. A contemporary wrote of Edward when he was still heir to the throne in the following terms:

> A lion by pride and fierceness, he is in inconstancy and changeabl-
> ness a pard [leopard], changing his word and promise, cloaking
> himself by pleasant speech. When he is in a straight he promises
> whatever you wish, but as soon as he has escaped he renounces his
> promise . . . The treachery or falsehood whereby he is advanced he
> calls prudence; and the way whereby he arrives wither he will,
> crooked though it may be, is regarded as straight; wrong gives him
> pleasure and is called right; whatever he likes he says is lawful. [The
> Song of Lewes]

The legacy of 'the covetous king' to his son was an empty treasury and an unwinnable war. His single-minded determination blinded him to the simple reality that the conquest of Scotland was beyond the means and capacity of his realm. His various campaigns strained the nation's resources to the limit and beyond. That the war in the north was a personal project can never really be doubted, for few of his noblemen shared Edward's enthusiasm for the enter-prise. To avoid the demands for political concessions that he faced from his magnates in 1294 and 1297, when he asked Parliament for additional taxation, he ran up an enormous burden of debt. At his death it has been estimated that he may have owed as much as £200,000, and the exchequer accounts were in chaos. The customs were mortgaged to the Italian banking house Frescobaldi, and money was owed to magnates, troops, courtiers, tradesmen, arti-sans and clerks. It is usual to blame the feckless and unfortunate Edward II for the disasters that were soon to overtake the English monarchy; but the simple fact is that the seeds were sown by the father and the harvest reaped by the son.

Edward I is not an attractive figure. His overbearing behaviour towards John Balliol, his conduct at the sack of Berwick and his pathological vindictiveness towards opponents all display a lack of chivalry and true nobility of character. He poisoned relations between England and Scotland to such a degree that his legacy cast a shadow far into the future. Nevertheless, he was the most formidable enemy Scotland ever had, and his death was greeted with relief by Bruce and his supporters. Few Scots had any doubts about the fate of his soul, for a rumour soon spread that an English knight had a vision of the late King being tormented by the demons in Hell. For Scotland the death of Edward I saw a new birth of freedom. Robert Bruce's time had come.

CHAPTER 5

The Winning of a Kingdom, 1307–1314

After the death of his father the new King, Edward II, led his army across the border on a rather aimless progress towards Cumnock in Ayrshire. From there he returned to England on 25 August, having achieved nothing, and breaking the oath of the swans.

Edward is usually condemned for abandoning his father's last campaign; but it's far from clear what the aims of this invasion were, other than to force the Scots into a pitched battle. Bruce had made it plain throughout the spring and summer that he no intention of making the same mistake that Wallace had at Falkirk. Moreover, Edward could not stay indefinitely in Scotland, for there were important matters of state to attend to: his father's funeral, his own coronation and his forthcoming marriage to Isabella of France. Parliament would also have to be summoned.

Before leaving for London the King did not neglect to make arrangements for the security of the north. He remained on the border until September, arranging for money and supplies. Amyer de Valence, now Earl of Pembroke, and the Earl of Richmond, were appointed as his lieutenants in Scotland; and special keepers of the peace were assigned to the northern counties of England, to be assisted, when necessary, by the local sheriffs. Even so, Edward was not the man his father was. Denholm Young in his introduction to the *Vita Edwardi Secundi* sums up his character and circumstances with admirable precision:

> Edward II sat down to the game of kingship with a remarkably poor hand, and he played it very badly. His father Edward I had left him with enormous commitments in Scotland and Gascony, and had unwittingly by subduing Wales, strengthened the Marcher lords. The finances were in extraordinary confusion. There had been mounting opposition to prerogative rule for the last decade. What is worse, when Edward of Caernarvon came to the throne in July 1307, though neither stupid nor criminal, he was not 'a man of business', but an aimless man without poise or sense of values. He had not been trained to rule: he had never really been let 'off the leash'. His laziness, incapacity, and lack of sympathy with his greater subjects gave opportunity to the baronial opposition—the successors of his father's

50

opponents of 1297—to air their grievances and seek the time honoured remedies.'

Edward had none of his father's strength of character and firmness of purpose. Most damaging of all, he lacked political judgement and the sense to maintain a balance of power and influence within the national community. Virtually his first act as King was to recall his close friend, the Gascon knight Piers Gaveston, exiled from England by his father. Edward's passion for Gaveston, whom he created Earl of Cornwall in 1308, and the favours he heaped upon him, caused considerable resentment amongst his other noblemen, and came close to wrecking the kingdom. The growing political crisis at home brought about by his relationship with Gaveston and his general incompetence prevented Edward from giving his full attention to Scotland for three of the most crucial years of the war. Not until 1310 was he able to return to the north, and by this many of the gains of the great offensive of 1303–4 had been lost and his Scottish allies destroyed.

The defence of Edward's interests in Scotland rested in the first place with the garrisons of the castles and fortified towns, supported by a small field army. His principal asset, however, was the support he received from the Comyns and their associates. Other Scots in English prisons were released on condition that they took up arms against Bruce. William Oliphant, the former defender of Stirling Castle and a Balliol loyalist, agreed to these terms, as did Thomas Randolph, Bruce's nephew, who had been captured at Methven.

Edward had reasonable cause to suppose that his allies, supported by English garrisons, would be strong enough to contain the army of Robert Bruce. In the south-east the castles were close enough to one another to offer strong mutual support, and Bruce had no siege equipment. In the north the Earl of Buchan, the leader of the Comyn party and the whole Scottish opposition to Bruce, together with his allies, the Earls of Ross and Sutherland, controlled a large part of Gaelic Scotland. The Earls of Angus and Dunbar had long been friends of England. In Galloway the MacDoualls and MacCanns were unlikely to be reconciled to Bruce; nor were the MacDougalls of Argyll.

But English strength was, in practice, illusory; for the anti-Bruce forces were too widely scattered and too static to be able to take effective counter measures against the King's small but highly mobile army. Action against Bruce's guerrillas required a high degree of co-ordination and first-class leadership. Edward's first mistake was to recall Pembroke and leave Richmond in sole command. His second mistake was to underestimate the military genius of Robert Bruce. In 1307 and 1308 Scotland underwent a brief but savage civil war in which Bruce destroyed his domestic opponents in a piecemeal fashion, largely free from English intervention.

Bruce decided to act quickly in the expectation that Edward would reappear in the summer of 1308. The first attack came in Galloway, the hereditary home of the Balliols, in September 1307. Here the fighting was so fierce that the local peasantry were compelled to flee over the border with their livestock to the refuge of Inglewood Forest in Cumberland. The ferocity of the attack is surely explained in part by the fate of Thomas and Alexander Bruce at the hands of the MacDoualls. The chief men of Galloway appealed in vain to Edward for help, and were forced to pay tribute to Bruce to obtain a truce; but they were only to have a brief respite.

Bruce now turned his attention to his chief Scottish enemy— John Comyn of Buchan, well entrenched in his powerful north-eastern earldom. His young lieutenant Sir James Douglas was left in the south to conduct operations in the area of Clydesdale, Douglasdale and the wooded country in the neighbourhood of Selkirk and Jedburgh. Douglas 'in great peril', according to John Barbour, the author of the epic poem *The Bruce*, moved swiftly, seizing every opportunity to pull the tail of the English lion, and making his own Castle Douglas one of the most perilous postings in Scotland. His guerrilla war in and out of the Forest did much to forestall any attempt by the English to assist Buchan in the north.

Bruce broke through the English-held lowlands and arrived in the Highlands in late September, heading for the Red Comyn's lands in Lochaber. His march across the mountains was supported by a fleet of galleys sailing up Loch Linnhe. John MacDougall of Lorne, son of the elderly Lord of Argyll, isolated and threatened by both land and sea agreed to a truce, allowing the King to continue on his great northern wheel towards Buchan. Inverlochy Castle, the Red Comyn's old Lochaber stronghold, fell sometime in October or November. Bruce continued in a north-easterly direction, marching up the Great Glen towards Inverness, capturing Urquhart Castle on the way, which was destroyed in accordance with the King's new policy. Inverness Castle was also razed, and the rapid advance continued into Nairn. The speed of Bruce's approach took the Earl of Ross by surprise and, feeling himself unable to face his enemy in battle, he concluded a truce to last to June 1308. The Earl tried to excuse his conduct in a letter to Edward II, saying that he had called out the men of the earldoms of Caithness and Sutherland as well as Ross but 'he [Bruce] would have destroyed them utterly if we had not made a truce with him'. Ross appealed to Edward for help, which never came. With his flank secure Bruce moved east towards Elgin and Banff. From there he turned south to settle his account with the Earl of Buchan. This time there would be no truce.

At this crucial point the King was overtaken by a life-threatening illness. The hardships he had endured since Methven were beginning to tell. This could not have come at a worse time: it was now winter and food was short; the Earl of Buchan was approaching, his forces supplemented by those of Duncan of Frendraught, sheriff of Banff, David de Strathbogie of Atholl and John Mowbray. Demoralised by the apparently fatal illness of their King many of Bruce's less hardy supporters deserted. With the King too sick to move further the army took up a defensive position at Slioch near Huntly. There King Robert, in the account of John Barbour of Aberdeen, was surrounded by 700 of his most dedicated partisans, now under the command of his brother Edward. The position was a strong one. Buchan's attempts to probe the defences on Christmas day 1307 failed, and he retired to seek reinforcements. When he returned on New Year's Eve he was unable to prevent Bruce and his men retiring in close order to cross the mountains towards Mar. No attempt appears to have been made to pursue the King and he was given time to recover from his illness. Early in the New Year he was strong enough to begin campaigning again. Attacks were made on strongholds throughout the north-east, and the castles of Duffus and Tarradale were destroyed. An attempt to capture Elgin Castle in April 1308 was only foiled by the intervention of John Mowbray.

The final conflict with the Earl of Buchan, who seems to have shown absolutely no skill as a military leader throughout this period, came at the Battle of Inverurie on 23 May 1308. Buchan's army was routed by Bruce's veterans—'they quickly turned their backs to go, and fled and scattered far and wide'. Buchan's men fled all the way to the castle of Fyvie, twelve miles to the north. The earl's own flight did not stop until he reached the safety of England, where he died childless later in the year. The Comyn claim to the earldom now passed to his eldest niece Alice, who by her marriage to Henry Beaumont brought much future anguish to Scotland.

After Inverurie Bruce proceeded to destroy the Comyn power base in Buchan, killing all those who remained loyal to the fugitive Earl. His men proceeded to devastate the earldom from end to end. The Comyn strongholds at Slains, Rattray, Dundarg, Kindear and Kelly were captured and destroyed, as were many homesteads. Livestock was slaughtered and stores of corn were burned. John Barbour has left a memorable description of these events:

> His men through Buchan he did send
> To burn and slay from end to end
> He ravaged it in such a way
> That fifty years beyond that day
> The Rape of Buchan still was grieved.

The Rape—or Herschip—of Buchan was for Bruce a grim political necessity: he could never hope to establish himself as king, or turn to face the English, with such an important area unsubdued in his rear. It also had the desired effect, for never again was Buchan to return to its old Comyn loyalties. The Earl of Ross, now completely isolated, submitted in October, soon to become one of Bruce's most loyal lieutenants. The Bishop of Moray, who had returned from Orkney, was appointed as guarantor for the Earl's good behaviour. Moray and his fellow bishop, Thomas of Ross, joined the Earl as the strongest pillars of King Robert's cause in the north.

With the north and east securely in his hands Bruce turned westwards to deal with the MacDougalls of Argyll. Alexander MacDougall, too old and sick to take part in the fighting, lay in his castle of Dunstaffnage. To his son John, who was also suffering from illness at this time, fell the task of deflecting the coming onslaught. In the summer of 1308 the MacDougalls took up position in the narrow Pass of Brander, where Ben Cruachan meets Loch Awe. John of Lorne, still recovering from his illness, observed the action from a galley on the Loch. His men lay on the hillside overlooking the narrow path through the pass. If they looked for a repetition of the Battle of Dalry they were to be disappointed, for Bruce had no intention of falling into so simple an ambush. A party of Highlanders, led by James Douglas, who had recently joined the King from the south, climbed higher up the mountain and positioned themselves in the enemy's rear. As the MacDougalls attacked they were caught in a vice, with King Robert coming up from below and the Black Douglas from above. The men of Argyll broke and fled. They were chased across the River Awe westwards all the way to the walls of Dunstaffnage, as John of Lorne escaped down the

Loch, eventually taking refuge in England, like the Earl of Buchan. The Lord of Argyll surrendered and did homage to Robert Bruce; but the following year he joined his son in exile and died in 1310 in the service of Edward II.

While Robert was over-running Argyll his last surviving brother Edward renewed the war in Galloway. Local resistance was stiffened by an English force led by Ingram de Umfraville and Amyer de St John. Edward Bruce defeated this army at a battle on the banks of the River Dee near Buittle Castle, the old Balliol stronghold, to which the enemy commanders fled for safety, while the Scots continued with a ruthless campaign against the remaining Balliol partisans. The interior of Galloway was subdued, although the English and the MacDoualls continued to hold a powerful line of coastal castles for some time afterwards. Edward Bruce was rewarded for his efforts when his brother named him Lord of Galloway, a distinction formerly held by John Balliol. The 'Rape of Galloway', however, was not as thorough as that in Buchan; for the area, which long enjoyed its own independent tradition within Scotland, was to nurture Balliol sympathies for many years. As late as the 1330s the men of Galloway rose to support Edward Balliol, who had come to Scotland to claim his father's lost inheritance.

By the end of 1308 there had been a remarkable shift in the balance of power in Scotland. All of King Robert's Comyn enemies had been destroyed and their lands lost. The survivors had no power base left in Scotland, and were only able to continue to fight as individuals in the English army. The advantages Edward appeared to enjoy in the late summer of 1307 were gone. North of the Tay there was virtually nothing left of the gains of the great offensive of 1303. Aberdeen Castle had fallen as had Forfar. Now only remote Banff Castle remained in English control. The capture of Forfar is especially noteworthy because it established a model soon to be repeated at the grander fortifications further south. An Angus man, Philip the Forester, approached the castle under cover of dark with a party of country people and used light scaling ladders to climb the walls and take the sleeping garrison by surprise. The castle was subsequently destroyed.

Huge areas of the country were now under Bruce's control, and he began to rule as King in the fullest sense of the term. As a sign of his confidence and prestige he summoned his first Parliament to meet at St Andrews in March 1309. All the earldoms of Scotland were represented, either by the earls in person or by representatives of the communities, with the exception of Dunbar, an area of Scotland still firmly under English control. Likewise, most of Scotland's bishops came in person. Glasgow and St Andrews, whose bishops were still in England, sent representatives. Many barons and knights also came, with the exception of those still loyal to Balliol.

The St Andrews Parliament is notable for two things: the resumption of Scotland's relations with France, and the solemn affirmation by the peers and clergy of King Robert's right to the throne. It also launched the enduring myth that John Balliol had wrongfully been imposed on the Scots by Edward I.

Philip the Fair must surely have been amazed by the astonishing resurrection of the ally he had so callously abandoned in 1303. He was now sufficiently confident that Scots independence had been recovered that he wrote to Robert requesting his participation in a planned crusade. Not surprisingly, both King and Parliament declined this invitation, pointing out that it was necessary to settle matters with the English first. But the most important task before the assembled dignitaries was to confirm in law Bruce's hold on a crown that he had won by force. In two separate declarations the clergy and nobles affirmed that Robert was the lawful heir of King Alexander III, and that he had succeeded to a throne that had wrongfully been denied to his grandfather by Edward I. By this declaration Parliament effectively dispossessed the Balliols, both father and son. John Balliol, in retirement in France, and nearing the end of his life, was obviously never going to return; but his son Edward, approaching manhood in comfortable English captivity, had now become the first and greatest of the 'disinherited'.

Amongst those present at the St Andrews Parliament was Thomas Randolph. He had been captured earlier in the year by James Douglas. Although he at first refused to serve with his uncle, criticising his guerrilla methods as contrary to honour, he later recanted and subsequently became one of Bruce's greatest generals, and a first-class exponent of a technique of warfare he had formerly despised.

By the spring of 1309 the civil war was over and Bruce was legally recognised as King by all but the rump of the Balliol/Comyn party. The remaining enemy garrisons in Scotland were now dangerously exposed. Edward II, deeply involved in a self-induced political crisis in his own land, had been unable to intervene. The confusion of the English is reflected in the rapid turnover of viceroys following the recall of the Earl of Richmond, which included Henry Beaumont for a very brief period. Most appear to have been unwilling to cross the border. Bruce was able to move round the country with complete ease, concentrating on the reduction of the castles and strongholds still in enemy hands.

In the years before Bannockburn these fortifications fell to Bruce like the leaves in autumn. Banff, Dundee and Dumbarton all fell at various points before 1314, as did many others of lesser note. In Galloway the last to hold out, Dumfries, was surrendered to King Robert in February 1313, by none other than Dungal MacDouall. Notwithstanding the fact that he had been responsible for bringing about the death of two of the king's brothers, MacDouall was treated with chivalry and allowed to go free to continue fighting with the English. But the toughest nuts to crack were undoubtedly the great strongholds of central and southern Scotland: Perth, Stirling, Edinburgh, Roxburgh and Berwick. Lacking siege equipment the Scots had no other weapons but courage, enterprise and audacity. The tactics employed by Bruce and his young lieutenants were the stuff of legends: surprise attacks were made in the dark when the garrisons were less alert; battlements were scaled with rope ladders fitted with grappling irons.

King Robert himself led the attack on the fortified town of Perth, commanded by Sir William Oliphant. Perth, considered to be the capital of Scotland at this time, was of great strategic importance to the English because of its dominant position in the centre of the country. Large sums had been spent on the improvement of its defences, and by 1312 it was enclosed by huge stone walls with towers placed at strategic intervals along the battlements. To the east the approach to the town was guarded by the River Tay, while the remaining three sides were surrounded by a deep moat. Oliphant was doubtless entrusted with its defence because of the respect he earned from the English by his conduct at the siege of Stirling Castle. At Stirling he had held out for three months against Edward I's great war machines; this time his experience was to be quite different. Towards the end of 1312 the town had been under siege for some weeks, but it was well provisioned, and Bruce could not afford to wait until Oliphant's stores ran out. He gave the order to lift the siege, and his men marched away from Perth, with the jeers of the jubilant garrison ringing in their ears. Believing the siege to be raised the defenders relaxed; but Bruce only withdrew a short distance, returning some days later under cover of darkness. On the night of 7–8 January 1313, after wading through the icy moat, where the water came up to the King's throat, the Scots scaled the walls and overwhelmed the unsuspecting garrison. Oliphant was sent once more into captivity, but later made his peace with King Robert. To mark his triumph the King ordered the walls of Perth to be razed.

On a similar night in February 1314 James Douglas took Roxburgh Castle using the same methods. Three weeks later Thomas Randolph, now Earl of Moray, captured Edinburgh Castle, seemingly impregnable on its high plug of volcanic rock. On the night of 14 March a diversion was created at the east gate while Randolph and his party climbed the steep northern precipice before scaling the walls. The guards were defeated and Randolph opened the gates to admit the rest of his troops. In keeping with agreed strategy both castles, amongst the finest in the land, were partially destroyed. Although similar attempts to take Berwick in 1312 and 1316 were frustrated, on the first occasion by the barking of a dog, the English hold on the south-east, which had remained constant since 1296, was now severely weakened. By the summer of 1314, apart from Berwick, only Stirling, standing in splendid isolation in the valley of the Forth, and Bothwell, in the Clyde valley, were still in English hands.

Edward had not been completely inactive during these years, but as so often in his career his efforts were fruitless. He came northwards with his favourite, Piers Gaveston, in September 1310 to escape his troubles at home. War brought no relief to the beleaguered King. Gaveston was eventually sent to strengthen the defences of Perth, while Edward hunted the elusive Bruce in southern Scotland. The author of the *Vita Edwardi Secundi* takes up the story:

> The King entered Scotland with his army, but not a rebel was found . . . At that time Robert Bruce, who lurked continually in hiding, did them all the injury that he could. One day, when some English and Welsh, always ready for plunder, had gone out on a raid, accompanied for protection by many horsemen from the army, Robert Bruce's men, who had been concealed in caves and woodland, made a serious attack on our men . . . From such ambushes our men suffered heavy losses. For Robert Bruce, knowing himself unequal to the King of England in strength or fortune, decided that it would be better to resist our King by secret [guerrilla] warfare rather than dispute his right in open battle.

By October Edward was in Linlithgow; but with his army demoralised by Bruce's hit-and-run tactics, and running seriously short of supplies, especially fodder for the war-horses, he returned to Berwick. Here he remained until the following summer, unwilling to give up the fight; or perhaps more to the point, unwilling to return to the carping of his baronial critics. He wrote to the Pope in frustration:

> Robert de Bruce and his accomplices, when lately we went into the parts of Scotland to repress their rebellion, concealed themselves in secret places after the manner of foxes.

Edward eventually returned to London in August 1311, accompanied by Gaveston, to whom he had given the empty title of 'Warden Beyond the Forth', having achieved absolutely nothing in his desultory ten-month campaign. His increasingly bitter dispute with his magnates, whose hatred of Gaveston was reaching a fever pitch, precluded any further intervention in Scotland for some time. Edward's failure was Robert's opportunity: in 1311 he led his first raid into England.

The Scots raid came in the wake of Edward's withdrawal. Bruce crossed the Solway on 12 August and harried the lands of the Lord of Gillsland, burning the town of Haltwhistle and much of Tyndale before returning north with a large booty of cattle—'But he had killed few men,' so says the Lanercost chronicler, 'besides those who offered resistance.' Scarcely was Bruce back in Scotland than he returned on another raid, this time crossing the eastern march into Northumberland, advancing by way of Harbottle, Holystone and Redesdale as far south as Corbridge . . . 'burning the district and destroying everything, and causing more men to be killed than on the former occasion.' The raiders continued down the Tyne valley, causing even more destruction. The communities of Northumberland, left defenceless by their King, had had enough and negotiated a short truce which was to last until February 1312 for the high price of £2,000. These raids had been highly lucrative in both booty and blackmail, and were soon to become a regular part of the Scottish war economy. In the following year there were raids into County Durham, Cumberland and Westmorland. More blackmail was paid in an effort to avert economic chaos. The situation in the northern counties became so bad that normal life could only continue by permission of the Scots. County Durham alone bought immunity on no less than eight occasions between 1311 and 1327, and at a high price. In 1313 even the threat of a further raid was enough to cause many northern communities to 'make an offer'. Failure or delay in payment resulted in prompt reprisals. Arrears in payments from the people of Cumberland in April 1314 brought Edward Bruce into the county on a campaign of reprisal. The Scots were often joined in these incursions by groups of English freebooters, a sign of the breakdown of law and order in the north. The government of Edward II, too preoccupied with its own problems, was largely indifferent to the sufferings of the town and country people of the north, so long as the castles resisted attack. Even King Edward was obliged to accept the payment of blackmail by his subjects north of the Trent and Humber, and the draining of English wealth into Scotland. A dangerous precedent had been established, and the way was clear for some on the border to consider a separate peace with Scotland.

With the winds of fortune blowing so firmly in his favour Bruce was pleased to receive the accession to his cause of some former enemies. John Mentieth, the betrayer of Wallace, joined the King before the St Andrews Parliament. In 1312 David de Strathbogie, Earl of Atholl, decided to switch allegiance to Bruce. Not only was his earldom restored but he was further rewarded by being appointed Constable of Scotland, a post that had been held by Gilbert de la Haye, one of the King's most faithful followers, who willingly yielded to political necessity. Bruce was also gratified by the return to Scotland of his old friend and ally, William Lamberton of St Andrews. Lamberton was released from prison on parole in 1308, and acted for sometime as an emissary for Edward II, before being allowed to return home in 1312, in time to witness some of the most dramatic events in Scottish history.

In 1313 Edward Bruce began the siege of Stirling Castle, commanded by a Scot, Sir Philip Mowbray. Unable to make any headway he agreed to a pact with Mowbray. The governor was to be allowed to hold the castle unmolested for a year. If no relief came by midsummer 1314 he agreed to surrender. By this rash treaty Edward Bruce undermined the strategy and tactics his brother had been diligently pursuing for the past six years. He may have believed that he had bought a cheap victory; for it was now two years since an English army had come to Scotland, and Edward had so recently been on the verge of war with his barons after the murder of Piers Gaveston in the summer of 1312. Yet this was a challenge that could not be ignored in the same way that the bleeding of northern England had been. Stirling was of vital strategic importance and its loss would be a serious embarrassment. The time allowed in the Bruce-Mowbray pact was ample for Edward to gather a powerful army. King Robert rebuked the folly of his brother, but felt bound to honour terms agreed. Mowbray had a breathing space and looked forward to the summer of 1314. In England Edward and his barons reached an uneasy peace and made ready: for at last the fox was coming out of his hole.

CHAPTER 6
Bannockburn and Arbroath,
1314–1320

Edward came to Scotland in the high summer of 1314 with the notional aim of relieving Stirling Castle; the real purpose, of course, was to find and destroy the Scottish army in the field and thus end the war. England, for once, was largely united in this ambition, although it should be noted that some of Edward's greatest magnates and former enemies, headed by his cousin Thomas of Lancaster, did not attend in person, sending the minimum number of troops they were required to by feudal law. Even so, the force that left Berwick on 17 June 1314 was impressive: it comprised between two and three thousand horse and seventeen thousand foot, at least two or three times the size of the army Bruce had been able to gather. The King was accompanied by many seasoned campaigners of the Scottish wars, headed by the Earl of Pembroke and veterans like Henry Beaumont, Robert Clifford and Marmaduke Tweng. The most irreconcilable of Bruce's Scottish enemies also came: Ingram de Umfraville and his kinsman the Earl of Angus, as well as others of the MacDoualls, MacCanns and Comyns. Most poignant of all came Sir John Comyn of Badenoch, the only son of the Red Comyn, who had grown up in England and was now returning to Scotland to avenge his father. This was a grand feudal army, one of the last of its kind to leave England in the Middle Ages. King Robert awaited its arrival just south of Stirling near the Bannock Burn.

Edward's army marched rapidly towards Stirling to be there before Mowbray's agreement expired on 24 June. Edinburgh was reached on the 19th and by the 22nd it was at Falkirk, only 15 miles short of its objective. Edward's host followed the line of the old Roman road, which ran through an ancient forest known as the Tor Wood, over the Bannock Burn and into the New Park, a hunting preserve enclosed at the time of Alexander III. Bruce's army had been assembling in the Tor Wood, an area providing good natural cover, from the middle of May. On Saturday, 22 June, with his troops now organised into their respective commands, Bruce moved his army slightly to the north to the New Park, a more heavily wooded area, where his movements could be concealed and which would, if the occasion demanded, provide cover for a withdrawal.

Bruce's army, like Wallace's before him, was chiefly composed of infantry armed with long spears. It was divided into four divisions. Thomas Randolph, Earl of Moray, commanded the vanguard, which was stationed about a mile to the south of Stirling, near the church of St Ninians; while the King commanded the rearguard at the entrance to the New Park. His brother Edward led the third division. By hereditary right the fourth was headed by Walter Stewart, the son and heir of James the Stewart; but owing to his youth and inexperience the real command was in the hands of his cousin, James Douglas. Bruce also had a light cavalry force of some 500 men under Sir Robert Keith, which was to play a small but crucial role in the coming battle. The army numbered some 5,000 men in all, gathered from the whole of Scotland: knights and nobles, freemen and tenants, town dwellers and traders, all hand-picked and trained for their task.

Since he landed in Ayrshire in early 1307 Bruce had demonstrated time and again that he was willing to take risks; but he was far from reckless in the gambles he accepted. He had no intention of chancing all on the outcome of a day, as Wallace had at Falkirk. Almost to the last minute the King was prepared to withdraw. He was persuaded to remain by news of the poor state of morale in the English army. But undoubtedly the most important factor in convincing him to make a stand was the ground which lay before him.

The Bannock Burn, over which the English army had to cross on the way to Stirling, and its sister streams flowed over the Carse of Stirling, a flat area of soft, peaty earth, before joining the River Forth to the north-east. The area was so criss-crossed by small waterways that it was known at the time as 'The Pows' or 'Les Polles' from an old Gaelic word, *pol*, meaning 'an area of muddy streams'. With the trees of the New Park covering Bruce's army to the west, the only approach apart from the Pows to the east was directly over the old road from Falkirk to Stirling. If this rout, virtually the only solid ground on which heavy cavalry could deploy freely, were to be denied to the English, they would have no choice but to wheel right to the north-east, on to the boggy ground of the Carse. To force Edward to take this route Bruce adopted similar tactics to those he used at the Battle of Loudon Hill: both sides of the road were peppered with small pits or 'pots', each three feet deep and covered with brush, which would force the enemy to bunch towards the centre on a dangerously constricted front. Once on to the Carse the English army would be caught in a kind of natural vice, as the main action on 24 June was to show, with waterways and marshes to the north, east and south. Such natural advantages were not easily obtained, and were unlikely to occur again.

It was on the old road that the preliminary actions of the Battle of Bannockburn took place on Sunday 23 June. For the English things started to go wrong even before the first blow had been struck. Sir Philip Mowbray, the commander of Stirling Castle, who had observed Bruce's preparations on the road, appeared in Edward's camp early in the morning, and warned of the danger of approaching the Scots directly through the New Park. Mowbray also pointed out that that there was no need to force a battle, as Edward was now close enough to the castle to constitute a technical relief in terms of the agreement with Edward Bruce. But even if the King was disposed to act on Mowbray's advice, it was already too late; for he was showing signs of losing control of his formidable but unwieldy host.

The vanguard under the Earls of Gloucester and Hereford, appointed to joint command by Edward after a quarrel about who would take the lead, a compromise that satisfied no-one, were already closing in on the Scots from the south, advancing in the same reckless manner that had almost brought disaster at Falkirk. Following the line of the Roman road, they crossed the ford over the Bannock Burn towards King Robert's division at the opening to the New Park. There now occurred one of the most memorable episodes in Scottish history. Sir Henry de Bohun, nephew of the Earl of Hereford, was riding ahead of his companions when he caught sight of the Scottish King himself. De Bohun lowered his lance and began a charge which carried him out of history and into legend. King Robert was mounted on a light horse and armed only with a battle-axe. As de Bohun's great war-horse thundered towards him he stood his ground, watched with mounting anxiety by his own army. With the Englishman only feet away Bruce turned aside, stood in his stirrups and hit the knight so hard with his battle-axe that he split his helmet and head in two. This small incident became in a larger sense a symbol of the war itself: the one side heavily armed but lacking agility; the other highly mobile and quick to seize the advantage. Rebuked by his commanders for the enormous risk he had taken the King only expressed regret that he had broken the shaft of his axe. Enormously cheered by their King's heroic encounter his division rushed forward to engage the main English force. For the English, so says the *Vita Edwardi Secundi*, 'this was the beginning of their troubles'. After some fierce fighting, in which the Earl of Gloucester was knocked off his horse, the knights in the vanguard were forced to retreat back to the Tor Wood. The Scots, eager to pursue, were held back by the command of King Robert.

In the meantime, another English cavalry force under Robert Clifford and Henry Beaumont skirted the Scottish position to the east and rode towards Stirling, advancing as far as St Ninians. Bruce spotted the manœuvre and ordered Randolph's schiltron to intercept. The action Randolph engaged in was to be a sampler of the main battle fought on the following day: unsupported by archers the horsemen were unable to make any impression on the Scots spearmen, precisely what happened in the opening stages of Falkirk. But the difference now was that the schiltron had learnt mobility and how to keep formation at the same time. The English squadron was broken, some seeking the safety of the nearby castle, others fleeing back to the army. The captives included Sir Thomas Gray, whose son and namesake was later to base his account of the Battle of Bannockburn in his book the *Scalacronica* on his father's memories.

The buoyant mood amongst the Scots was only slightly dampened by later reports of the treachery of the Constable of Scotland—David de Strathbogie, Earl of Atholl. Strathbogie had formed an intense dislike of Edward Bruce, who seduced and then abandoned the earl's sister, and remembered he was the son-in-law of the Red Comyn. On his way south, supposedly to join King Robert and the rest of the Scottish army, he attacked Bruce's base camp at Cambuskenneth Abbey, killing the commander, Sir William Airth, and many of his men, before running off some of Bruce's supplies, and finally fleeing into permanent English exile. Strathbogie was later condemned as a traitor and his earldom was granted to Bruce's nephew, John Campbell, the son of his sister Mary and Sir Neil Campbell of Lochawe. The office of Constable reverted to Gilbert de la Haye of Errol.

• News of the day's defeats soon spread, causing considerable unease in the main body of the English army, still approaching Stirling from the south. The experience of the vanguard confirmed the intelligence brought to Edward by Sir Philip Mowbray: Bruce's preparations had made the direct approach to Stirling too hazardous. It was now late in the day. The army needed to rest and the horses had to be watered. Having failed in a frontal attack Edward made the worst decision of all: after consulting with his commanders he ordered the army to abandon the highway and cross the Bannock Burn to the east of the Scots in the New Park onto the firm but restricted ground between the Bannock and Pelstream burns, an area known as the Carse of Balquhiderock, where he made ready to spend the night of the 23–24 June. It was a prelude to disaster.

After knocking down houses to obtain materials for rudimentary bridges to help them across the streams of the Carse, the knights and at least part of the infantry took up position north of the Bannock Burn. With the marshy ground close to the waterways churned up under the hoofs of the horses, and fearful of a sudden Scottish attack, the army spent an uncomfortable and sleepless night preparing for the following day. Sir Thomas Gray describes the scene thus: 'The King's army . . . debouched upon a plain near the water of Forth beyond Bannockburn, an evil, deep wet marsh, where the said army unhorsed and remained all night, having sadly lost confidence and being much disaffected by the events of the day.' The general mood was so bad that King Edward ordered heralds to travel the camp, explaining that vanguard had only been involved in some unimportant skirmishing, and that victory was assured. News of the despondency in Edward's camp was brought to Bruce by Sir Alexander Seton, a Scots knight defecting from the English. Bruce had been heartened by the day's successes, but he was still on the verge of ordering a withdrawal westwards into the Lennox, where the terrain was too difficult for the English knights to follow, rather than take the risk of confronting the main enemy force, humbled but still immensely powerful. Seton's report helped him to change his mind. The King now made the most important decision in his life. He had defended his position well and learned much from Randolph's attack. He would neither withdraw nor would he wait for the enemy: when dawn came Scotland would take the offensive.

Not long after daybreak on 24 June 1314, Robert Bruce, King of Scots, ordered the most momentous advance in the nation's long history. Prior to this he rode amongst his troops, speaking words of encouragement, saying in Barbour's rhyming account:

> . . . that for our lives,
> And for our children, and our wives,
> And for our freedom, and our land,
> In battle we are forced to stand.

The spearmen moved steadily forward, resembling the ancient Macedonian phalanxes of Alexander the Great, towards the English, cramped in a narrow neck of land between the Forth to the north and the Bannock Burn to the south and east. The English soldiers were well accustomed to Scots guerrilla warfare, and while they had feared a sudden night attack, the last thing they expected was to see their enemy take the offensive in broad daylight. King Edward was most surprised of all to see Bruce's army emerge from out of the cover of the woods: 'And when the King of England saw the Scots thus take on hand to take the hard field so openly and upon foot, he had wonder and said, What! Will yon Scots fight?' As Bruce's army drew nearer they paused and knelt in prayer. Edward was even more amazed. 'They kneel to ask for mercy,' Barbour reports him as saying. Ingram de Umfraville, the former Guardian, who now stood by Edward's side, knew his fellow countrymen better. 'They ask for mercy', he replied 'but not from you. To God they pray, for them it's death or victory.'

Perceiving the danger of the English position both Umfraville and Gilbert de Clare, Earl of Gloucester, urged the King to delay giving battle. Edward promptly turned on Gloucester and accused him of cowardice. Angered by this taunt Gloucester mounted his horse and led the vanguard in a ruinous charge against the leading Scots division, commanded by Edward Bruce. The Earl, the last of the de Clares, was killed on the forest of Scottish spears. He died in the company of John Comyn of Badenoch, Sir Robert Clifford and many other prominent knights. King Robert ordered Randolph and Douglas forward in support of his brother, while he held his own division in reserve. The remaining English battalions were now so tightly confined that they had to bunch together in a single mass, with infantry impotently trapped behind the cavalry. The very size and strength of the great army was now proving to be a major liability. If Edward had been a bad king he was now showing himself to be a worse general. He must have heard his father talk many times of his triumph at Falkirk. But the archers who had enabled the cavalry to penetrate Wallace's schiltrons were now confined with the rest of the infantry. With casualties high and mounting Edward at last managed to deploy a company to the north of the Scots; but they were unsupported by cavalry or spearmen and were quickly driven off by the charge of Sir Robert Keith and the Scottish light horse, which Bruce had held back for just such an eventuality. The bowmen fled back in panic to their own lines, only to be beaten up by their comrades.

Bruce now committed his own division to an inexorable and bloody push into the disorganised English ranks. The King's schiltron was the flower of Gaelic Scotland, bringing together the men of Carrick in the south to the men of Argyll and the Isles in the north, many under the command of Angus Og, who had offered Bruce much needed help in the desperate summer of 1306. They joined a battle that had reached its climax. All the reserves were now committed; the whole Scots army was now fighting side by side across a single front. A small force of Scottish archers added to the panic and misery in Edward's army, which was now so tightly packed that if a man fell he was immediately crushed underfoot. The knights began to give ground as the rear ranks did their best to escape back across the Bannock Burn. With the English ranks beginning to break a great shout went up from the Scots, who hitherto had fought in grim silence—'Lay on! Lay on! Lay on! They fail.' This cry was heard by Bruce's camp followers, the poor folk of Scotland, who had been at the rear with the baggage on Coxet Hill. They promptly gathered weapons and banners and charged forward, shouting 'Upon them now! They shall all die!' To the English army, already failing, this appeared like a fresh reserve and they lost all hope. The end had come and Edward, whose personal bravery in battle had done nothing to make up for his fatal mistakes, was forcibly taken from the field by the Earl of Pembroke aided by Giles d' Argentan and the rest of his personal bodyguard. Once the King was free from immediate danger d' Argentan—called 'the third best knight in Christendom'—returned to the battlefield to meet death with honour.

Edward's enforced flight ended the remaining order in the army; panic spread and defeat turned into a rout. In trying to recross the Bannock Burn the English suffered their greatest casualties. The *Lanercost Chronicle* says: 'many nobles and others fell into it with their horses in the crush, while others escaped with much difficulty, and many men were never able to extricate themselves from the ditch' Just to the north the King arrived with his bodyguard at the gates of Stirling Castle seeking refuge, only to be refused entry by Sir Philip Mowbray, who was now compelled to surrender by his agreement with Edward Bruce. Edward, in the company of Henry Beaumont, managed to circle round the victorious Scots to the west, escaping to the south and east with James Douglas in close pursuit. He eventually arrived at Dunbar Castle, where he was admitted by his ally Earl Patrick, the son of the man who fought under the banner of Edward I. From there he took ship to England, ready to face the silent contempt of Thomas of Lancaster and all those who remained safely at home.

From the carnage of Bannockburn the rest of the army escaped as best they could. Sir Marmaduke Tweng remained in hiding until the following day, when he surrendered in person to King Robert. The Earl of Pembroke, acting with considerable coolness, managed to take charge of a large body of frightened Welsh infantry, leading them across the border to safety. Many others were attacked and killed by the country people as they fled south. Scotland had won the greatest triumph in her history; England had experienced one of her worst defeats. The author of the *Vita Edwardi Secundi* laments: 'O famous race unconquered through the ages, why do you who used to conquer knights, flee from mere footmen? At Berwick, Dunbar and Falkirk you carried off the victory, and now you flee from the infantry of the Scots . . . the hand of the Lord was not with you.' Bannockburn had joined the earlier battle at Courtrai as a milestone towards a new age in warfare. Their example was to be followed in the next year when the Swiss defeated the Austrian knights at the Battle of Morgarten. In his *History of the English Speaking Peoples* Sir Winston Churchill says of the Battle of Bannockburn: 'No more grievous slaughter of English chivalry ever took place in a single day. Even Towton in the Wars of the Roses was less destructive. The Scots . . . feat in virtually destroying an army of cavalry and archers by the agency of spearmen must . . . be deemed a prodigy of War.' The long day of feudal cavalry was over; thirty years later the English took this lesson to France.

After the battle Stirling Castle capitulated and its defences were razed. Philip Mowbray entered Robert's service, and proved himself to be a loyal lieutenant. The Earl of Hereford, fleeing from the battlefield, took refuge in Bothwell Castle, along with the Earl of Angus, Sir John de Seagrave, Sir Anthony de Lucy, Ingram de Umfraville, Maurice of Berkley and others, only to fall captive to Bruce when it was promptly surrendered to Edward Bruce by its commander, Walter FitzGilbert. Hereford was a particularly valuable captive. Robert was able to exchange him for his queen, Elizabeth de Burgh, his daughter Marjory and his sister Christian. His other sister, Mary, had been released in a prisoner exchange some two years before. Donald, Earl of Mar, Bruce's nephew and former ward, was also given the chance to return to Scotland, but he preferred to remain in England, having formed a close personal attachment to Edward II. There is no mention in the exchange of Henry Beaumont's captive, Isabel of Buchan, to whom Bruce owed so much, and she must be presumed to have died some time prior to this. Bruce also obtained the release of Robert Wishart, now blind from his long years in English prisons. The gallant old bishop died a free man in a free Scotland in November 1316. The other captives were held to ransom, although Bruce was prepared to show considerable generosity towards his defeated enemies. Sir Marmaduke Tweng was allowed to go home without ransom, as was Ralph de Monthermer, step-father of the dead Earl of Gloucester. Bruce spent a night of silent vigil over the body of Gloucester, his cousin, before sending his remains and those of Robert Clifford home to their families for burial.

In the November after the battle the Scots Parliament met at Cambuskenneth Abbey and passed sentence of forfeiture on all who held land in Scotland but continued to fight against the King. Thus ended the 'aristocratic international' which had been a feature of feudal Britain since the time of Henry I of England and David I of Scotland. Landowners could no longer have divided political loyalties: they had to choose one side or the other. The new class of 'disinherited' were men on the English side, usually with Comyn and Balliol associations, who refused to accept the new realities; men, in other words, who wished to remain loyal to the King of England but continue to hold estates and titles in Scotland. Chief amongst the disinherited was Henry Beaumont, who escaped from Bannockburn along with King Edward, who laid claim to the earldom of Buchan in right of his wife, Alice Comyn. The leading Scot to be disinherited was David de Strathbogie, the former Earl of Atholl. Strathbogie never made his peace with King Robert, and died in exile in 1327. His son, also called David, grandson of the Red Comyn, laid claim to the earldom of Atholl, as well as part of John Comyn's Lochaber lands in right of his mother, Joan Comyn. Beaumont and Strathbogie were later to find common cause under the banner of Edward Balliol.

Few battles in history are truly decisive, and Bannockburn was no exception to this general rule. The war was nowhere near an end; for King Edward, who had none of his father's skill and all of his stubborn pride, refused to recognise the country's independence or Bruce's royal title. But it certainly resolved the issue in Scotland itself, for as the *Lanercost Chronicle* states: 'After the aforesaid victory Robert de Brus was commonly called King of Scotland by all men, because he had acquired Scotland by force of arms.' Even old enemies like Patrick de Dunbar, Earl of March, hurried to make their peace with the victorious king. Notwithstanding the fact that he had robbed the King of his greatest prize when he assisted the flight of Edward II, March was graciously received and repaid the King with loyal service.

With the country almost completely free of the English and their allies, King Robert had time to turn his attention to pressing political matters, chief amongst which was the question of the succession. Parliament met at Ayr in April 1315 to settle this important matter. As yet the King had no legitimate male heir. The times were considered too dangerous to allow the succession to pass to his daughter Marjory, now betrothed to Walter Stewart. Marjory agreed to waive her rights to the throne in favour of her uncle, Edward Bruce. If Robert died without a male heir the crown would pass to Edward and his male heirs. Failing this the succession would revert to Marjory and her male heirs. The Earl of Moray was named as regent if the crown should fall to a minor. With this settled Robert turned once more to the further prosecution of the war.

The disaster at Bannockburn once again exposed northern England to attack; and a war that previously had swept as far north as the shores of the Moray Firth was now carried as far south as the gates of York. Virtually unmolested Bruce and his lieutenants raided Cumberland, Northumberland, Durham, Westmorland, Lancashire and Yorkshire. The raiders came mounted on small horses designed to give them maximum mobility. All fighting, however, was done on foot. These small horses were called hobins, and from them the raiders acquired the name of 'hobelars'. Hobins and hobelars caused as much confusion and anxiety in the north of England as the Viking longships had in the ninth century. Scots tactics also became bolder, and lightning attacks were made against strongholds. Bruce attempted to take Carlisle in the summer of 1315, building a few siege engines for the purpose; but the town was ably defended by its commander, Andrew Harclay, and the Scots were forced to withdraw. Despite the misery and economic hardship caused by these incessant raids the heart of English power lay beyond the reach of the Scots south of the Humber, and Edward did nothing either to defend the north or to end the war. Clearly more drastic measures were required.

For the Lion

Since the time of Henry II the kings of England had also claimed to be lords of Ireland. English settlers had taken roots in Ireland, chiefly along the eastern seaboard north and south of Dublin. But the native Gaelic chieftains still enjoyed a large measure of autonomy, especially in the north and west, and English control was often of a fluctuating nature. With the opening of the Wars of Independence Edward I had made heavy demands on the Irish for both men and materials, pushing the country close to the point of financial ruin. King Robert, who long maintained political and personal contacts with the men of Ulster, decided to exploit Irish discontent to open a second front against England. He sent envoys to the native Irish kings and clergy with letters invoking the common ancestry of the two nations and offering to help them recover their liberty. A response was received from the O'Neils of Ulster, asking for aid against the English and offering the crown of the High Kings of Ireland, hardly theirs to give, to his brother, Edward Bruce. It might be thought that this was a perilously narrow base for a new military adventure; for as always in Gaelic politics, the enemies of the O'Neils would be bound to be friends of the English; but it was enough for the aims King Robert had in mind. Edward Bruce and Thomas Randolph of Moray landed with an expeditionary force at Larne near Carrickfergus Castle on 25 May 1315, ready to conjure up the spirit of the 'Celtic International'.

Edward Bruce was joined by a number of the local chieftains and won some early successes against the Anglo-Irish aristocracy. He won his first engagement at the Moiry Pass in Armagh and sacked Dundalk on 29 June. Bruce was able to exploit disputes between his two leading opponents—the Earl of Ulster and Edmund Butler, the Justiciar of Ireland—and defeat them in a piecemeal fashion. The Earl of Ulster, King Robert's father-in-law, was routed at Connor in County Antrim on 10 September, after which the Ulster English fled to the safety of Carrickfergus Castle, where they were besieged. Roger Mortimer of Wigmore was defeated at Kenlis towards the end of December; and Edmund Butler was routed at the Battle of Skerries in Kildare on 1 February 1316. Edward Bruce was confident enough to be crowned as High King of Ireland at the hill of Maledon near Dundalk on the 2 May 1316.

Edward Bruce's successes in Ireland raised the threat of a grand Celtic rising against the English, and a possible Scots invasion of Wales from across the Irish Sea. King Robert had recaptured the Isle of Man from the English after Bannockburn; and although it

72

was retaken by his old enemy, John of Lorne, to whom Edward had given the grand title of Admiral of the Western Seas, it was recovered once more in 1317 and remained in Scots hands until 1333. Scots privateers under the command of Thomas Dun attacked English shipping in Holyhead and raided Anglesey. The abortive rising of the Welsh under Llewelyn Bren may have helped to give some colour to the rumour of a Scots invasion. But shortage of resources and the re-establishment of English naval supremacy in the Irish Sea made this a highly unlikely prospect.

Although King Robert came to Ireland himself in early 1317, to assist his brother in a royal progress round the island, the whole episode was becoming an expensive and rather pointless side-show. Apart from defeating the Red Earl of Ulster once more—who was soon suspected of treachery because of his family connection with the Bruces—the progress round the island achieved very little. Apart from the O'Neils of Ulster few of the native Irish were prepared to support the High King, preferring to concentrate on clan feuds. Bad weather had also brought famine to Ireland and the rest of western Europe at this time, and war simply added to the misery. King Robert only remained until May, when he returned to Scotland with the Earl of Moray, having made no progress in the face of English intransigence and Irish indifference. Edward Bruce was left to manage as best he could on his own.

Edward Bruce continued to try to enforce his authority, but was soon drawn down by the treacherous quicksands of native Irish politics. The supposed kinship between the Celts failed to material-ise to any significant degree, and for most Irish the Normanised Scots were little better, if not worse, than the English settlers with whom they were familiar. A Connaught tract of this time refers to 'Scottish foreigners less noble than our own foreigners.' Edward Bruce's control was limited to the north, and the threat he posed to English power finally ended when he was killed in battle at Faughart near Dundalk in October 1318 by an Anglo-Irish force led by John de Bermingham. The death of King Robert's brother enabled the English to inflict their last indignity on the Bruce family: Edward's body was beheaded and quartered. The quarters were sent to the four principal towns of Ireland and the head to Edward II. De Bermingham was named Earl of Louth by the grateful King. The treatment of Edward Bruce's remains invites contrast with that accorded by King Robert to the dead Gloucester. But the native Irish, who on the whole failed to rise above their petty quarrels, were glad that the day of the High King had come to an end. By way of obituary the Irish Annals say of him that he:

> was the common ruin of the Gaels and Galls of Ireland . . . never was a better deed done for the Irish than this . . . For in this Bruce's time, for three years and a half, falsehood and famine and homicide filled the country, and undoubtedly men ate each other in Ireland.

Although Edward Bruce's enterprise was a failure, English power in Ireland had been severely weakened in the time he spent on the island. Over the rest of the Middle Ages English domination steadily shrunk to little more than the Pale of Settlement around Dublin; and it wasn't until the time of Henry VIII that it began to expand again.

The death of Edward Bruce required a new Act of Succession. The King's daughter, Marjory, who had been killed in an accidental fall from her horse in March 1316, had left a baby son, Robert Stewart. On the 3 December 1318 Parliament assembled at Scone and settled the succession on the infant Robert should his grandfather die without a male heir. Once again Randolph was named as Guardian for the period of any royal minority. In the event of his death the guardianship of the kingdom was to pass to Sir James Douglas. Bruce's grandson was destined to become the first of the Stewart kings of Scotland; but it was to be over fifty years before he was able to claim his inheritance.

The border war had not been neglected during the Irish episode. James Douglas continued to be active, winning a number of engagements against the English in 1316, including an important one at Skaithmuir near Coldstream, and was named Lieutenant of Scotland when the King and Randolph went to Ireland. Goaded beyond endurance, and frustrated by the indifference or impotence of their King, a group of north-country Englishmen organised their own seaborne attack on Scotland. Ships were assembled on the Humber to carry their little army to the shores of Fife. The local militia were frightened off, but the attempted invasion was beaten back when William Sinclair, the Bishop of Dunkeld, took to horse and led the militia back into battle. Sinclair's heroism was especially commended by Bruce and earned him the appellation of 'the King's Bishop.' An attempt by Thomas, Earl of Lancaster, now the leading figure in the English government, to organise an 'official' invasion in 1316 came to nothing when Edward refused to participate, in revenge for Lancaster's conduct during the Bannockburn campaign.

By early 1318 Berwick was the only Scottish stronghold left under English control. Bruce started to lay siege to this important strategic centre shortly after Bannockburn; but the walls built since the time of Edward I were too strong, and the town resisted all attempts at capture. By the beginning of 1316, however, the Scots blockade had brought the inhabitants close to starvation, and it is reported that they were reduced to consuming the flesh of dying horses. Supply ships were intercepted by John Crabb and other Flemish privateers in the pay of the Scots. If the men of Berwick looked south in hope of catching sight of a relief army they were disappointed, for none ever came. Even so, fresh supplies must have got through, because the continuing resistance forced Robert to begin the construction of siege engines in December 1317. But it was treachery, not bombardment, that led to the fall of Berwick. Piers of Spalding, an English burgess, had been insulted by the commander of the garrison. In revenge he assisted an assault party led by James Douglas and Thomas Randolph over a section of the wall he was guarding on the night of 1 April 1318. After a battle through the streets the Scots managed to gain control of the town. The castle was starved into submission some weeks later. Spalding was given an estate in Angus as a reward by the grateful Bruce; as far away as possible, one assumes, from the revenge of the English marchmen.

The borders of 1296 had now been restored. Contrary to his usual policy Bruce did not order the destruction of Berwick's defences, because of the military and economic importance of the town and its close proximity to the English border. The reasoning behind this decision is understandable, but in time to come Berwick became Scotland's Achilles Heel, when the direction of the country's affairs was in the hands of less skilful men. Bruce was fully aware of the risk he was taking and set about improving the town's defences. He appointed his son-in-law, Walter Stewart, in whom he had considerable confidence, as warden of both the town and castle. Stewart summoned his friends and followers to assist him. He also recruited John Crabb, a skilled military engineer as well as a pirate.

The capture of Berwick was clearly a challenge that the English could not ignore. Rather than wait for his enemies to respond, King Robert followed up his success by leading yet another punishing raid into northern England. The castles at Harbottle, Wark and Mitford in Northumberland were all captured. Facing little opposition, the raiders moved south into Yorkshire. Northallerton, Boroughbridge and Knaresborough were all consumed by fire.

Ripon was only spared after the citizens promised to pay a considerable sum in blackmail. When the raiders returned north they took with them a large quantity of livestock as booty. In impotent frustration William Melton, the Archbishop of York, once more proclaimed sentence of excommunication against Robert Bruce.

The fall of Berwick had a sobering effect on King Edward and his magnates. Amyer de Valence managed to arrange a temporary reconciliation between the King and his chief opponent, Earl Thomas of Lancaster. In a spirit of artificial harmony king and earl came north together with a sizeable army in the summer of 1319 to retake the town. Queen Isabella accompanied Edward as far as York. Vigorous assaults were made on Berwick by land and sea, but Walter Stewart, ably assisted by John Crabb, conducted a heroic defence, beating back all attacks. However, he could not be expected to hold out indefinitely. King Robert had no intention of leading a direct attack on the powerful English army, which in Barbour's words 'might well turn to folly'. Rather, he supported the Stewart by ordering Douglas and Randolph to lead a large force of hobelars on a diversionary raid into Yorkshire. It was rumoured that one of the aims of this raid was the capture of Queen Isabella in York. As the Scots approached the town Isabella was quickly sent south by water, taking refuge at Nottingham. Because there were no troops in the area to face Douglas and Randolph the Archbishop of York hastily improvised a militia of townsmen, priests and monks, perhaps hoping to emulate the exploits of his illustrious predecessor Archbishop Thurstan at the Battle of the Standard. From the gates of York Melton's homeguard advanced bravely to intercept the battle-hardened Scots. The outcome was inevitable. When the two forces met at Myton-on-Swale on 20 September 1319 the men of York were cut to pieces. Yorkshire was now totally undefended and at the mercy of the Scots. News of the 'Chapter of Myton', so called because of the large number of clergy slain, caused serious disputes in the English army at Berwick. Edward and the southerners wanted to continue the siege; but Lancaster and the northerners, anxious to defend their homes, refused to remain. With a third of his army gone Edward had no choice but to abandon the siege of Berwick.

The campaign had been another fiasco, and England was more divided than ever. It was widely rumoured that Lancaster was guilty of treason—the raiders appeared to exempt his lands from destruction—and the King's new favourite, Hugh Despenser the elder, alleged that he told the Scots of the Queen's presence in York. Edward was now closer than ever to open conflict with his baronial enemies. To make matters worse, no sooner had the army disbanded than Douglas came back over the border and carried out a destructive raid in Cumberland and Westmorland. The King had little option but to ask Bruce for a two-year truce, which was granted shortly before Christmas. Embittered by his repeated failures against the Scots, and with his arms now at rest, Edward persuaded the Pope to take up the offensive on his behalf.

Ever since the murder of John Comyn the Holy See had been distrustful of Robert Bruce and his rebel bishops. Sentence of excommunication had been repeated at intervals against Bruce and his followers. When Clement V died in 1316 the new Pope, John XXII, was keen to launch a crusade. Edward's representatives told him that only the intransigence of the Scots 'rebels' prevented England giving its full support to the venture. In response John issued a bull, *Vocatis Nobis*, commanding England and Scotland to accept a two-year truce. Two cardinals, the Bishop of Corbeil and the Archdeacon of Perpignan, were appointed to carry John's letter to the Scots. Robert received the envoys with grace and good humour, but refused to accept correspondence addressed to 'the noble Robert Bruce, acting as King of Scots' on the grounds that there were other men of this name in Scotland, and it would be wrong to open letters that might be intended for them. The envoys tried to side-step this difficulty by arguing that the Pope could not be seen to take sides in the struggle by recognising Bruce as King. Robert demolished this assertion, saying that the Pope and the church of Rome were in fact taking sides by addressing Edward II as King while continuing to deny him the same title. 'If you had brought letters in this manner to other kings', Bruce continued 'you might well have received a more savage reply.' The Cardinals were forced to return to Pope John with their mission unfulfilled.

Already angry at the failure of King Robert and the Scottish church to obey papal decrees the Pope was only to willing to participate in Edward's schemes, attacking the rebel bishops of a rebel king. In November 1319, shortly before Bruce agreed to the English truce proposal, Pope John summoned the bishops of St Andrews, Dunkeld, Aberdeen and Moray to appear before him at Avignon to give an account of the situation in Scotland. When they ignored the summons they were all excommunicated as, once again, was King Robert, whom the Pope now addressed as 'Governor'. In place of the bishops, Pope John was sent one of the most stirring manifestos of all time—the Declaration of Arbroath.

The Declaration takes the form of a letter addressed to the Pope and issued from the Abbey of Arbroath in April 1320. The authorship is unknown, but it is thought to have been drafted by the Abbot of Arbroath, Bernard of Linton, who was also the King's chancellor. In it the community of Scotland declares its loyalty to King Robert who 'endured every peril to rescue his people and inheritance out of the hands of the enemy'. The letter continues, 'To him in defence of our liberty we are bound to adhere'. But the pursuit of freedom transcended even the particular cause of King Robert, for

> if he should give up what he has begun, and agree to make us or kingdom subject to the King of England or the English, we should exert ourselves at once and drive him out as our enemy and a subverter of his own rights and ours, and make some other man who was well able to defend us our King; for, as long as one hundred of us remain alive, never will we on any conditions be brought under English rule. It is not for glory, nor riches, nor honours that we are fighting, but for freedom alone, which no honest man gives up but with his life.

King Robert's own son and successor, David, would one day come to learn the meaning of these brave words. It most certainly caused the Pope to pause in reflection; for shortly after he received it he recommended that Edward and Robert make a final peace. He also bestowed on Bruce the elevated but ambiguous title of 'Regent of the Kingdom of Scotland'. This only postponed the inevitable, and in 1324 he finally recognised him as King.

CHAPTER 7
Northampton, 1321–1329

As the truce of 1319 drew to a close the political situation in England was explosive. In December 1321 Lancaster was ready to take up arms against the King and his favourites, the Despensers. Rumours of treason now took on flesh as the rebel earl sent his agents to James Douglas and the Earl of Moray to negotiate an alliance between Scotland and the English baronial opposition. It seems unlikely that Bruce had much confidence in Lancaster, who referred to himself as 'King Arthur' in his negotiations with the Scots, but he was quick to take advantage of the threat of civil war in England. Scarcely had the truce expired in January 1322 than Douglas, Moray and Walter Stewart came over the border on a large-scale attack on the north east. The three commanders fanned out across the region: Douglas to Hartlepool, Moray to Darlington and the Stewart to Richmond. Lancaster with his army at Pontefract did nothing to stop them.

With royal power in the north threatening to disintegrate completely Andrew Harclay, the governor of Carlisle, came south to meet Edward, who was coming north in the hope of destroying the hated Lancaster. Harclay urged immediate action against the Scots; but Edward decided that the attack on Lancaster and his allies took priority. In reply to Harclay the *Vita Edwardi Secundi* reports the King as saying: 'You may know for certain, Andrew, that if Robert Bruce threatens me from behind, and my own men, who have committed such enormities against me, should appear in front, I would attack the traitors and leave Robert Bruce alone.' Harclay returned with orders to raise the levies of Cumberland and Westmorland and intercept the rebels before they joined with the Scots.

When Lancaster and his associates the Earl of Hereford, Sir Robert Clifford and John Moubray left Pontefract and moved north to escape the King they were intercepted on 16 March by Harclay, who had taken up position at the bridge across the River Ure at Boroughbridge. Lancaster had to force this passage before linking up with the Scots, or risk being caught between Harclay and Edward, advancing rapidly from the south. There now followed one of the seminal battles of English military history, whose importance has often been overlooked. Harclay showed himself to be a brilliant student of the lessons of the Scottish wars. He protected the bridge with a body of spearmen arranged in the Scottish schiltron fashion, while the nearby ford was covered by archers. His force was all on foot and made ready to meet the rebels in a defensive position. Hereford led the direct attack on the bridge, while Lancaster attempted to outflank Harclay by leading his cavalry across the ford. Hereford was killed by a spearman and Clifford was wounded and captured, after which the attempt to clear a passage across the bridge was abandoned. Lancaster fared no better at the ford, where his horsemen were 'cut up by a shower of arrows.' The attack was abandoned, and the following day, with much of his force deserting, he surrendered to Harclay. He was taken to Edward at Pontefract and executed without trial, in much the same way as Piers Gaveston in 1312. Clifford and Moubray were also condemned as traitors. Meanwhile, the Scots raiders slipped back across the border.

Harclay had defeated the rebel earls using a skilful combination of infantry, dismounted men-at-arms and archers. The Battle of Boroughbridge therefore marks an important departure in English battle tactics, which hitherto had been based on the mass charge of heavily armoured knights. It was to be ten years, though, before this success was repeated, when the new tactics were used in a fully evolved form at the Battle of Dupplin Moor. Harclay also deserves the credit of being the first Englishman to make extensive use of the hobelar. He was rewarded by a King grateful for the seldom tasted prestige of victory by being named Earl of Carlisle and Warden of the Marches.

Boroughbridge was a new beginning for Edward. The tactics had been Harclay's, but the strategy had been his. The baronial opposition had been defeated and tainted with treason; the King had at last enjoyed his long awaited revenge for the murder of his beloved Piers. This was the high point of his reign, and, emboldened by this rare triumph, he decided to embark on what was to be his last invasion of Scotland. It was to be a disaster. Edward seems to have learned nothing from the Battle of Boroughbridge. He abandoned Harclay's use of mounted archers and summoned an army of cavalry and foot spearmen.

While Edward's army gathered at Newcastle King Robert, together with James Douglas and the Earl of Moray, entered England on 1 July with a new raiding party, advancing deep into the undefended counties in the west. The raiders rode through Cumberland, crossing the Duddon Sands into Furness. At Furness Abbey the abbot bought immunity. The raiders continued to use the sands at low tide, crossing into the heart of Lancashire, setting fire to both Lancaster and Preston, before recrossing the border on 24 July in time to prepare for Edward's invasion.

By the time Edward was ready to begin his advance in early August Bruce was more than ready. He adopted the same tactics Wallace had in 1298: crops were destroyed and livestock removed. In all of Lothian the English are said only to have found one lame cow, causing the Earl of Surrey to remark 'This is the dearest beef I ever saw.' But unlike 1298 the Scots army was withdrawn over the Forth, to Culross in Fife, well beyond the reach of the English. Thomas Gray describes the campaign thus:

> The King marched upon Edinburgh, where at Leith there came such a sickness and famine upon the common soldiers of that great army, that they were forced to beat a retreat for want of food; at which time the King's light horsemen were defeated by James de Douglas. None dared leave the main body to seek food by forage, so greatly were the English harassed and worn out by fighting that before they arrived at Newcastle there was such a murrain in the army for want of food, that they were obliged of necessity to disband.

Beyond the destruction of Holyrood Abbey near Edinburgh the invasion had achieved precisely nothing. More seriously, the effect on national morale of the ignominious retreat of a starving army was almost as bad as the defeat at Bannockburn. Worse was to follow; for, as always, Edward's retreat was a signal for yet another Scottish attack.

Bruce crossed the Solway to the west soon after Edward returned to England. The boldness and speed of the Scots raid soon exposed the King to danger, even in his own land. Edward had taken up residence at Rievaulx Abbey in Yorkshire with Queen Isabella, when the Scots approached from the north-west in mid-October. Their progress was blocked by a powerful English force led by John of Brittany, Earl of Richmond, on Scawton Moor, between Rievaulx and its sister abbey at Byland. To dislodge him from his strong position on the high ground Bruce employed similar tactics to those used against John of Lorne at the Battle of the Pass of Brander. As Moray and Douglas charged uphill a party of Highlanders climbed up the cliffs on the English flank and attacked Richmond in the rear. Resistance soon crumbled and the Battle of Old Byland turned

81

into a rout. Richmond himself was made prisoner, as were Henry de Sully, Grand Butler of France, Sir Ralph Cobham—'the best knight in England'—and Sir Thomas Ughtred. Edward, 'ever chicken hearted and luckless in war', was forced to make a rapid and undignified exit from Rievaulx, fleeing in such haste that all his personal belongings were left behind. Edward ran to the safety of York, while Queen Isabella took ship at Tynemouth despite the roughness of the weather, the second time in three years a queen of England had been forced to take to her heels. Edward had now drunk the cup of humiliation down to the sourest dregs. 'After Byland', says Sir Thomas Grey 'Scots were so fierce and their chiefs so daring, and the English so cowed, that it was no otherwise between them than as a hare before greyhounds.'

The defeat at Old Byland left northern England almost completely defenceless. With their impotent King stubbornly refusing to make peace, many northern communities hurried to make their own private agreements with the Scots. With the permission of Archbishop Melton the monks of Bridlington opened negotiations to secure immunity from attack. Their example was followed by Henry Beaumont's brother, Louis de Beaumont, the Bishop of Durham. The heads of many other religious foundations were also given permission to make private treaties. But by far the most damaging to Edward's prestige was the approach to the Scots made by Andrew Harclay, the new Earl of Carlisle, because Harclay sought peace rather than simple immunity. Harclay's overtures to Bruce were the result of a simple observation. In the words of the *Lanercost Chronicle*: 'the said Earl of Carlisle perceived that the King of England neither knew how to rule his realm nor was able to defend it.'

Harclay made a secret visit to Bruce at Lochmaben Castle in January 1323, and negotiated a draft peace treaty. The document bears a strong resemblance to the official treaty of 1328: Bruce was to be recognised as King of Scotland, free from any claim of English supremacy; the Scots would pay an indemnity of £27,000, the approximate value, one assumes, of the blackmail extorted from northern England since 1311; a marriage would be arranged between Bruce's heir and a leading member of the English royal family; and there would be no restoration of the disinherited in either realm. This was the basis of a national agreement, which Harclay promised to put to King Edward; but he also allowed for some private insurance by including a clause allowing for the protection of his own estates in the event of further Scottish raids. Harclay's negotiations were no more than a recognition of political reality; unfortunately for him, they were also treasonable.

When Edward learned of the draft agreement he was incensed. Harclay was arrested, tried and condemned as a traitor. Yet Edward had nothing with which to counter the Bruce-Harclay talks. He was now almost completely discredited, and while he doggedly refused to recognise Bruce as King, he had no alternative but to open up his own negotiations with the Scots, which concluded with both sides agreeing to a thirteen-year truce in May 1323. When the matter was discussed in council at Bishopthorpe near York Henry Beaumont, hitherto one of Edward's closest associates, argued against the acceptance of any truce which disregarded the claims of the disinherited, for whom he was now the leading spokesman. Edward overruled Beaumont and the two quarrelled. Beaumont retired from the court to continue his intrigues in exile, eventually joining forces with Edward's estranged wife Isabella and her lover Roger Mortimer, Lord of Wigmore. The long truce was welcomed as a much-needed breathing space for both countries, for the economies of northern England and southern Scotland had both suffered grievously over the preceding years. However, it settled none of the outstanding issues between the two nations and only postponed the final reckoning. Talks held at York in November 1324 to secure a final peace came to nothing because Edward could not accept that Bruce was King of an independent Scotland.

Despite his quarrel with Beaumont, Edward did not altogether abandon the disinherited card. Angered by the Pope's recognition of Bruce as King in early 1324 Edward drew virtually the last arrow from his quiver. In July and again in August 1324 he commanded the long-forgotten Edward Balliol to come to England from his ancestral estates in France, where he appears to have been living in obscure retirement since 1320. The exact purpose of this visit is unknown, and nothing came of it. At the very least Edward is likely to have seen in Balliol a way of weakening Bruce's hold on Scotland: if he was not able to defeat him by force of arms, he might well be able to challenge his legitimacy. That Bruce's kingship was not beyond such a challenge had been shown by a shadowy attempt to replace him in Scotland in 1320 with William de Soules, the grand nephew of the former Guardian, who had Comyn associations. In any event, this was a game that was only to be played out in the succeeding reigns in both England and Scotland.

The invitation to Balliol must have appeared as an ominous foretaste of future English intentions. King Robert's marriage had been fruitless for many years, but in March 1324 Queen Elizabeth finally gave birth to a son called David in memory of King David I, who had invited the Bruce family to Scotland many years before. Bruce was more anxious than ever to strengthen the security of the realm and to secure an uncontested succession. In 1326 the Franco-Scottish alliance was renewed with King Charles IV at Corbeil, and Scotland linked its fate to one of the great European powers. Strong diplomatic representations were also made to secure full papal recognition: the excommunication on Bruce was finally lifted in 1328, and in the following year Pope John issued a bull authorising the crowning and anointing of Bruce and his successors as kings of Scotland. This came too late for Robert; but his son David was to be the first monarch in Scottish history to receive at his coronation the full honours of medieval kingship.

The truce of 1323 ended sooner than anyone expected, and in a fashion that no-one can have anticipated. In the years after Boroughbridge Edward steadily squandered all the advantages he gained by the destruction of Lancaster and his party. Having learned nothing from the case of Piers Gaveston, he elevated his favourites the Despensers, both father and son, beyond all reasonable bounds. Inevitably such conduct incited the hatred of the remaining magnates, especially on the Welsh marches, where the Despensers were attempting to build up a power base. But fatally for them, and for the King, it also incited the hatred of Queen Isabella, who had long despised Edward's homosexual friends.

In 1325 the Queen was sent on a diplomatic mission to her brother, King Charles IV. While in France she formed a secret relationship with Roger Mortimer of Wigmore, an enemy of the Despensers, who had been in exile since 1323. Isabella then arranged for the heir to the throne, her twelve year-old-son, Edward of Windsor, to come to France to do homage on behalf of his father for the Duchy of Aquitaine. With the young Prince under her control the Queen soon declared that she would not return to England so long as the hated Despensers remained in power. Assisted by Roger Mortimer, now openly displayed as her lover, and other noble exiles, Isabella planned to invade England and remove the Despensers by force. King Charles, conventional enough to be shocked by his sister's relationship with Mortimer, refused to participate in her schemes, but she obtained the help of the Count of Hainault, after agreeing to the marriage of his daughter, Philippa, and Prince Edward. The Queen and Mortimer recruited a small army and sailed for England in September 1326, landing at Orwell on the Suffolk coast.

Isabella and Mortimer were taking a great chance coming to England, for the force at their disposal was extremely modest; but they were clearly well aware of the mood of the country: almost no one, it turned out, was prepared to fight for Edward and the Despensers. London declared for the Queen, and a mob killed Walter Stapledon, the Bishop of Exeter, one of Edward's last remaining supporters. The King was forced to flee to the west with the Despensers and his few friends, who included Donald of Mar, hotly pursued by the vengeful Queen. Edward and the Despensers were soon captured. The Despensers were executed, while Edward was imprisoned in Kenilworth Castle, and forced to abdicate in January 1327 in favour of his young son. Donald of Mar escaped back to Scotland, where he was graciously received by his uncle, who immediately restored his earldom and allowed him to plot the restoration of Edward II.

From Kenilworth Edward was moved to the dungeons of Berkeley Castle where he was murdered in September 1327. Edward II failed both as a king and as a soldier; but he was in many ways a deeply unfortunate rather than an unsympathetic figure. He was called to a role in life that he had not been prepared for and was totally unsuited to play. But play it he did against a background of insurmountable political, military and financial problems bequeathed to him by his father that would have broken even the strongest of men. He 'kept faith' with his father by continuing the struggle in Scotland, ultimately at great personal cost to himself. In his *History of England* John Lingard contrasts the reigns of the first two Edwards thus:

> The first Edward had been in disposition a tyrant. As often as he dared, he had trampled on the liberties of his subjects; and yet he died in his bed, respected by his barons and admired by his contemporaries. His son, the second Edward, was of less imperious character; no acts of injustice or oppression were imputed by his greatest enemies; yet he was deposed from the throne and murdered in prison.

It is surely Edward II's greatest misfortune that he was called to lead a country at war at a time when the usefulness of the old feudal military order was passing away, and when he was confronted with enemies as formidable as Robert Bruce, Thomas Randolph and James Douglas. His son came to maturity when a new set of military ideas was taking shape, and after Scotland's greatest captains had passed into history.

Edward II's son, now fourteen years old, and completely under the control of his mother and Mortimer, was crowned King Edward III on 1 February 1327. King Robert was immediately distrustful of the new regime, even though Mortimer and Isabella seemed genuinely to have desired a continuation of the temporary peace. It's possible that Robert decided to take advantage of the political uncertainty in England to force a recognition of his position in Scotland. Mortimer and Isabella had unwisely referred to 'Robert and his adherents' in their unilateral attempts to renew the truce, thereby reminding Bruce of his true status in English eyes. Most important of all, time was running out for the ailing King, and it was imperative that his long struggle was successfully concluded before he died. On the very day that Edward was crowned Bruce launched a surprise attack on Norham Castle, thereby signalling that he no longer felt bound to adhere to the truce of Bishopthorpe. Matters soon came to a head.

The final campaign of King Robert's reign was fought as a great game of political and military chess. The King opened the moves himself, leading an expedition to Ulster in April 1327, taking advantage of the disorders arising from the recent death of the Red Earl, and thereby releasing, once again, the spectre of a Celtic alliance. This was followed on 15 June by a large cross border raid by Moray and Douglas. With them came Donald of Mar, anxious, no doubt, to rescue his imprisoned friend and patron. Also present was James Stewart, the younger brother of Walter, who had died the previous year; and Archibald Douglas, the younger brother of Sir James. They ravaged Weardale and an adjacent valley. The French chronicler John Froissart has left a striking account of the kind of men Moray and Douglas led, and the hardships they endured:

> The Scots are tough . . . When they make forays into England, they cover sixty to seventy miles at a stretch, either by day or by night . . . They never take transport on wheels with them, because of the wild mountains they have to cross in Northumberland . . . their habits are so austere that in time of war they subsist for quite a long time on half cooked meat, with no bread, and river water, without wine . . . And as they know they will find plenty of cattle in the country where

they go, they take no provisions with them, except that each carries a flat stone under his saddle flaps, and a little bag of oatmeal behind the saddle: when they have eaten so much meat that their stomachs feel weak and ill, they put the stone on a fire and mix a little oatmeal and water. When the stone is hot, they lay this thin paste on it and make a little cake, like a biscuit, which they eat to ease the stomach.

As the Scottish hobelars continued on their destructive passage through Weardale, a large army under the nominal command of the young Edward III left York on 10 July to intercept them. The King brought with him a large party of soldiers from Hainault, countrymen of his intended wife Philipa, one of whom, Jean le Bel, wrote an account of the campaign. Continuous rain made the pursuit difficult, and the English, much more heavily equipped than their opponents, floundered around for some time unable to make contact with the agile Scots. The country through which they passed had suffered heavily in the wars. Le Bel describes it as 'a savage land full of desolate wastes and great hills, and barren of everything except wild beasts'. Frustrated by their failure to catch up with the Scots, the English commanders decided to take up position at Haydon Bridge on the Tyne, hoping to block any attempt by Moray and Douglas to return to Scotland. They waited for the Scots in vain. The weather continued wet and miserable; provisions began to vanish and morale plummeted. After waiting for over a week at Haydon Bridge, the army abandoned this position and took to the road once more, finally catching sight of their opponents on 1 August on the southern bank of the River Wear.

The Scots were in a good position and declined all attempts to draw them into battle. After a while they left, only to take an even stronger position at Stanhope Park, a hunting preserve belonging to the Bishop of Durham. From here on the night of the 4 August Douglas led an assault party across the river in a surprise attack on the sleeping English. Le Bel describes what happened:

> The Lord James Douglas took with him about two hundred men-at-arms, and passed the river far off from the host so that he was not perceived; and suddenly he broke into the English host about midnight crying 'Douglas!' 'Douglas!' Ye shall all die thieves of England'; and he slew or seized three hundred men, some in their beds and some scarcely ready; and he stroke his horse with the spurs, and came to the King's tent, always crying 'Douglas!', and stroke asunder two or three cords of the King's tent.

The attack caused considerable confusion, and Edward only narrowly escaped capture. His own chaplain was killed in his defence. A further assault was expected on the following evening, and the English were kept on edge by frequent false alarms. But on the night of the 6/7 of August the Scots outflanked their anxious enemies, and escaped to the north, following a rout through a treacherous marsh. By the time the English realised that they had been given the slip the Scots were well out of their reach on their way to the border. Once again English arms had been humiliated, and the King is said to have wept in impotent rage. The army retired to York and disbanded.

When confronted by men like Moray and Douglas, guerrilla leaders of genius, the English fared badly. However, in organisational and tactical terms it should be noted that all of the lessons of the Scottish wars had now been fully absorbed. The army was no longer a 'feudal host' in the thirteenth century sense of the term. Many had been recruited for pay, including several thousand mounted archers—hobelars—armed with the longbow, who became the basis of a new military class of professional soldiers. Moreover, at the outset of the Weardale campaign the government gave instructions that even the greatest noblemen would have to be ready to fight on foot. Henry Beaumont and David de Strathbogie were both present on the campaign, and would soon have an opportunity to prove themselves to be skilled practitioners of the new techniques of battle.

Weardale had been a tactical defeat for the English and Bruce followed it up with the final part of his great offensive—the invasion and conquest of Northumberland. After forcing the English seneschal of Ulster, Henry Mandeville, to conclude a year-long truce, in which Mandeville formally recognised Bruce as King, he returned to Scotland and made ready to cross into England for the last time. In early September King Robert crossed the Tweed and began the siege of Norham Castle, assisted by the Flemish military engineer, John Crabb. Free from any threat for the time being from the English army, Bruce had the leisure to conduct a systematic assault, and John Crabb busied himself building siege engines. While the King was at Norham Moray and Douglas raided extensively in the surrounding countryside, attacking the castles at Alnwick and Warkworth. Those who could hurried to make terms with the Scots. The sense of unease in English government circles was heightened by rumours that Bruce intended to annex

Northumberland, a cherished ambition of Malcolm Canmore and his successors.

While London was often indifferent to the sufferings of those who lived north of the Trent and Humber, it could not afford to ignore the potential dismemberment of England. Short of money—the abortive Weardale campaign had cost a staggering £70,000—and fearful for their grip on power, Mortimer and Isabella decided to sue for peace. Henry Percy, Lord of Alnwick, and William of Denum, both seasoned negotiators, were sent to find King Robert at Norham on 9 October. The King was delighted to receive them and retired to Berwick to consider the matter. From there he issued his terms, which were almost exactly the same as those of the Harclay treaty of 1323. Bruce agreed to peace provided he and his heirs were recognised unreservedly as rulers of Scotland, free from any kind of homage or claim to feudal supremacy. The peace was to be cemented by a marriage between David, Prince of Scotland and Edward's sister Joan of the Tower. The King sweetened the pill by offering to pay an indemnity—'for the sake of the peace'—of £20,000, the whole amount to be paid within three years of the conclusion of peace, £7,000 less than he had been prepared to pay under the Harclay agreement. He also offered England a military alliance, saving his obligation to the King of France under the Treaty of Corbeil. Finally, he proposed that that those who fought on the English side would not seek the restoration of lost lands in Scotland, nor would Scots nobles make similar demands of England; the 'disinherited', in other words, would remain just that.

Towards the end of October Edward agreed that discussions should proceed on the basis of the terms outlined by Robert. These talks were held at Newcastle. In February 1328 the Scots representatives came to York, where King Edward and his lords were meeting in Parliament. From here Edward issued letters patent renouncing his claim to Scotland, and finally recognising Bruce's title. Finally, an English delegation came to Edinburgh on 10 March, empowered to make a final peace. The Treaty of Edinburgh was signed on 17 March 1328, largely on the basis of the terms put forward by King Robert at Berwick. The Edinburgh treaty was ratified by the English Parliament at Northampton on 4 May, and in consequence is generally known as the Treaty of Northampton.

The peace may have been a just one, but it was far from popular in England, even in the northern shires, where people had most reason to welcome the end of the long war. It was also flawed in two important respects: the continuation of Scotland's French alliance, and the silence on the question of the disinherited. Bruce was fully aware that he had made peace with an increasingly unpopular clique around Mortimer and the Queen Mother, and therefore Scotland may have need of future French assistance. There were obvious dangers in this, though, because of unresolved disputes between England and France in Gascony and the Low countries. Any future Anglo-French quarrel would automatically involve Scotland.

The problem of the disinherited was even more vexed. In the peace negotiations King Robert proposed that there should be no rein-statement of men who fought on opposite sides in the war. But because of the strength and influence of the disinherited lobby in England the final treaty failed to address the issue. Henry Beau-mont, now a master of political intrigue, had been joined by Henry Percy, Thomas Wake of Liddel, and William de la Zouche in keeping the question alive in official circles. Their efforts met with a measure of success: for when Queen Isabella attended her daughters wed-ding to David Bruce in July 1328, she used the occasion to make representations on behalf of the disinherited lords. Her efforts on behalf of Henry Percy were successful, as he was given leave to seek restoration of those lands where he could prove a hereditary right. She may also have obtained some concessions on behalf of the others, although these were not observed. In any event, progress on the matter was clearly too slow for Beaumont and Wake, who by the end of the year could be numbered amongst Mortimer and Isabella's principal opponents.

It was widely felt that the Treaty of Northampton had been a humiliation for England, and Roger Mortimer was held to blame. At the Northampton Parliament a number of leading magnates had refused to give their assent to the treaty, Henry of Lancaster, brother of the rebel earl, foremost amongst them. The government of Mortimer and Isabella was also becoming as irksome to many nobles as that of Edward II and the Despensers. Lancaster retired from Northampton to his estates in the midlands, refusing to attend the Salisbury Parliament in October, where Mortimer was created Earl of March. By the end of the year he had risen in rebellion with the support of the earls of Norfolk and Kent. He was joined by his son-in-law, Thomas Wake of Liddel, Henry Beaumont, David de Strathbogie, now married to Beaumont's daughter Katherine, Henry Ferrers and Thomas Rosselin, the nucleus of the disinherited party, and soon to be prominent supporters of Edward Balliol. The rising was short lived, and when Lancaster submitted in January 1329, Wake and Strathbogie also made their peace with the government. Not so Henry Beaumont, who was specifically excluded from the royal pardon of 29 December, along with Thomas Rosselin, and forced to go into exile, and there continued to plot Mortimer's downfall. When the Earl of Kent was arrested in March 1330, and charged with conspiring to restore Edward II, whom he had been deluded into believing was still alive, he alleged at his trial that Beaumont had met him in Paris and told him that his plot would be supported from Scotland by the armed intervention of the deposed King's friend, Donald, Earl of Mar. Kent was executed and Beaumont would never be allowed to return to England for as long as Mortimer and Isabella held on to power.

The disinherited were a very distant threat when King Robert died in his manor house at Cardross near the Firth of Clyde on 7 June 1329. His life's work was complete: Scotland was free and his infant son would ascend her throne unchallenged as King David II. The gallant Earl of Moray became Guardian of Scotland for the duration of David's minority. In accordance with his master's last wishes the ever loyal James Douglas—the good Sir James—carried Bruce's heart on crusade. Douglas was killed on 25 March 1330, fighting the Moors of Granada on behalf of King Alfonso XI of Castile and Leon. He died as he had lived—following King Robert's heart into the thickest part of the battle.

A few years after King Robert's death his essential military teachings were circulated in verse form:

> On foot should be all Scottish war
> Let hill and moss their foes debar
> Let woods for walls be bow and spear
> That enemies do them no deir.[harm]
> In safe places go keep all store,
> And burn the plainland then before.
> Then shall they pass away in haste,
> When they shall find the land lie waste.
> With wiles and wakings of the night,
> And Muckle noises from on height,
> Them shall ye turn with great affray,
> As they were chased with sword away.
> That is the counsel and intent
> Of Good King Robert's Testament.

For the Lion

It was to be a cause of considerable regret that this sound advice was soon to be forgotten. Two years after the King's death Edward Balliol was persuaded to leave his French estates for the last time and come to England. A new game was about to begin.

CHAPTER 8
A Disputed Throne, 1329–1332

Edward Balliol is an elusive and neglected figure in Scottish history; yet he cast a long shadow over the years that followed the death of Robert Bruce. For he came like the ghost of Banquo to spoil the feast of Scottish independence. It was he who revived a cause that had been dormant for almost a quarter of a century. He led a small party of adventurers to an astonishing victory over superior forces at the Battle of Dupplin Moor, and for a brief season brought Scotland to its knees, a task that had been beyond Edward II and all the power of England. And yet his quest was ultimately to prove as empty as his father's tabard. He was fated to pass into history as a Quisling king, whose collaboration with Edward III in the dismemberment of Scotland damned the Balliol cause for ever.

The Second War of Independence which Balliol began when he invaded Scotland in August 1332 has also suffered from historical neglect. There are understandable reasons for this: it lacks the drama and romance of the wars of Wallace and Bruce, and there was, for Scotland anyway, little of the high glory of Stirling Bridge and Bannockburn. Rather, the country recovered its freedom in a prolonged and dour struggle; by a combination of its own efforts and the declining interest of Edward III in the northern war after he turned his covetous eyes on the rich pastures of France. In the end there was no dramatic conclusion to the Anglo-Scottish war: it simply ran out of steam. Nevertheless, the second phase of the fight for independence tested and resolved all of the issues that had remained outstanding at the end of the first, by simple exhaustion if by no other process. By the late 1350s Scotland had, in retrospect, overcome the greatest challenge to its existence that it ever faced, or would ever face again. The Second War of Independence was not, therefore, a postscript to the first but an integral part of the whole struggle. Just as the Treaty of Bretigny in 1360 and the Treaty of Troyes in 1420 are now viewed merely as episodes in the Hundred Years War, so the Treaty of Northampton is surely best seen as a pause in Scotland's own war of national survival.

Edward Balliol is clearly a figure of some importance; but it's difficult to decide if he was the author of his own ambitions or little more than a lever for the designs of others. He took no part in the first war, and it is doubtful if he had any military experience before he came to Scotland. The driving force behind the adventure of Edward Balliol was the irrepressible Henry Beaumont, the arch conspirator of the disinherited. George Ridpath, whose book *The Border History of England and Scotland* was published as long ago as 1810, had no doubt of this: 'The lord Henri Beaumont, a man of high prowess, ripe in years, and of great experience in affairs both civil and military, is always celebrated as the chief in contriving and co-ordinating this remarkable enterprise.' It was Beaumont who formed a 'party' of the disinherited in the period after the peace of Northampton; he who encouraged Balliol, with Edward III's approval, to leave his French estates and come to England. He was also a seasoned campaigner, who had been present both at Bannockburn and Boroughbridge and learned much from both encounters. It is almost certain that he was the architect of Balliol's victory at Dupplin Moor; and he is likely to have advised Edward III of the tactics that brought him the first great military success of his career at the Battle of Halidon Hill, an exact foretaste of the later triumph at Crecy. Beaumont provided much of the financial support that allowed the impecunious Balliol to descend on Scotland at the head of an army of freebooters. His principal loyalty was to himself and then to Edward III; for, as time was to show, Edward Balliol, King of Scots, was a convenient hook on which he hung the cloak of his ambitions.

Beaumont first made contact with Balliol when he was in exile in France. Balliol grew into manhood as a state prisoner in England in the years after 1296, and appears to have been there as late as 1320, when he figures on a list of the Scots adherents of Edward II. Thereafter he was allowed to go into permanent retirement on his estates in Picardy, for which he did homage to the kings of France after the death of his father. By the mid-1320s the English government, having failed to subdue Robert Bruce by military means, was becoming aware of Balliol's potential as a pretender to the Scottish crown, and he was invited to England with increasing frequency by successive regimes. It is possible that he may have been present on the Weardale campaign of 1327, but the evidence is not conclusive. There is nothing in the records to suggest that prior to Beaumont's approach he had shown any desire to recover his father's lost throne. His efforts, such as they were, were directed at the recovery of the estates that his father had forfeited to the crown by his treason to Edward I. Edward I had in fact allowed for this possibility when, after awarding Balliol's confiscated estates to Guy Beauchamp, Earl of Warwick, he left it open to a future government to restore these lands to Edward Balliol. After the King's death Balliol petitioned his successor for the return of his hereditary lands in England and Galloway. Nothing came of this. A further petition was submitted in 1313, when Balliol scaled down his request and simply asked for the return of at least some of his English lands, on the grounds that his father's French estates were so heavily mortgaged that he was unable to support himself financially. Again he was disappointed. Unlike his chief lieutenant Henry Beaumont, whose English lands, confiscated by Roger Mortimer, were restored by Edward III, Balliol was to remain permanently disinherited in England. Impoverished in France and landless in England Balliol was at last persuaded to turn to Scotland.

The opportunity for Balliol and Beaumont came with the downfall of Roger Mortimer in October 1330. The young King had grown restive under Mortimer's tutelage and increasingly angry at his arrogance. On the night of 19 October, with the help of William Montagu, Edward entered Nottingham Castle secretly and took Mortimer prisoner. He was sent to London where he was tried and executed. Edward's mother, Queen Isabella—the she wolf of France—was sent into long retirement, and the King began to rule in his own right.

The tasks before the seventeen-year-old monarch were immense. England was badly divided by over twenty years of discord, political mismanagement and factional strife. The economy was weak, and respect for the king's law at a particularly low level. There was unfinished business in both Scotland and France. The nation had to be united in a common purpose, and war was to provide an ideal catalyst in achieving this end.

Edward III was far closer in character to his grandfather than his father; but he lacked something of the first Edward's tenacity and strength of purpose. Above all, he lacked his grandfather's intensely legalistic frame of mind: while he was anxious to safeguard what he believed to be his rights, all political considerations were ultimately subordinated to his pursuit of profit and martial glory. Edward III was one of history's great opportunists, eager to seize any advantage that presented itself, but often unwilling to make the prolonged and laborious effort required to consolidate his gains. The prizes he won in Scotland and France were startling but transitory; and the noon-day glory of his reign was eventually to sink into a disappointing twilight.

In assuming power Edward was mindful of the support he had received from Henry Beaumont. He would also have been aware that while Beaumont was a useful friend he could also be a dangerous enemy. His shifting loyalties since 1323 had all been dictated by his overriding desire to recover the earldom of Buchan. But Edward embraced the cause of the disinherited for reasons more subtle than simple gratitude: for Beaumont's tireless plotting eventually provided the occasion to set aside the peace of 1328.

Before the end of 1330 Edward started to make strong diplomatic representations on behalf of Beaumont and Wake who, after the settlement of the Percy claim, were the only two noblemen to be officially recognised as disinherited by the English and Scottish governments. He wrote to his young brother-in-law David Bruce in December, requesting the restoration of the lands of the 'Earl of Buchan' and the 'Lord of Liddesdale'. The Scots were reminded that King Robert had promised that these outstanding claims would be settled in addition to that of Henry Percy. But Edward must have realised that there was little chance of the Scots accepting Beaumont and Wake into their midst. The lands restored to Percy were strategically unimportant, and he had not been allowed to lay claim to the earldom of Carrick, awarded to his father by Edward I in 1306. It would make little sense to hand over important lands in the west march and the north-east of Scotland to men whose personal and political loyalties lay with a potential enemy, and who were widely known to be vehement opponents of the Treaty of Northampton. The Guardian, Thomas Randolph, was obviously conscious of this and Edward's requests were effectively ignored. Beaumont now began to seek restitution by other means.

Aside from those for whom the English government was prepared to make diplomatic overtures there was a large class of 'unofficial' disinherited, men whose families had been on the wrong side in the Scottish civil war. First amongst these was David de Strathbogie, the pretender Earl of Atholl, grandson of the Red Comyn. As well as the earldom of Atholl Strathbogie laid claim to half of John Comyn's Lochaber lands, in right of his mother Joan. The other half of Lochaber was claimed by Richard Talbot, an Englishman who married Elizabeth Comyn, John Comyn's second daughter. The others included Gilbert de Umfraville, who laid claim to the earldom of Angus, once held by his family; Henry Ferrers who claimed lands in Galloway; and Walter Comyn, son of William Comyn of Kilbride in Lanarkshire. This group was augmented by those who had been displaced as a result of participation in the anti-Bruce Soules conspiracy of 1320, principally the sons of Roger Mowbray—Geoffery, John and Alexander. Apart from these there seems to have been a group of minor people who had fought on the losing side and who were dependent on small handouts from the English exchequer. Their names are not recorded, but are likely to have included the MacDoualls and MacCanns of Galloway. Taken together these men represent the rump of the Balliol/Comyn party. In 1331 they found in Henry Beaumont a leader who was rich and influential enough to give shape to their dreams.

With the payment of the final instalment of the Scots indemnity in 1331 Edward had no further reason to preserve the *status quo*. He made no secret of his dislike of the Treaty of Northampton, which he liked to believe had been forced upon him during his minority; but he was not as yet willing to be cast in the role of an aggressor. The disinherited offered a way of challenging the legitimacy of the peace settlement, while allowing Edward to preserve the outward forms of neutrality. Throughout this period Edward was something of a 'sleeping partner' in the schemes hatched in the mind of Henry Beaumont. Some time between 1330 and 1331 Beaumont conceived a plan to invade Scotland with a private army headed by himself and the 'rightful' King—Edward Balliol. Edward had nothing to lose by this and much to gain: he would clearly extract a high price for his secret co-operation, but would be able to disassociate himself from the enterprise if things went wrong; at the very least he would benefit from the destabilisation of Scotland. Beaumont's scheme was bold to the point of foolhardiness; but it seems reasonably certain in view of the modest size of the army he was eventually able to recruit that both he and Edward reckoned on at least some support for Balliol from a native 'fifth column'.

The first contacts between Balliol and Beaumont had been made in 1330. In 1331 these approaches became more serious as Beaumont finalised the details of his plan. In June both he and David de Strathbogie crossed the Channel to visit the exile in Picardy. Beaumont returned in August and again in November, when he was accompanied by Walter Comyn. The *Brut Chronicle* contains a colourful story, not repeated in any other source, that Balliol had incurred the displeasure of the King of France, and had to be rescued from imprisonment by the pleadings of Henry Beaumont.

What is certain is that he was finally persuaded to leave France and come to England in the winter of 1331. He was settled in the manor of Standal in Yorkshire, a property belonging to Beaumont's sister, Isabella, the lady Vesci. Standal manor now became something of a court in exile. Donald of Mar, who had been granted permission to come to England, is alleged to have visited Balliol and greeted him as the rightful King of Scotland. After settling the 'king from over the water' in Yorkshire, Beaumont visited Edward: 'So came Sir Henry of Beaumont', says the *Brut Chronicle* 'to Kyng Edward of Engeland and praiede him, in way of charite, þat he wolde grant of his grace unto Sir Edward Balliol þat he moste safliche gone bi land from Sandall for to conquere his ritz heritage in Scotland.' Edward would allow him to go—by sea, not by land. No official meeting is recorded between Edward and Balliol, but he must have at some-time over the winter learned the price he was expected to pay for the King's tacit support. Letters issued at Roxburgh in November 1332 make it plain that he met Edward sometime between the winter of 1331 and the summer of 1332 to pay homage for the kingdom he hoped to win.

An atmosphere of impending doom dominated Anglo-Scottish relations towards the end of 1331. Randolph was fully aware of the growing menace. Parliament met at Scone and it was agreed that the coronation of David Bruce proceed as quickly as possible. Towards the end of November the seven-year-old boy was crowned and anointed by James Bennet, Bishop of St Andrews, as David II, King of Scots. The occasion was a triumphant postscript to the War of Independence, with all suggestion of subordination to England gone. But it was also in a sense the final act of a heroic age. Randolph stood alone, the last of the great captains. Of the church-men Wishart was long dead, and had recently been joined by William Lamberton and David Murray. Their loss would soon be felt.

The Lanercost Chronicle says of David's coronation; 'About the feast of St Andrew's day David son of the late Robert de Bruce was anointed and crowned King of Scotland, and it was publicly pro-claimed at his coronation that he claimed right to Scotland by no hereditary succession, but in like manner as his father by conquest alone.' It doesn't seem very likely that this extraordinary declaration was ever made; but if it was it would have acted as a *causus belli*—an invitation to the 'legitimate' party to test their claim by force of arms.

In the spring of 1332 Edward was playing a double game. He made one final official approach to Randolph on the unsettled claims, whilst allowing the disinherited lords to raise money and assemble their forces. Sir Thomas Gray describes Edward's final contacts with Randolph memorably:

> The lords who had been disinherited in Scotland for the cause of himself (King Edward) and his predecessors made supplication to him that he would restore them to their inheritance which they lost on his account, or allow them to take their own measures. The King referred this matter to the Earl of Moray, . . . which earl replied . . . demanding that he (King Edward) should allow them to take their measures and let the ball roll.

Randolph's own preparations were thorough: he concentrated men and weapons in the east of Scotland in anticipation of invasion. To be ready, the Guardian, now seriously ill, took up residence at the castle of Musselburgh on the south side of the Firth of Forth and waited.

Beaumont and his associates were busy making their own final arrangements for the planned expedition. They raised the necessary cash by leasing their English manors with royal permission. Edward was still not willing to countenance an open breach of the peace. In March 1332 he ordered the sheriffs of the northern shires to prevent a cross-border invasion, while he did nothing to stop men, materials and ships being gathered in the Yorkshire sea ports. Local officials, well aware of what was going on, were presumably instructed not to interfere.

The private army that waited to sail in the tense summer of 1332 was an odd assortment of individuals. Besides Balliol and the Comyn partisans there were a number of English knights, who clearly came with Edward's approval. Chief amongst these was Ralph de Stafford, created Earl of Stafford in 1351, who may have served as Edward's surrogate on the campaign. Also present were Fulk Fitzwarren, Thomas Ughtred—who had been captured by the Scots at the Battle of Old Byland—Nicholas Beche, Robert Winchester and Walter de Mauny. Few of these gentlemen had any outstanding claims in Scotland, and were presumably attracted by adventure or possible grants of land. There were also a number of mercenaries, including a small party of Germans. The size of the force assembled cannot be established with any real accuracy, but the sources all agree that it was fairly modest: the *Bridlington Chronicle* suggests a figure of 500 men-at-arms and 1,000 foot; Henry Knighton, prone on occasions to wild exaggeration, puts forward a figure of 300 men-at-arms and 3,000 foot; while Lanercost, probably the most reliable, suggests a total force in the region of 1,500 to 2,800. All agree that by far the largest proportion of footmen were archers, armed with the longbow. By mid July all preparations were complete and Balliol's little armada of some eighty-eight ships waited for the right moment to sail. It came with the news that the Earl of Moray had died at Musselburgh on 20 July 1332. Poison was suspected; but it usually was when great men died suddenly.

The disinherited were quick to take advantage of Scotland's leadership crisis. Their small fleet sailed out of the Yorkshire ports of Ravenser, Barton and Hull on 31 July, headed by Edward Balliol, but under the real command of Henry Beaumont. Just over a week after they sailed, and after they landed in Scotland, King Edward, 'having been informed that Henry Beaumont and others are preparing to invade Scotland', took the precaution of appointing Henry Percy as Warden of the March, with power to raise the northern levies in case of Scots retaliation. He was obviously concerned that the Scots would see through the pretence, and view the whole endeavour not as a private affair but as an act of English aggression. He then awaited the outcome.

At this critical moment the Scots magnates gathered at Perth to appoint a successor to Randolph. It was only after some heated discussions that they chose Donald, Earl of Mar, on 2 August. Mar appears to have been chosen because of his close family relationship to the boy King—they were cousins—and because there was really no one else qualified to fill the post. If the choice was not surprising it does not appear to have been greeted with much enthusiasm. Mar had spent much of his adult life in England, and was known to have been sympathetic to the disinherited, many of whom he would have known personally. He was also suspected by some of treasonable associations with Balliol. Although he had taken part in the Weardale campaign, events soon showed that he had poor leadership and even poorer military skills. Suspicion over his motives and loyalties did much to contribute to the coming disaster at Dupplin Moor.

At about this time Balliol's fleet entered the Firth of Forth. For a few days he held the tactical advantage; for the Scots, uncertain where their enemy intended to land, were forced to divide their forces in two, to allow for a descent on the northern or southern shores. The southern command was given to Patrick de Dunbar, Earl of March, the same earl who helped Edward II escape from

Scotland after Bannockburn. Donald of Mar held the command in the north. The disinherited finally came ashore on 6 August at Kinghorn in Fife, on the northern shore. A local force under Duncan, Earl of Fife, Alexander Seton, son of the warden of Berwick Castle, and Robert Bruce, illegitimate son of the late King, attempted to oppose the landing, but the English longbows provided an effective screen, covering the landing of the men-at-arms led by Henry Beaumont. Alexander Seton was killed, and his companions were forced to flee to the interior of Fife. The English landed the rest of their men and equipment unopposed. Edward Balliol was able to set foot in Scotland, a country he had been taken from thirty six years before, when he was probably no older than the child King whose throne he had come to seize. With the landing complete the ships were sent north to round Fife and enter the Firth of Tay. From this it was clear that the army intended to march on Perth, and Beaumont presumably had it in mind that the ships would provide a means of escape if things went wrong. The only way now was forward; there could be no retreat.

CHAPTER 9

Edward Balliol, the Autumn King, 1332

From Kinghorn Balliol and Beaumont's small army advanced on Dunfermline, where Robert Bruce lay buried. There they found some of the stores and weapons the late Guardian had ordered to be gathered. After Dunfermline the march continued northwards towards Perth. On 10 August they camped at Forteviot, just south of the River Earn, a few miles short of their objective. To the north of the river Donald of Mar had taken up position with a much stronger force on the heights of Dupplin Moor. The disinherited now faced one Scottish army in front with another fast approaching from the rear. Patrick of Dunbar had reacted quickly to the news of the Kinghorn landing, and set off in rapid pursuit with the southern army, crossed the Forth and reached Auchterarder, only a few miles distant from the camp at Forteviot. For Balliol and Beaumont the situation was desperate: they were in danger of being crushed between Mar's anvil and Dunbar's hammer. The expected Scots support for King Balliol had not materialised; and his former friend and ally, the Earl of Mar, was clearly determined to fulfil his role as Guardian. Drastic measures were required.

In view of their predicament it comes as no surprise that morale in Balliol's camp began to sink. According to Thomas Gray the disinherited lords were so dismayed by the size of Mar's army that they accused Henry Beaumont of having betrayed them with false promises of Scottish support for Balliol. But Beaumont, the most experienced soldier on either side, reacted to this dangerous situation with coolness and precision. It was obvious that he could not wait for Dunbar to link up with Mar. He would therefore cross the Earn, as Douglas had the Wear in 1327, and launch a night attack on his superior foe. Mar would then be forced into battle before the southern army arrived.

On the opposite bank of the river the Scots had a clear view of Balliol's ludicrously small army. Mar was so confident of his strength and the superiority of his position that he did not even bother to set a watch, and his army settled down on the night of

10–11 August, relaxed enough to spend much of the time drinking, convinced of an easy victory the following day. At midnight on 10 August, unobserved by the carousing Scots, Sir Alexander Mowbray led a picked force across a nearby ford shown to him by the sole traitor from the Scots camp, one Murray of Tullibardine.

After crossing the ford Mowbray climbed up the rising ground towards Gask, where he immediately attacked the slumbering Scottish camp followers, in the mistaken belief that he had encountered the main Scottish host. He learned his mistake at daybreak on 11 August; but by that time the rest of the army had safely crossed the Earn and taken up a strong defensive position on some high ground at the head of a narrow valley. Mar had been outflanked. Learning of the rapid approach of the main Scots force, Balliol's army was ordered to form a line, with the archers projecting outwards on both flanks and the men-at-arms in the centre, the whole formation resembling a half moon. All were dismounted, save for a small group of Germans to the rear. Beaumont now made ready to employ tactics that had been demonstrated in outline at Boroughbridge ten years before, which in their fully evolved form were to allow the English to dominate the battlefields of Britain and western Europe for the next hundred years.

The Scots were angry that their enemy had been allowed to carry out so simple a manoeuvre under their very noses. Lord Robert Bruce made no secret of his conviction that Mar's incompetence was evidence of treachery. Mar denied this, and like Gloucester at Bannockburn, resolved to be the first into battle. Lord Robert claimed this honour for himself and both charged off to destruction, followed by their disorganised schiltrons, all semblance of generalship gone. Bruce and Mar's wild charge was met by a great cloud of arrows, cutting through the air with the whisper of death, and falling on the Scottish flanks. Each bowman was so skilled, and could fire with such speed, that he had several arrows in the air at one time. The badly armoured Scots with their unvizored helmets had no protection against the repeated volleys. Bruce's battalion, pushing through the storm of missiles, was the first to make contact with the enemy centre, forcing Beaumont and the men-at-arms to yield some ground. But the arrow fire was so unrelenting and fierce that his flanks converged towards the middle 'blinded and maddened', as if seeking shelter from a storm. The front units were pushed forward on to Beaumont's spears. Retreat or redeployment was made impossible by the arrival of Mar's schiltron, charging down the narrow glen, and straight into the rear of Lord Robert's men. The crush was so great that many fell never to rise again. Probably as many were killed under the feet of their own comrades as they were by the murderous and unceasing arrow fire. In his brief extract on the life of Henry Beaumont in '*The Book of the Illustrious Henries*' the chronicler and historian John Capgrave describes the carnage at Dupplin:

> In this battle . . . more were slain by the Scots themselves than by the English. For rushing forward on each other, each crushed his neighbour, and for every one fallen there fell a second, and then a third fell, and those who were behind pressing forward and hastening to the fight, the whole army became a heap of the slain.

The bodies of the Scots were piled so high above each other that it is said they reached the height of a spear. The English surrounded the bloody heap, thrusting in their swords and spears, so that no one could be taken out alive. Scots losses were heavy: Mar and Bruce were both killed, as was Thomas Randolph, the former Guardian's son, the Earl of Mentieth and Alexander Fraser, the High Chamberlain, together with many others of all ranks. Ironically Robert Keith, who scattered Edward II's archers at Bannockburn, was also among the slain. The exact number of dead is unknown, but estimates range from a low of 2,000 to a high of 13,000. English losses were very light, amounting to no more than thirty-three knights and men-at-arms, of whom the chief were John Gordon and Reginald de la Breche. Not one archer is said to have been killed, for their crossfire had pushed the hand to hand fighting into a narrow front in the centre. The Earl of Fife tried to lead the survivors of Mar's army on an orderly retreat, but this turned into a rout after Beaumont and the others took to horse, charging off in pursuit. Many who escaped the carnage inflicted by the archers were cut down by the cavalry. The Earl of Fife was taken prisoner.

The Battle of Dupplin Moor was the worst Scottish defeat since the Battle of Falkirk, thirty four years before, far exceeding the setback at Methven. The losses were heavy, but they could be made good, and Dunbar's army, probably as strong as Mar's, was still in the field. However, the worst casualty of all was the national confidence that had grown from the successive victories of King Robert, which had produced an illusory sense of invulnerability. After Dupplin the Scots rarely gained the upper hand against the English in battle. Once again the nation had tasted serious defeat, and the effect it had on morale surely explains Dunbar's reluctance to engage Balliol's tired little army in battle. In his classic study, *The History of War in the Middle Ages*, Sir Charles Oman says of Dupplin: 'The Battle of Dupplin forms a turning point in the history of the Scottish wars. For the future the English always adopted the order of battle which Balliol and Beaumont had discovered. It was the first in a long series of battles won by a skilful combination of archery and dismounted men-at-arms.' Beaumont may have per- fected the technique, but the honour of discovery surely belongs to the long dead Andrew Harclay.

Mar's army had been destroyed and the victory was later claimed to be the work of God; but Dunbar's army was still perilously close, and not willing to test God's forbearance for a second time, Balliol and Beaumont marched on the undefended town of Perth. The defences which had lain in ruins since King Robert captured the town in 1313 were hastily repaired with wooden palisades protected by ditches. Perth was well provisioned, with sufficient stores to withstand a siege. These stores were augmented by a raid on nearby Methven. Balliol's men then dug in to await an imminent attack.

It was some days, though, before Dunbar, accompanied by Sir Archibald Douglas, the younger brother of Sir James, arrived at Perth. Balliol's position was weak, yet no attempt was made to rush his rudimentary defences. The sight of the unburied dead on Dupplin Moor is likely to have had a sobering effect on Dunbar and his men. Rather than face the English arrows Dunbar decided that it would be more prudent to begin a blockade.

Balliol's army was now far from its English base, and although well provisioned, it could not expect to hold out indefinitely in such an isolated position. The only access the disinherited had to the outside world was the sea route via the Firth of Tay, guarded by Beaumont's ships. It was imperative that this link be cut if Dunbar's siege was to have any chance of success. With this task in mind, John Crabb, the many talented Flemish seaman and engineer in the service of Scotland, led a small flotilla from Berwick to attack the English fleet in the Tay. The two forces met in a naval engage- ment on 24 August. Although the English heavily outnumbered the Scots by a factor of eight to one, Crabb's force attacked with courage and determination, capturing Henry Beaumont's own flagship, the *Beaumondscogge*, killing all those within. But the English eventu- ally managed to gain the advantage, and most of the Scots flotilla was destroyed. The survivors sailed off with the *Beaumondscogge* as their sole prize, while John Crabb escaped ashore. Balliol's supply rout was secure.

This second defeat caused Dunbar, running short of supplies himself, to raise his half hearted siege of Perth and retire south. His departure was hastened by a new crisis in his rear: for Balliol's invasion had, at last, led to a small but important rising in his favour. The men of Galloway had taken arms on behalf of their hereditary lord on hearing of his predicament in Perth. Raphael Holinshead explains:

> Whereof when they of Galloway had advertisement, because the king was their special lord and chief governor, they assembled together under the conduct of the Lord Eustace de Makeswell (Maxwell), and invaded the lands of those Scotsmen that had besieged their lord king, Edward Balliol, and by that means constrained their adversaries to leave their siege.

The leader of the rising, Sir Eustace Maxwell of Caerlaverock, had previously been indicted for his part in the Soules conspiracy against Robert Bruce, but had been acquitted. His true loyalties were now clear.

This rebellion so near to the English border could not be ignored, and the Scots leaders were forced to descend on Galloway. Andrew Murray of Bothwell and Avoch, the son of Wallace's colleague of 1297, was chosen to replace Mar as Guardian. The bulk of the Scots army had now disbanded, and Murray led the remainder against the men of Galloway. He was joined by Dunbar, Archibald Douglas and John Randolph, the second son of the great Randolph and now the new Earl of Moray, in the attack on Maxwell and his supporters, the descendants of the MacDoualls and MacCanns who fought for Balliol in 1307 and 1308. In one corner of Scotland the civil war between Bruce and Balliol had been rekindled. The fighting was so fierce that many people were forced, as in the past, to flee their homes and seek refuge in remote places.

Lord Hailes, in his book, *The Annals of Scotland*, says that with the departure of Dunbar from Perth Balliol was in possession of Scotland. This was an illusion: Balliol and his men were only in possession of the ground they stood on. Yet it was obviously one to which Balliol and Beaumont were subject. Balliol's position certainly appeared strong. His enemies were defeated and dispersed; the news of the Galloway rising came as a welcome relief; and the captured Earl of Fife, brother of the same Countess Isabel who came to Scone to lead Bruce to the throne in 1306, was persuaded to change his allegiance and bring some of the local gentry over to Balliol. But the factor that convinced him that he had indeed subdued Scotland was undoubtedly the adherence to his cause of a number of important churchmen, who appear to have accepted the astonishing verdict of Dupplin Moor as divine judgement. James Bennet, the Bishop of St Andrews, left Scotland after Dupplin and died in exile; but the Bishop of Dunkeld, William Sinclair, who had repulsed an earlier invasion of Fife, came out in favour of Balliol, as did the abbots of Dunfermline, Coupar, Inchaffray, Arbroath and Scone. Sinclair, the most senior Scottish churchman to declare for Balliol, was appointed to officiate at the planned coronation; and the man who had once been honoured by Robert Bruce as 'my own bishop' was now to be King Balliol's bishop. In general, the church in the Second War of Independence was to provide little of the guidance, inspiration and leadership that it had in the first.

With the welcome support of the Bishop of Dunkeld and the Earl of Fife Balliol now had all the elements of a traditional Scottish coronation. He was duly accompanied by his followers to Scone, where on 24 September 1332 he was crowned and anointed by Sinclair as Edward 1, King of Scots. This tense and unhappy occasion was accompanied by none of the joy that had been evident at the coronation of David II the previous November. Despite the accession of Fife and Dunkeld Balliol and his small army were isolated in a sullen and hostile country. At the banquet after the coronation ceremony it is said that the guests remained fully armed, save for their helmets. There was good reason for this; for it is also said that the local people attached themselves to Balliol more from fear than love. The terror of the new regime soon spread, and the priors of St. Andrews wrote of 'the lordship of Edward Balliol and Henry Beaumont' and their inability to collect the dues from the church at Fordun 'for fear of the said Lord Henry.'

The general lack of enthusiasm for King Balliol clearly gave rise to some concern amongst the disinherited about the security of their conquest. Galloway, too far away from Perth for comfort, was the only part of Scotland to demonstrate its old Balliol/Comyn loyalties. There was no equivalent rising for Beaumont in Buchan, or Strathbogie in Atholl or Lochaber. The sense of isolation was heightened by the fact that there had been no contact with England for several weeks. It was now vital that Balliol re-establish communications with his feudal superior to consolidate his newly won crown. The army therefore prepared to leave Perth and march south towards the English border. On the way it would pass through Galloway to assist the beleaguered Balliol partisans.

Before leaving Perth in late September Balliol appointed the Earl of Fife as his warden, charged with the defence of the town. In one sense at least this was not an unusual choice, as the Earl commanded a significant degree of local support. But he was also a very recent convert to the Balliol cause. The reasons for his change of loyalties are unknown: amongst other considerations he was presumably anxious to avoid being kept prisoner, with the eventual prospect of ending up in an English dungeon. No other commander of note was left to strengthen the Earl's resolve. Balliol's force, of course, was of modest size, and he could not take the risk of leaving a large garrison that any of the disinherited lords would obviously have demanded. Besides, no Englishman is likely to have welcomed the prospect of remaining in Perth in such uncertain circumstances.

While the main Scottish army had left with Dunbar some forces clearly remained in the vicinity observing the movements of their enemy. No sooner had Balliol left Perth than the patriots took the offensive. Fife seems at best to have offered only a token defence, and on 7 October the town was stormed by a force under the command of Sir Simon Fraser, cousin of the companion of Wallace, Robert Keith, grandson of Bruce's cavalry commander, and John Lindsay. Fife and his daughter Isabella were taken prisoner and sent to Kildrummy Castle. However, his apostasy was not viewed seriously, and he was soon released. Also taken prisoner was Murray of Tullibardine, who had helped the disinherited ford the River Earn. He was executed as a traitor. The rudimentary defences erected by Balliol and Beaumont were destroyed. The fall of Perth was later attributed to treachery on the part of the Earl of Fife by the English chroniclers. The records are silent on the fate of Beaumont's little armada: it presumably left the Tay and returned to England when Balliol quit Perth, or after the town was retaken by the Scots.

On leaving Perth Balliol's army came to Glasgow. From there it travelled in a south westerly direction through Ayrshire, where Balliol received the homage of some local landowners at Irvine, before turning eastwards across the River Cree into Galloway, where its appearance came as a welcome relief to his hard pressed supporters, who had been fighting under the leadership of Duncan MacDouall and Patrick MacUlach, as well as Eustace Maxwell. Balliol's enemies were soon scattered, some taking refuge in England, which was still adhering to the outward forms of neutrality. From Galloway Balliol moved in an easterly direction, towards the old border fortress of Roxburgh, accompanied by Eustace Maxwell and other local supporters. His progress was closely shadowed by a guerrilla force under the Guardian and Sir Archibald Douglas, waiting for an opportunity to attack. There was a brief skirmish at Jedburgh, from which Murray had to withdraw. A further opportunity to take the offensive came just after the disinherited reached Roxburgh. Believing that Balliol had gone to nearby Kelso, leaving the bulk of his army at Roxburgh, Murray attempted to cut him off by destroying the bridge across the River Tweed. The plan backfired. Murray and the Flemish freebooter, John Crabb, were both taken prisoner and sent to captivity in England. He was replaced as Guardian by Archibald Douglas. The circumstances of Douglas's appointment are unknown; but he was presumably chosen for his relationship to the late Sir James, and for the personal courage he had demonstrated to date. As far as military skill is concerned his elevation was to prove even more disastrous than that of Donald of Mar.

Balliol took up residence in the partially ruined fortress of Roxburgh. He remained here for several weeks, awarding lands to some of his English supporters, including Sir Thomas Ughtred. These grants, though, were all of a fairly minor nature; for the cake could only be properly divided when Balliol had a much firmer grip on the kingdom. Much depended on the attitude of Edward III. Balliol's most important act at this time was his attempt to define his relationship to the English King. He was clearly aware that he could not expect to hold Scotland with his present strength for long. Winter was coming; many of his party would wish to return to their homes; and money to pay the mercenaries was likely to be running short. It was therefore essential that King Edward abandon his neutrality and agree to give open support to his protégé. Balliol outlined the price he was willing to pay for this support in the Declaration of Roxburgh.

The Declaration takes the form of two open letters, issued on 23 November 1332. In these Balliol openly recognised Edward as his feudal superior, confirming that he had already performed an act of homage and sworn fealty to his liege lord. He further promised to assist England in military operations both at home and abroad, in return for which he asked Edward's help in maintaining him and his heirs as kings of Scotland. It should be remembered that even

Balliol's spineless father had balked at the English king's demands for overseas service. In case Edward retained any concerns about the fate of his young brother-in-law, Balliol promised to provide for the 'deposed' David Bruce, and to marry the King's sister Joan, on the assumption that, in view of her age, she could only be considered as 'betrothed' to David.

All of this was important, but the real meat of the Declaration lay in the promise of major territorial concessions. In return for Edward's aid to date Balliol promised to cede to the English crown the town, castle and county of Berwick. This was to be supplemented by further grants of land up to the value of £2,000. Theses lands were to be in those parts of Scotland adjacent to the English border, and were to be separated from Scotland forever and annexed to England. The true extent of this promise was not to be fully known until early 1334; but the implication was clear enough: Edward Balliol would be the client king of a dismembered Scotland. The terms of the Roxburgh Declaration were conveyed to England by Henry Beaumont and David de Strathbogie, who left Scotland some time after the letters were issued to attend the English Parliament at York. Edward subsequently issued letters of protection on behalf of Beaumont, allowing him to return to Scotland on a diplomatic mission, connected, one assumes, with Balliol's promised concessions. Before this mission could be carried out the disinherited had been scattered like chaff in the wind.

In England the news of Balliol's victory at Dupplin Moor caused great excitement when Parliament gathered at Westminster in early September. Edward had probably been expecting at most some kind of revolution on behalf of Balliol, and a renewal of the civil war. That Balliol and Beaumont would, without assistance, defeat a powerful Scots host in battle and force the country's government into hiding, was surely the last thing on his mind. He had planned to go to Ireland; but in view of the remarkable events in Scotland it was agreed that he make his way to northern England to be prepared for any contingency that might arise. Although the news from Scotland was good it was generally felt that Balliol had not cut all the heads off the hydra. Parliament readily agreed to grant the King further subsidies for the security of the border.

Shortly after he arrived at York Edward learned of Balliol's coronation. Events in Scotland were moving fast, and on the advice of his magnates the King summoned another Parliament to assemble in York in early December. In the meantime, Edward made

110

himself ready to grasp any opportunity that arose to increase his influence north of the border. When he learned of the death of James Bennet, the Bishop of St Andrews, in October he quickly wrote to the Pope suggesting his own nominee, Robert Ayelston, Archdeacon of Berkshire, as a replacement, notwithstanding the fact that St Andrews was the principal see of an independent country. The Pope failed to act on Edward's request. A further approach was made in March 1333, but in view of the tense political situation, and the growing likelihood of war between England and Scotland, the Pope declined to make any appointment. The see was to remain vacant for nine years.

England had already undergone a partial mobilisation by the time Parliament met on 4 December. Attendance was poor and the opening session was delayed until 8 December to allow for late comers. Although the numbers present had not greatly improved by that date, matters were too pressing to postpone debate any longer. The lords and prelates were formally notified of the terms of Balliol's Roxburgh Declaration. brought to them by Henry Beaumont. Representatives also came from King David, who throughout the summer and autumn seems to have remained in the west at Cardross or Dumbarton Castle. The Scots asked for assistance from an 'ally' against the disinherited, but these approaches were rejected, the King's council being of the opinion that he was not obliged to act against his own subjects, who had taken action to recover what was rightfully theirs.

In the interval between the Westminster and York Parliaments King Edward had been considering how he could best profit from the crisis in Scotland. Ironically, the speed of Balliol's success came close to being the cause of his undoing. Edward, observing how quickly Scotland had been overcome, no longer felt himself bound by any prior commitment he had made to Balliol. Even the generous concessions promised in the Roxburgh letters were no longer enough to satisfy the King's emerging ambitions: rather than accept a slice of the cake he now wanted to take the bakery itself. At the opening session of the York Parliament Geoffrey Scrope, Chief Justice of the King's Bench, and one of Edward's leading advisors on foreign policy, argued the King's case. Scrope began by saying that the peace of 1328 had been imposed on Edward when he was a minor and against his will. This being the case the situation was, in terms of feudal law, precisely as it had been in 1296: Scotland, in other words, was still a forfeited fief of the English crown. Scrope proceeded to remind the members of the transgressions of the former King John Balliol against the present King's grandfather, and pointed out that the government was not in any way bound to support the cause of Edward Balliol. It was open to the King either to accept the promises made in the Roxburgh Declaration, or to claim the whole realm of Scotland for himself. Edward clearly wanted Parliament to endorse the latter; but the majority of those present were reluctant to embark on a fresh Scottish adventure. They avoided making a decision by claiming that they were not representative enough, owing to the absence of a number of import-ant magnates and prelates. Parliament was then prorogued to reassemble at York on 20 January 1333, when the question would be considered again, this time it was hoped by a more representative assembly. However, when the lords came again to York the situation in Scotland had undergone a dramatic change.

In the second week in December King Balliol moved from Rox-burgh to Annan, a town belonging to his patrimonial estates, near the Solway Firth on the west march, where he intended to spend the Christmas season. The reasons for the move from the relative safety of Roxburgh Castle are not entirely clear: it's reasonable to assume, though, that Balliol wished the additional security that the proximity to Galloway offered, especially, as it seems, most of his leading supporters appear to have gone back to England. While at Annan Balliol was gratified to receive the submission of some of the local landowners, headed, remarkably, by Alexander Bruce, the Earl of Carrick, the natural son of Edward Bruce. These submissions did much to increase his sense of security. The armed force Balliol had at this time is unknown, but it seems to have been very modest. The patriots, gathering to the north of Annan, were quick to take advantage of King Balliol's weakness and complacency.

At Moffat a large company of mounted Scots gathered under the command of the Guardian and the Earl of Moray. They rode through Annandale on the night of the 16–17 December, past the sleeping walls of Lochmaben Castle. By dawn they arrived at Annan, and took Balliol, who appears not to have taken the precaution of posting sentries, by complete surprise. Balliol's extreme compla-cency was later excused on the grounds that there was a truce in operation at the time, causing him to drop his guard. This story only appears in the chronicles of Hemingburgh and Walsingham, written well after the events in question; there is no mention of this important fact in the most reliable, and pro-English, contemporary accounts—the *Scalacronica* and the *Lanercost Chronicle*. Indeed, Lanercost simply says of the Scots raiders: 'They found the King (Edward Balliol) and his people in bed, like those who were too confident in the safety secured through many different victories already won.'

Balliol's men were quickly overwhelmed, many being slain in their beds. Among the killed were Sir John Mowbray, Sir Walter Comyn and one Henry Balliol. The latter is often described as Edward Balliol's brother, even though there seems to be absolutely no contemporary evidence for this assertion (Thomas Gray specifically says that John Balliol 'had but one son'). Alexander Bruce only narrowly escaped death by the intervention of the Earl of Moray. Without having time to get fully dressed, Edward Balliol saved himself by making a hole in the wall of his chamber and finding a horse in the confusion. He escaped, so says the Scots chronicler Bower, 'on a sorry jade, with neither bridle nor saddle, one shank booted and the other bare.' Balliol rode, seemingly alone, to the safety of the English border. 'He escaped with much difficulty to Carlisle', says Sir Thomas Gray 'many of his people being slain, and all of his followers being driven out of Scotland, to begin their conquest all over again.' Balliol had reached the heights and plunged the depths, all in a space of six months; he arrived in England, a regal beggar, and held out his hands to Edward III.

The enterprise of the disinherited had failed, and so died the illusion that a small party of determined men could hold a kingdom against the will of the vast majority of its people without substantial foreign aid. Edward could have saved himself much future trouble by acting as an arbiter and pacifying the unsettled border. However, the genie of greed was out of the bottle, and the promises made by Balliol at Roxburgh were simply too tempting to be set aside. The time had come to stop the pretence and take up arms.

CHAPTER 10
Halidon Hill, a Barren Triumph, 1333

Balliol spent Christmas at Carlisle, where he was well received by Lord Dacre and the local population, pleased by his exploits against the Scots. His unexpected arrival in England had a sobering effect on Edward, causing him to scale down his ambitions. Scotland was after all not going to be the easy prize he had imagined. Edward was now prepared to greet Balliol as an ally, and to settle for that part of Scotland he had been promised in the Roxburgh Declaration. As a first step towards this Balliol, of course, would have to be restored to his throne. For the next four years most of the King's attention was taken up by the Scottish question; and as a mark of his preoccupation, York became the temporary capital of England, just as it had in the time of Edward I.

When Parliament reassembled on 20 January 1333 it proved no more willing to endorse a military adventure. But Edward's mind was made up. Losing patience he dismissed the assembled noblemen and decided on a unilateral course of action. The Treaty of Northampton was to be disregarded, and Edward Balliol was openly recognised as King of Scotland. A few days after the lords of Parliament dispersed military preparations were firmly underway. The disinherited were assisted in their own preparations for a fresh invasion of Scotland, royal subsidies being paid to Edward Balliol, Henry Beaumont, David de Strathbogie and others. In return, Balliol confirmed the sweeping terms of the Roxburgh Declaration in letters issued at Burgh in February 1333. These letters were carried to Edward by Balliol's lieutenants, Alexander Mowbray and John Felton, who were also empowered to swear on oath that he would adhere to their provisions. Balliol was now given leave to raise forces for a cross border invasion, which had been denied to him the previous year.

Edward had other reasons for renewing the war besides territorial gain and martial glory. A weakened Scotland with a compliant king would cease to be a threat to the English rear in the event of a quarrel with France. Scotland was also an attractive economic prize. Her economy had recovered from the dislocations of the First War of Independence, and foreign trade, especially in the export of wool, was buoyant. In the years between 1327 and 1333 at least 5,500 sacks of wool were exported annually from the eastern seaports. Berwick was by far the most important of these, accounting for an annual export of some 1,800 sacks. The customs dues collected here averaged £640 a year, constituting the largest single item in the crown's revenues. Berwick alone would be worth the expense of a campaign.

Edward's preparations for war blinded him to all political caution. He was getting ready to set out on an enterprise which, if successful, would rob Scotland of a large proportion of her most economically productive territory, and force her to accept a foreign aristocracy headed by an alien king. The experience of Edward's grandfather should have shown him that Scotland could not be won on the outcome of a single battle; and despite the transitory success of Dupplin Moor, Balliol had proved that he had insufficient support in the country to be able to stand on his own. Edward was therefore committing England to a war that could only be won by a considerable expenditure in men and materials. Time was to show that Edward III had neither the patience nor the stamina to sustain the effort required.

At the beginning of 1333 the atmosphere on the border was tense. England was openly preparing for war. In Scotland the Guardian, Archibald Douglas, made arrangements for the defence of Berwick. Weapons and supplies were gathered, and the defence of the town was entrusted to Sir Alexander Seton, whose son had been killed at Kinghorn the previous year. Command of the castle was given to Patrick de Dunbar, Earl of March. These preparations were complete by the time Balliol crossed into Roxburghshire on 10 March. Besides the disinherited lords he was accompanied by a number of English magnates. His first target was the small fortress of Oxnam, defended by Robert Colville, which was quickly overwhelmed. Balliol then advanced towards Berwick and invested the town and castle, while David de Strathbogie devastated the surrounding countryside. The deceptions of the previous year were gone, and Balliol was now quite openly acting in the English interest. The Second War of Independence was now firmly underway.

The new war was to be a grim and bleak contest between participants of unequal strength. The major pitched battles— Halidon Hill and Neville's Cross—were both disasters for Scotland, exceeding anything the country had experienced in the first war.

But the Scots were fortunate because Edward III seldom demonstrated the same ruthless determination as his grandfather. His only serious attempt to campaign north of the Tay in 1336 was a shadow of the first Edward's great invasions of 1296 and 1303–4. His one attempt to conduct a winter campaign in 1334–5 failed because it had no clear aims, and because most of his countrymen were reluctant to submit themselves to the harshness of the Scottish climate. When he finally accepted that the country could only be held by a strong line of fortifications he no longer had the resources to carry this policy to a conclusion.

The Scots started the war seemingly forgetting all of King Robert's teachings. After the catastrophe of Halidon Hill resistance was very weak. Even so, it never died out completely, as it did from time to time in the first war. Andrew Murray, after he returned from English captivity in 1334, reacquainted Scotland with the benefits of scorched earth tactics backed up by unceasing guerrilla warfare. He was never to enjoy the prestige of great victory as his father, Wallace and Bruce had done; but it was his tenacity, and the example he set, that finally broke the back of the English occupation.

There appears to have been no Scottish force in the neighbourhood of Berwick to prevent Balliol's siege taking hold. The Guardian's response was to launch a brief and rather pointless cross border raid into Gilsland on the western border on 22 March. All he achieved was a reprisal raid two days later by Sir Anthony Lucy, and the first minor Scottish reverse at the 'Battle of Dornock', where William Douglas, the commander of Lochmaben Castle, later to achieve infamy as the 'Knight of Liddesdale', was taken prisoner. Dornock, according to Andrew Wyntoun, provided a foretaste of the coming disaster at Halidon Hill. The Guardian's actions also provided fuel for Edward's propaganda, allowing him to write to the King of France denouncing the Scots as aggressors. Balliol's action at Berwick was, needless to say, ignored.

Edward arrived at the border in May after leaving his Queen, Philipa, in the safety of Bamburgh Castle on the Northumberland coast. His army then crossed into Scotland to join Balliol at the siege of Berwick, and was met there by a strong naval squadron. By the time Edward arrived his ally had been at Berwick for some two months, and had been so far unmolested that he had been allowed to place the town under close siege. Trenches had been dug, the town's water supply cut and all communication with the hinterland ended. The Guardian's inactivity contrasts sharply with the swift

Scots reaction to the siege of 1319. Douglas seems to have spent the time after the Gilsland raid gathering a large national army; otherwise life continued as normal. There was no scorched earth policy; and in the south east, the area closest to the battle front, normal commercial activities were carried on much as before. English raiders scoured the countryside foraging for supplies, apparently free from any threat of retaliation. One party penetrated as far as Haddington in East Lothian: they arrived on market day, killed all the traders and sacked the town.

But Berwick itself continued to defy all Balliol's attempts at capture. Sensing the depth of Scots hostility to the pretender King, the English noblemen, according to the author of the *Anonimalle Chronicle*, spoke to the defenders, ' saying that the town ought to be given over to them to the use of the King of England and not to the use of Sir Edward Balliol.' But Edward Plantagenet was no more attractive to the Scots than his namesake and protégé. So the struggle continued.

With the arrival of King Edward the attack on the town began in earnest. The King brought with him the Flemish engineer John Crabb, captured the previous year at Roxburgh, who had helped Walter Stewart defend the town against Edward II in 1319. To save his life he now changed sides, and used his invaluable knowledge of Berwick's defences to assist the bombardment. Aside from the usual siege engines the defenders may also have been subject to some elementary cannon fire; if so, this is likely to have been the first time such equipment saw active use in the British Isles. But the real damage was done by the huge stones lobbed in by the catapults, which caused considerable destruction in the town. Nevertheless, the walls built by the English, and strengthened by Robert Bruce, were strong, and the defenders continued to hold out. In late June an attempt was made to take the town by a double pronged assault from land and sea. When the tide came in the English warships drew alongside the walls, joining the landward attack. William Seton, the second son of the warden, Sir Alexander Seton, was killed attempting to resist the naval squadron. His comrades attempted to set fire to the English flotilla, but they only succeeded in setting the town itself ablaze. As the buildings burned the warden had no choice but to seek a truce to deal with this emergency. This was granted provided he agreed to surrender the following day. When the fire was at last brought under control Seton changed his mind and Edward ordered the attack to recommence.

Despite the warden's defiance the defenders were close to exhaustion, and a further truce had to be sought on 28 June. Seton and Dunbar now promised to surrender if they were not relieved by 11 July. Edward agreed; but this time he was determined that Seton should keep his bond, insisting on the surrender of twelve hostages, to include the warden's last surviving son, Thomas Seton.

Scotland was now faced with exactly the same situation that England had before Bannockburn: as a matter of national pride Archibald Douglas would have to come to the relief of Berwick, just as Edward II had come to the relief of Stirling. The army the Guardian had spent all too long gathering was now compelled to take to the field, with all initiative lost. However, Douglas's force was an impressive representation of the nation's strength and unity, with men coming from all corners of the realm. As always with medieval armies the precise number of troops is difficult to estimate: it is possible, though, that it was at least as strong as that of Bruce at Bannockburn, or perhaps even stronger. Douglas now began his belated march towards the English border.

In an attempt to draw Edward away from Berwick the Scots entered England on 11 July, the last day of Seton and Dunbar's truce. They advanced eastwards towards the little port of Tweedmouth, just south of Berwick on the English side of the River Tweed. The town was destroyed in the sight of the English army, but Edward did not move. A small party of Scots led by Sir William Keith managed with some difficulty to make their way across the ruins of the old bridge to the northern bank of the Tweed. Keith and some of his men were able to enter the town by the Briggate, but the others were killed or captured by William Montagu. Douglas chose to regard this as a technical relief of the town, and the defenders confirmed this by replacing Seton as warden with Keith. Messages were sent to Edward calling on him to depart, with the added threat that if he failed to do so Douglas would take his army south and lay waste to England. Again the King refused to accept the challenge, and Douglas made his way south to Bamburgh Castle, where Queen Philipa was in residence, perhaps hoping for a repetition of the events leading to the Chapter of Myton. Whatever concern Edward may have had for the safety of his wife, he knew that Bamburgh was strong and could easily withstand a siege. The Scots, moreover, did not have the time to construct the kind of equipment that would be necessary to take the fortress by assault. For Berwick, on the other hand, time was definitely running out.

Edward refused to consider Keith's entry into Berwick as a relief in terms of the agreement of the 28th of June. As that truce had now expired, and the town still refused to surrender, he ordered the hostages to be hanged before the walls, beginning with Thomas Seton, who died in the sight of his parents. Thereafter, a further two were to be hanged every day for as long as the garrison refused to capitulate. Edward's determination had the desired effect. To save the lives of those who remained the defenders agreed to a third truce, promising to surrender the town and castle if they were not relieved by Tuesday, 20 July. Everything now hinged on a Scots victory in battle. Sir William Keith was allowed to leave Berwick in the company of Sir William Prendergast and Sir Alexander Gray to carry news of the terms of the latest truce to the Guardian in the neighbourhood of Bamburgh. Whatever doubts Douglas may have had about facing the English in open battle after Dupplin Moor were stilled by Keith, who reassured him that his army was stronger than Edward's. Keith is also reputed to have threatened to surrender the town forthwith if Douglas refused to accept Edward's challenge. Having lost all freedom of action the Guardian set off northwards into the teeth of the wolf.

Edward and his army took up position on Halidon Hill, a small rise of some 500ft two miles to the north west of Berwick, which gives an excellent view of the town and surrounding countryside. From this vantage point he was able to dominate all of the approaches to the beleaguered port. Any attempt by Douglas to by-pass the hill and march directly on Berwick would have been quickly overwhelmed.

Crossing the Tweed to the west of Edward, Douglas reached the town of Duns in the county of Berwick on Sunday, 18 July. On the following day he approached Halidon Hill from the north west, ready to give battle on ground chosen by his enemy. It was a catastrophic decision. The Scots chronicle of Pluscarden describes the scene:

> They (the Scots) marched towards the town with great display, in order of battle, and recklessly, stupidly and inadvisedly chose a battle ground at Halidon Hill, where there was a marshy hollow between the two armies, and where a great downward slope, with some precipices, and then again a rise lay in front of the Scots before they could reach the field where the English were posted.

Douglas's approach was observed by Henry Beaumont, who would have fully briefed Edward on the tactics used at Dupplin Moor when the two men met at York the previous December. The order of battle the King now employed mirrored those used by Beaumont, allowing for some variations because of his superior strength. The army was divided into three divisions, comprising infantry, men-at-arms and knights. All made ready to fight on foot in a defensive position. The division on the left was commanded by Edward Balliol, the centre by the King and the right nearest to the sea by Thomas Brotherton, the Earl of Norfolk and Earl Marshall of England, and Sir Edward Bohun. Beaumont was stationed in Brotherton's division. Standing on the flank of each division were six supporting wings of archers, those on the right being commanded by Strathbogie and Gilbert de Umfraville. The bowmen projected slightly forward in wedge formation to offer maximum use of supporting crossfire, an arrangement that was later to be adopted on the battlefield of Crecy. Edward was required to take no further action other than wait for the Scots; for if Douglas refused to give battle, as caution and good sense surely demanded, the English would win Berwick by default.

Douglas's army was also divided into three divisions. The men-at-arms had dismounted to join the spearmen, leaving their horses with the grooms some distance to the rear. The divisions were drawn up in the traditional schiltron formation: Douglas commanded the left; Robert Stewart, Robert Bruce's grandson and the future King of Scotland, commanded the centre, and the Earl of Moray the right. As Pluscarden says, to engage the English they had to advance downhill, cross a large area of marshy ground and then climb up the northern slope of Halidon Hill. Although the Scots spearmen had proved their worth when faced with cavalry at Stirling Bridge and Bannockburn, the battles of Falkirk and Dupplin Moor had shown how vulnerable they were to arrow fire. Not only was the ground bad, but it must have been obvious to the Guardian as he looked towards the massed ranks of Edward's archers that this was not going to be a cavalry battle. The prudent course of action would have been to withdraw and wait for a better opportunity to fight; but this would have meant the automatic loss of Berwick. Douglas's delays and mismanagement forced Scotland to fight what was perhaps the most disadvantageous battle in her history, exceeded only by the even more disastrous Battle of Flodden two centuries later.

No sooner had the Scots entered the marsh at the foot of the hill than the arrows began to rain, and the air filled with their sinister whine. They continued to descend in great clouds as the schiltrons freed themselves from the marshy ground to begin the ascent up Halidon Hill. Having lost all momentum they moved slowly upwards, so tightly packed that even the most indifferent archer could not fail to hit his target. The fire was so intense that the Scots turned their faces away as if walking into a storm of sleet. The Lanercost chronicler writes: '. . . the Scots who marched in the front line were so wounded in the face and blinded by the multitude of English arrows that they could not help themselves, and soon began to turn their faces away from the blows of the arrows and fall.' Casualties were heavy, with some of the finest troops falling dead or wounded on the lower reaches of the hill. The survivors crawled upwards through the arrows and into the spears.

The Earl of Moray's depleted schiltron was the first to make contact with Edward Balliol's division on the left of the English army. The Stewart followed, advancing to meet King Edward in the centre. Douglas's men were the last to approach the top of the hill. But even before the Stewart and Douglas arrived Moray's front ranks were having the worst of the hand to hand fighting with Balliol. With the arrows continuing to fall the schiltron broke, retreating rapidly downhill. Panic spread to the centre and left. With English arrow fire directed towards the flanks the Scots bunched in a disorganised mass towards the centre, much as they had done at Dupplin Moor, as if each man was trying to escape death behind the body of his comrade. Those to the rear began to run back towards the marsh away from the killing ground. Scots honour was saved by the Earl of Ross and his highlanders who, like the Spartans at Themopolaye, fought to the death in a gallant rearguard action.

With Ross gone the English knights mounted their horses and rode off in pursuit of the fugitives. It is said that the survivors who made it back to camp found that the grooms had fled with their horses; but at least some must have remained, for Robert Stewart, the Earl of Moray and the Earl of Strathearn all managed to escape Edward's murderous hunt, presumably not on foot. Few of the other magnates escaped, and a large number of ordinary soldiers were slaughtered with sword, axe and mace. The hunt only ended at dusk, when the knights returned to Halidon to take the measure of their triumph. The battlefield was a grim place for Scotland. The Guardian lay dead together with five earls: John Campbell of Atholl, King Robert's nephew, Alexander Bruce of Carrick, Macolm of Lennox, Hugh of Ross and Kenneth of Sutherland. Also killed was

William, Lord of Douglas, son and heir of the great Sir James, who had fought in the Stewart's division. They died in the company of the nameless commons of Scotland, who fell in their thousands. English casualties were light. The following day Berwick surrendered and Edward celebrated the occasion by having the few Scots prisoners from the battle beheaded.

The news of Halidon sent shock waves throughout southern Scotland. Edward soon received the fealty of several landowners in the area of Berwick. Fearing destruction the important religious foundations at Melrose, Kelso, Coldstream, Eccles and Coldingam all hurried to submit. In England the victory, the first for many years, brought a great boost to the morale of the nation. Bannockburn had finally been revenged. The patriotic poet, Laurence Minot, was exultant:

> A little fro that foresaid toune (Berwick)
> Halydon-hill that es the name
> Thaire was crakked many a crowne
> Of wild Scottes, and alls of tame;
> Thaire was thaire banner born all doune.

Other balladeers celebrated the restoration of national pride:

> Scottes out of Berwick and Aberdeen
> At the Burn of Bannock ye were far too keen,
> King Edward has avenged it now, and fully too, I ween.

Edward III's victory at the Battle of Halidon Hill was a more devastating blow for Scotland than his grandfather's at Dunbar. After Dunbar most of the nobles had been captured and lived to continue to fight another day; after Halidon most of the country's natural leaders were dead, and the few who remained were in hiding. Scotland was prostrate. It was said at the time that the English victory had been so complete that it marked the final end of the northern war. However, five years after the event the chronicler Adam Murimuth wrote:

> And so, men freely declare that the Scotch wars had been brought to their close, that nothing remained of the Scotch nation that was willing or able to defend or govern itself. Yet they were wrong as the sequel showed.

The time that had passed before Murimuth wrote these words had shown Halidon to be a barren victory. For Edward did little to exploit his success; and Scottish resistance, although weak, was not fully subdued. A great opportunity had passed never to come again. Dupplin and Halidon had virtually destroyed the governing class of Scotland. A determined push by Edward in the summer and autumn of 1333 might conceivably have extinguished the last flames of national resistance. It was not to be so.

Confident in the completeness of his victory the King was content to leave Balliol the task of conquering Scotland, with a force no greater, perhaps, than that which had descended on Fife a year before. He may have believed that the Scots, humbled by the rout at Halidon, were more likely to accept their 'king' if he arrived with his own power, rather than in an English baggage train; if so, it was a serious miscalculation, and one he would soon come to regret.

CHAPTER 11

The Shifting Sands of Fortune, 1333–1335

The immediate task before Edward was to take possession of Berwick as the first instalment of the lands promised to him by Balliol. Henry Percy was appointed as the keeper of both the town and castle. The former keeper of the castle, the Earl of March, always one to follow the prevailing wind, changed sides and was compensated for his loss by being allowed to repair his castle at Dunbar at English expense. Edward came to regret his generosity. The former warden of the town, Alexander Seton, also changed allegiance, despite the fact that he had now lost all three of his sons in the cause of Scotland and King David. Berwick was to be the main English base in Scotland for over a hundred years. It only passed back into Scottish hands for a brief twenty year period in the fifteenth century, before it was lost again; this time forever.

After settling matters at Berwick Edward returned south to join Queen Philipa at Bamburgh. From there he returned to London to bask in the sun of his first triumph in war. Most of his soldiers also went home. Edward Balliol left Berwick on a journey north to reclaim his kingdom. The army of the disinherited passed without opposition into central Scotland. Balliol took up residence at Perth, which now became his capital.

King Balliol now enters a period of about a year's length in which he appeared to exercise at least some royal authority in a country which now had two kings. His occupation of Perth and central Scotland was certainly more secure than it had been in 1332. He was sufficiently confident to summon his first Parliament to Scone in September 1333, where the disinherited proceeded to harvest the fruits of their labours. Those who supported the Bruce party were to be the new disinherited. Balliol revoked and quashed all the deeds and grants of Robert I, 'ordaining and commanding,' so says the *Lanercost Chronicle* 'that all that he (Robert) had granted should be restored to such of the original and true heirs who had not born arms against him in the aforesaid war.' Many of the native gentry came to Scone to offer homage to the new King. The greater the investment in King Balliol's cause, the greater the reward: Henry Beaumont was named Earl of Moray as well as Earl of Buchan, and he was appointed Constable of Scotland. David de Strathbogie, the Earl of Atholl, was also to be the new Stewart of Scotland in place of the forfeited Robert; and Richard Talbot was to be Lord of Mar (curiously, not Earl). The Red Comyn enjoyed a posthumous triumph over his enemies.

To the Parliament at Scone also came Henry Percy and Ralph Neville at the head of a powerful English embassy to remind King Balliol of the pact with the devil he had concluded at Roxburgh. Beaumont and Strathbogie, the two most important props of Balliol's regime, were also recruited by Edward to join this embassy, as if to remind Balliol where the ultimate loyalties of his most powerful noblemen rested. This matter was to be considered again at Balliol's second, and last, Parliament, which met in Edinburgh in February 1334.

It's difficult to be sure just how much of Scotland the Balliol party did in fact control in the late summer of 1333. Perhaps all of central and south east Scotland was firmly in King Balliol's peace. Fife was firm, with garrisons at St. Andrews and Cupar Castle, the latter commanded by the cleric William Bullock, soon to be named as Balliol's chancellor. Galloway was certainly loyal, but not completely secure until the fall of the old Bruce stronghold of Lochmaben Castle. Henry Beaumont was able to return to Buchan in the north east where, according to Andrew Wyntoun, he repaired the old Comyn stronghold at Dundarg on the Aberdeenshire coast, destroyed by Robert Bruce in 1308, sometime in 1333 or 1334:

> The Beaumont went intil Buchan;
> And there, Dundarg of lime and stane
> He made stoutly, and therin lay.

As well as establishing a base at the island castle of Lochindorb in Moray, Strathbogie was able to take steps to confirm his position as the new Stewart of Scotland. He took control of Renfrewshire, the island of Bute in the Firth of Clyde and the Cowal Peninsula in Argyll, all part of the hereditary Stewart lands. Alan de Lisle, an Englishman, was appointed by Strathbogie as sheriff of Bute and Cowal, and garrisons were established at Dunoon and Rothesay castles.

And yet even at its most secure Balliol's rule has an impermanent character: attendance of the native nobility at his two parliaments was extremely weak; no accounts have come down to us from William Bullock, his chancellor; and he never issued his own coinage. Throughout this whole period there was a small body of patriots who would not be reconciled to his rule; but there also seems to have been an even larger group who remained on the sidelines, supporting neither one party nor the other, simply waiting to see how things turned out. The far north, the west central highlands and the Isles appear to have been controlled by the 'neutral party'; men like John of the Isles, chief of the MacDonalds, who was to be courted unsuccessfully by both sides.

The nature of Balliol's kingship was made clear to his subjects from the outset: his freedom of action was always highly circum-scribed, as the affair over Malise, Earl of Strathearn, demonstrates. Malise was one of the fortunate few to escape the carnage of Halidon Hill. His earldom was forfeited by the new regime and awarded to John de Warenne, Earl of Surrey and Balliol's cousin. In 1334 Malise seems to have made an attempt to make peace with Balliol, who began to consider restoring his earldom. When Edward learned of this he wrote to Balliol in March 1334 in vaguely menacing terms, advising him to undertake no such measure. He also wrote to Henry Beaumont, his principal aid in Scotland, asking him to oppose any attempt to restore the forfeited earl.

In the dark summer of 1333 the Bruce cause was kept alive by the garrisons of a few scattered castles, that seem to have escaped the late King's policy of reducing strongholds. In Richard Talbot's lands of Mar, the lady Christian Bruce, sister of King Robert and wife of Andrew Murray, held Kildrummy Castle. In the south-west John Thomson held the island fortress of Loch Doon in Carrick. Alan de Vipont held Loch Leven Castle, uncomfortably close to Balliol's own capital, while Robert Lauder held Urquhart by Loch Ness. The two most important castles still in the hands of the Bruce loyalists were Lochmaben, which commanded the west march, and Dumbarton under Malcolm Fleming, which dominated the upper reaches of the Firth of Clyde. It was to Dumbarton that young King David and Queen Joan took refuge after Halidon, presumably from the nearby Bruce manor house at Cardross. Here they remained throughout the dangerous winter of 1333/4, to be joined by Robert Stewart, who managed to escape from his hideout on Bute in a rowing boat, with only the clothes he wore and his family charters.

Lochmaben fell to an Anglo-Scottish force led by David de

Strathbogie and Edward Bohun in November 1333, and was to serve as the symbol of English mastery in Annandale for the next fifty years. The other castles, however, remained in the hands of the supporters of King David throughout the war. They were too widely scattered to represent an immediate danger to Balliol, but as long as they resisted, and King David remained at liberty, he could not really be regarded as the rightful King of Scotland. Rather than ignoring them Balliol may simply have lacked the men and equipment necessary for their reduction without further English assistance. Any additional help from Edward would obviously depend on Balliol fulfilling his promise of November 1332.

It would appear that King Balliol was beginning to drag his heels slightly over the sweeping terms of the Roxburgh Declaration. For now that his position was slightly more secure he had the leisure to consider the political damage the wholesale English annexation of southern Scotland would undeniably do to his cause. Edward lacked the wisdom and good judgement to appreciate the dilemma. If he had settled for Berwick, which he already possessed, it's quite possible that the remaining pockets of Bruce resistance could have been stamped out, and England would have been able to settle its problems with France free from any Scottish entanglement. But Edward was unable to look beyond the immediate prospect of territorial enlargement. On 30 May 1333 he had taken possession of the Isle of Man, awarding it absolutely to his close confidant, William Montagu, and without any apparent reference to Edward Balliol, although the island had formed no part of the Roxburgh concession. To put additional pressure on Balliol to fulfil the terms of his bargain he quite deliberately reminded him of the vulnerability of his position in November 1333, when he issued safe conducts to leading representatives of the Bruce party, including Sir Malcolm Fleming. Clearly the issue raised by the Roxburgh Declaration could be postponed no longer.

There were signs in early 1334 that all was not well in Scotland. Balliol was not able to attend the York Parliament in February because of alleged disturbances on the islands of the Firth of Clyde; although this may simply have been a convenient excuse, allowing him to preserve some royal dignity by avoiding attendance at an English assembly. Conditions were certainly secure enough for Balliol's own Parliament to met at Holyrood Abbey at Edinburgh on 10 February 1334. The church was well represented, with more than half the bishops in attendance including Glasgow, Aberdeen,

Dunkeld, Galloway, Ross, Dunblane and Brechin. Balliol and King Edward's victories were clearly seen as signs of divine grace. The magnates did not seem so sure, for they were seriously underrepresented. Apart from the 'reinherited' the only Scots earl in attendance was Patrick of Dunbar, and the only other Scots of note were Alexander Seton and William Keith. Representation was made up by a number of Englishmen.

As at Scone the previous September a strong English embassy appeared, this time headed by Geoffrey Scrope, to remind Balliol of the contract he had entered into with Edward. Two days passed before they received an answer. We have no record of the debate, but it may be that Balliol and his supporters considered ways of minimising the damage that Edward's demands would cause. It is possible that the churchmen, who after all were not of the disinherited party, fought some kind of delaying action. But the outcome was inevitable given the loyalties of most of those present, and the contribution Edward had made to the cause of Henry Beaumont and the other Anglo-Scottish lords. On 12 February letters were issued ratifying the Declaration of Roxburgh. Parliament approved the cessation of Berwick and Berwickshire and agreed to further substantial territorial concessions, although these were not specified. It was also agreed that Balliol should pay further homage to Edward at a date and time to be decided.

Balliol finally met Edward at Newcastle on 12 June 1334, and the full extent of the Roxburgh promise became known: almost all of English speaking Scotland was to be surrendered, eight counties in all, including the three Lothians, Roxburgh, Selkirk, Peebles, Dumfries as well as Berwickshire—all that King Malcolm II had won at the Battle of Carham three hundred years before, and more. In giving up these lands Balliol made no allowance for his own hereditary estates in Dumfriesshire. Edward was gracious enough to order the return of some these lands on 18 June; the remainder being similarly returned in December 1335. These were, of course, returned to Balliol in a personal capacity and not to Scotland. Balliol would now have a divided rule as King of Scotland and the English Lord of Galloway. The letters authorising the disposal of southern Scotland were witnessed by the chief noblemen of the Balliol party. They were joined by the Archbishop of York and the bishops of Durham and Carlisle. No Scottish churchman signed. On 19 June Balliol performed an act of homage to what was left of his truncated kingdom. To sweeten the pill Edward promised to maintain Balliol and his heirs as Kings of Scotland, and further agreed to abandon any claim to jurisdiction in Scotland and the right to hear Scots appeals before the English courts, the very matter that led to the ruin of Balliol's father.

It is difficult to accept that Scotland would have been able to survive as a national entity after the permanent loss of the south and south east. Not only were these the richest and most fertile lands in the country, but they were vital to the defence of the realm. Scotland would have been extremely vulnerable to any future English aggression, and its quite likely that the history of late medieval and early modern Scotland would have followed the pattern of piecemeal conquest and subjugation that was to be the fate of Ireland. The news of Balliol's dismemberment of Scotland would have been passed to all corners of the kingdom by the ecclesiastics who attended the Parliament in February. Before long the forces of resistance, which had been in partial hibernation, began to stir. But a more immediate threat awaited Balliol. He returned to Scotland in the summer of 1334 to the news that the King of France was at last taking an interest in the fate of his northern ally.

After Halidon Hill the Earl of Moray had been able to escape to France in the company of those prelates who refused to follow the example of the Bishop of Dunkeld. In Paris he began to plead the cause of King David. King Philip VI, the first of the Valois kings of France, was at first reluctant to involve himself in a quarrel seemingly lost. Moray persisted, and was rewarded in early 1334 by Philip's recognition that there may still be life in the Bruce cause. After a slightly shaky start Philip VI was to prove himself a better friend to Scotland than Philip IV had ever been. As a first step he agreed to offer asylum to King David, an act that was bound to be viewed in a hostile light by the English. Moray was given a gift of 1,000 marks to fit out a ship with which to return to Scotland and bring David and Joan to France. They arrived with their little court in Normandy in May 1334, and were well received by King Philip, who allowed them to settle in Chateau Galliard, Richard Coer de Lion's old stronghold on the River Seine near Rouen. This was to be David and Joan's home for the next seven years.

The arrival of David Bruce in France brought a definite change in Anglo-French relations. Edward had recently sent an embassy to France charged with settling the outstanding disputes in Gascony. Once these had been dealt with he even proposed to join with Philip on a crusade, a project close to the French King's heart. But Philip surprised the ambassadors by refusing to consider any treaty that did not also address the Scottish question. Philip's new firmness presented Edward with an unforeseen dilemma: if he hoped to recover the lands his father had lost in France he would have to abandon Balliol and his newly won territories in Scotland. Some time after the failure of the English embassy the French ambassador at the papal court explained to Pope John XXII, the recipient of the Declaration of Arbroath, the commitment his country had made to Scotland in the Treaty of Corbeil. The Pope, who clearly saw this as a potential cause of war, replied that France was rich and her riches were desired by others. The Anglo-Scottish conflict was to be one of the tributary streams flowing in to the great torrent known as the Hundred Years War.

Edward was quick to take possession of his new Scottish domains. The English border was now pushed up to the Firth of Forth, and a full administration was established, headed by a chamberlain, chancellor and justiciar. Once again Edward was absurdly optimistic in assuming that the people of southern Scotland would readily settle down to this alien government. Scotland was a country with which he had only recently been at war; yet the new officialdom was supported by an extremely modest occupying army. When William Pressen took possession of the partially ruined castle at Jedburgh he had with him ten men-at-arms and ten hobelars. In Dumfries, William Wessington, the new sheriff, did slightly better with fifteen men-at-arms and thirty hobelars; but his colleague Gilbert Burden, the sheriff of Peebles, had only eight men-at-arms and twelve hobelars.

Edward's attempt at occupation on the cheap invites contrast with his grandfather's in newly conquered north Wales in 1283, an area not much greater in size than that which the English now controlled in southern Scotland. Edward I had secured the principality of Wales by constructing a ring of castles headed by Caernarvon, Conway and Harlech. This, of course, had been ruinously expensive, and Edward III could nor afford to build on this scale in Scotland; but he made no effort at this time even to repair the castles that had been partially demolished by Robert Bruce. In the whole of the eight counties the only castles of note in English hands were Berwick in the east and Lochmaben in the west. The ring of castles, headed by Edinburgh, which had enabled Edward I and Edward II to hold the south east of Scotland for so long, remained in a state of ruin, with the possible exception of Jedburgh. The failure to make proper arrangements for the security of the south east was a serious error of judgement, only exceeded by the failure to attend to security in Balliol's satellite kingdom. By neglecting to provide Balliol with the means of reducing the remaining Bruce strongholds Edward effectively negated the success of Halidon Hill, with serious consequences for both kings. In the great national uprising of 1334 English administration in the south east vanished as quickly as it had come, and many of the recently appointed officials fled for their lives to the safety of Berwick.

By the time Balliol returned to Perth in the summer of 1334 Dumbarton Castle had become the centre of national resistance. It was from here that Robert Stewart struck the first blow by setting out to recover his ancestral lands from Strathbogie. Together with Dougal Campbell of Lochawe he gathered a small company of men and launched a seaborne attack against Dunoon Castle in Cowal. The defenders were overwhelmed and Stewart established his own garrison. News of this blow soon spread to the loyal Stewart tenants on the Isle of Bute. Led by John Gibson, and armed with no more than the stones they found scattered upon a hillside, they attacked and defeated Strathbogie's sheriff, Alan de Lisle, and took possession of Rothesay Castle. The Stewart was able to return to Bute in triumph after the 'Batayle Dormag'—the Battle of the Casting Stones—and arranged for the security of the newly won castle. In the meantime, guerrilla bands began operations in the old Bruce territories of Kyle and Annandale.

When John Randolph, Earl of Moray, returned from France with the welcome news of King Philip's renewed interest in the Bruce cause, plans for a major counter offensive began to take shape. A council of war was held at Dumbarton and it was decided to open up operations in the south west of Scotland. In late July 1334 a little fleet under the joint leadership of Moray and Stewart left Dumbarton and crossed the Clyde into Renfrewshire. With them came Laurence of Abernethy and William Douglas of Liddesdale, recently released on ransom from English captivity. The Stewart was welcomed as a liberator by the people of Renfrew, and the army, no doubt swelled by fresh recruits, advanced down Clydesdale, encountering little resistance. In Cunningham Balliol's sheriff, Sir Godfrey Ross, was compelled to change sides. So, in a very short period of time, almost all of south west Scotland north of Galloway was in the hands of the patriots, demonstrating the extreme superficiality of Balliol's rule. Scottish government was re-established, and the Stewart and Moray became joint Guardians in the name of King David. From Carrick the fighting continued into Galloway. As always the contest here was bloody and bitter. It also seems to have been further complicated by a minor civil war amongst the adherents of Edward Balliol. His concessions to England appear to have caused Duncan MacDouall to come over to the Bruce party with many other people of Galloway. However, the supporters of Balliol and King Edward were rallied by Eustace Maxwell, who managed to maintain an effective resistance in eastern Dumfriesshire.

Scottish operations continued into those areas nominally under English rule, bypassing King Balliol in nervous isolation at Perth. By the end of the year of the eight ceded counties only Berwickshire remained fully under English control. The *Lanercost Chronicle* reflects on the magnitude of the crisis: 'The number of Scots in rebellion against their King [Edward Balliol] increased daily, so that before the feast of St Michael [29 September 1334] nearly the whole of Scotland rose and drove the King to Berwick.' Balliol's kingdom was disintegrating, along with all the gains of Halidon Hill.

In the midst of the growing crisis Balliol sent Thomas Ughtred to Edward pleading for help. The King underestimated how dangerous the situation had become, and no immediate help arrived. Events were moving fast, and by the time Edward decided to intervene directly it was already too late.

It was obvious from the urgency of his appeal to England that Balliol lacked the means to deal with the uprising on his own. His best policy in the circumstances would have been to hold together his small party of adherents until English help arrived. But as his kingdom contracted to a small area of central Scotland, the carpet was pulled from under the feet of the desperate King by the very men who brought him to Scotland from France. His rule ended not in battle but ironically in a dispute over land: 'King Balliol . . . being the first himself to open the way to his own ruin, by imprudently occasioning discord amongst his most powerful friends.' (Joshua Barnes *The History of Edward III*)

The matter concerned the lands of John Mowbray, killed at Annan in December 1332. Mowbray left three daughters, amongst whom his land should rightfully have been divided. However, their inheritance was claimed by their uncle, Alexander Mowbray, whose claim was favoured by Balliol. In this he made the mistake of alienating his most powerful nobles—Henry Beaumont, David de

Strathbogie and Richard Talbot, who all took the part of the daughters. This dispute, serious enough for Balliol's prospects, had acquired a kind of Byzantine unreality: for the lands in question were no longer under his control. Yet, with astonishing blindness to the reality of the situation, the matter was allowed to come to a head at Balliol's council in Stirling on 24 August, when Beaumont's objections were finally overruled.

With the Bruce loyalists closing in the disinherited now fell apart. Beaumont and the others in a fit of umbrage resolved to abandon the King they had taken such trouble to make, and like so many Achilles return to their individual tents, taking no further part in the King's defence, and allowing the patriots to pick them off piecemeal. Of the three only Henry Beaumont was able to complete his journey to Dundarg Castle in Buchan. Strathbogie was intercepted on the way to his own castle at Lochindorb and chased into the countryside of Lochaber, where he was forced to yield to the Earl of Moray on 27 September. Strathbogie decided to save his life by switching his allegiance to King David, a defection that was to do the Bruce cause little good. On his way to the Highlands Richard Talbot was frightened by the growing signs of insurrection, and decided that England offered a better refuge. In early September he was trapped near Linlithgow and forced to surrender after a brief fight. Talbot was taken to Dumbarton Castle. He was finally ransomed in April 1335 and left Scotland, seemingly never to return.

Now almost alone at Stirling Balliol faced one final humiliation. Andrew Murray had recently been allowed to ransom himself from his English prison, an act which showed that Edward's greed greatly outweighed his political wisdom. At this point Alexander Mowbray, whose desire to keep hold of his lands took priority over his loyalty to King Balliol, became aware of the strength of the prevailing wind, and abandoned the man who had supported him at such great personal cost to himself. Both he and his brother Geoffrey, the English sheriff of Roxburgh, joined Murray in taking action against Balliol. Mowbray proceeded to rob him of his money and royal furniture. In desperation Balliol fled across the border after narrowly escaping a raiding party sent to catch him, taking refuge at Ravensworth in late September 1334. He arrived in England virtually destitute, thus proving to Edward and all the world that he had been unable to make good his claim to be the ruler of Scotland. The illusion of Balliol's kingship came to an end that autumn: from this time forward he was to be little better than a figurehead.

When King Edward set out from Newcastle in November 1334 to try to retrieve something from the summer debacle, the auguries were not good. Almost all had been lost. Only Patrick de Dunbar, Earl of March, and Henry Beaumont, closely besieged by Murray and Mowbray in remote Dundarg, remained loyal. Winter campaigns were never popular, and the army he brought with him was not strong enough for a major offensive. To attract more recruits a joint proclamation was issued in his name and that of Edward Balliol holding out the prospect of unlimited looting. Still the number of troops remained disappointingly small. Only a very limited operation was possible.

To rectify some of the errors of 1333 Edward advanced on Roxburgh and set about repairing the ruined castle. While the large company of builders he brought with him went to work the King remained here throughout the winter of 1334-5, appealing for reinforcements that never came. What he hoped to do if he had sufficient force has not been revealed; at the very least he is likely to have wished to march to the relief of Henry Beaumont and the garrison of Dundarg, estimated to have numbered some 300 people, including women and other non-combatants. As Edward's small army froze in the winter gales at Roxburgh, Beaumont's position was becoming desperate. Murray was making use of a siege engine which caused extensive damage, partially destroying the main tower. Under continual attack, running short of supplies and with no sign of a relief force Beaumont was compelled to surrender on 23 December. After a brief imprisonment he was ransomed and returned to England in time for the summer campaign of 1335. While he came back to Scotland it is uncertain if he ever again returned to Buchan. Dundarg Castle was destroyed for the second and last time in its history.

With the fall of Dundarg the only result of Edward's winter war was the repair of Roxburgh Castle. In a final attempt to lure the Scots into battle he conducted a limited campaign in the border area. Edward advanced into the forest of Ettrick, while Balliol led a force from Carlisle to Peebles, all to no avail. Balliol was keen to continue the winter operation, although to what end is not at all clear. He also asked that Edward put political considerations before the short term prospect of financial gain, and ransom no more prisoners of war. This served as something of a disguised reprimand; for both must have been mindful of the release of Andrew Murray, the victor of Dundarg, and the consequence this had for the cause of both kings. Edward agreed with Balliol's observation; but ironically it was the ransom of a greater individual than Murray that was ultimately to bring Balliol's pretence to an end.

The most damaging side effect of the Roxburgh campaign was the defection of Patrick of Dunbar. Whilst on the borders the English forces had raided indiscriminately in the surrounding countryside, not bothering to inquire about the political allegiance of the owners. Dunbar's lands were ravaged, and unable to obtain proper compensation, he abandoned his erstwhile allegiance and rejoined the Bruce party. His castle at Dunbar was shortly to become a major nuisance to the English forces in Lothian.

When Edward's army finally disbanded in February 1335, he returned to Newcastle to be met by a French embassy demanding to know the reasons for his continuing aggression in Scotland and support of Edward Balliol, a man who had no right to the throne, over his own sister and brother-in-law. The King managed to control his feelings and simply declined to give a reply. Not wishing a direct confrontation with King Philip he allowed the envoys to proceed to Scotland. As a consequence of the ensuing diplomatic coming and going an Anglo-Scottish truce was concluded to last until the mid-summer of 1335. This undoubtedly suited Edward, who used the pause in fighting to make preparations for a great summer offensive, which he probably conceived before leaving Roxburgh. The projected campaign was intended to be a final knock out blow, designed to correct the mistakes of 1333 and end the Scottish war once and for all.

CHAPTER 12
For the Lion, 1335–1336

Throughout the spring and early summer of 1335 King Edward made preparations for war. As early as March recruiting officers throughout England were ordered to have troops ready for the summer. Extensive naval preparations were made by John Howard, Edward's admiral, who assembled ships of all sizes in the eastern seaports. Despite the truce there was no relaxation of the naval blockade of Scotland. Recruiting officers were also busy in Ireland, where the Justiciar, John Darcy, was busy raising troops and gathering ships to join Edward in Scotland.

Parliament assembled at York on 27 May to learn that Edward's preparations for the summer were virtually complete. By the second week in July the King had over 13,000 men under arms at Newcastle. He was joined there by Edward Balliol from Carlisle. A council of war was held and it was decided that Scotland would be enveloped in a vast pincer movement by land and sea. The army was divided in two: Edward was to command the invasion of Scotland from Carlisle, while Balliol moved northwards from Berwick. Balliol's progress would be supported by a strong naval force moving up the east coast towards the Firth of Tay; while in the west Darcy's expedition from Ireland would support the King's left flank by an advance into the Clyde estuary.

Scotland was ill prepared for Edward's great invasion. The country had not yet recovered from the upheavals of 1334, and government authority was weak. The two Guardians, Robert Stewart and the Earl of Moray, seem to have drifted apart and gathered rival parties around them. In April 1335 a Parliament was held at the castle of Dairsie near Cupar in Fife, to try to agree a common strategy to deal with the expected summer invasion. This was not a happy occasion. Strathbogie had formed an intense dislike for the Earl of Moray, who forced his submission the previous autumn. He appeared at Dairsie, according to the chronicler John Fordun, with a large force, proceeding to conduct himself in an arrogant and overbearing fashion. Strathbogie was a strong personality, and Robert Stewart seems to have come under his influence, despite the fact that he had so recently been dispossessed by him. The divisions were such that Scotland was to face Edward's invasion without a united leadership. Parliament did, however, agree to return to Bruce's neglected scorched earth policy, and avoid direct contact with the superior English force. The people of southern Scotland were told to take their livestock and moveable goods to seek refuge in the hills. Scotland's military forces would shadow the invader to seek an opportunity to attack when the advantage was greatest.

As the truce drew to a close the people of Scotland prepared themselves for the coming blow. By early summer there was an atmosphere of tense expectation. A number of religious communities sought protection against destruction by applying to King Edward for certificates of immunity. The waiting finally came to an end when Edward began his advance in the second week of July. The King pushed into south west Scotland with the earls of Cornwall, Warwick, Hereford and the Count of Juliers He was also accompanied by Henry Beaumont and Henry of Lancaster, son of the elderly Earl of Lancaster and husband of one of Beaumont's daughters, Isabella. Edward advanced into Scotland unopposed, destroying everything in his path. In the east Balliol re-entered his twice lost kingdom at the head of a large English force. He was accompanied by his cousin, the Earl of Surrey, and the earls of Arundel, Oxford and Angus, together with the lords Percy, Neville, Berkeley and Latimer.

The purpose of the campaign was to destroy the Scottish resistance in the field, rather than to take castles. Edward marched up Nithsdale, by-passing Loch Doon Castle, still held for King David, and overran Carrick, Cunningham and Kyle. Meanwhile, Balliol moved quickly up the east coast into Lothian, leaving the Earl of March's castle at Dunbar unmolested on his right flank. Like a plague of biblical locusts his army consumed everything it found in its path. Edward's letters of immunity did nothing to protect Newbattle Abbey or Manuel Nunnery from desecration at the hands of Balliol's men. In the Firth of Forth the abbey on the island of Inchcolm was destroyed by the English navy, which then proceeded to sail north into the Tay, landing at Dundee, setting the town and its Franciscan friary alight. The looting and destruction of the friary caused the English author of the *Lanercost Chronicle* to drop his usual patriotic cloak to express his disapproval in a brief flourish of Christian solidarity.

On 23 July Balliol's force encountered their first serious obstacle at the small fortress of Cumbernauld to the north east of Glasgow, which lay directly across the path of their advance. The garrison under Sir David Mareschal refused to submit, managing to hold out for five days. They were finally compelled to surrender after the tower was set on fire. Some two hundred men were taken prisoner. There were also some women amongst the captives, most notably the wife of Sir Philip Mowbray and the widow of Sir Archibald Douglas. Apart from Sir David and the constable of the tower, all other male members of the garrison were hanged. Balliol was able to continue on his way towards his rendezvous with Edward. Towards the end of July the arms of the great pincer closed at Glasgow, having caught nothing of substance in their embrace. From there the combined force advanced on Perth.

The attack from Ireland, suggested to Edward by Balliol while they were at Roxburgh, was late in starting. Although the idea had been sound, the whole expedition was poorly co-ordinated; and when it finally got underway in late August its precise task was unclear. The chief objective may have been the Bruce stronghold at Dumbarton; but it would be necessary, first of all, to take the castle of Rothesay, garrisoned the previous summer by Robert Stewart. Rothesay was bombarded by a siege engine, but it did not fall. Thereafter the Irish campaign seems to have petered out, although there were still some Irish troops on Bute and Arran as late as mid October. Balliol appears to have made an attempt to link up with the Irish for a possible attack on Dumbarton in an expedition he and Henry Beaumont led from Perth westwards 'beyond the mountains'. Nothing more is known of this.

The Irish campaign in the Clyde estuary was well conceived but badly executed. The late arrival of the force commanded by John Darcy could have been compensated by some kind of co-ordinating action. However, poor communications made this practically impossible. The events of 1334 had clearly shown that Dumbarton was the paramount centre of Scottish resistance; yet despite the considerable force, both English and Irish, that Edward had at his disposal in the late summer of 1335, no serious attempt was made to capture this important stronghold, aside from Balliol's rather vague foray. The failure of the Irish expedition mirrors the strategic failure of the campaign as a whole.

The driving force behind the Scots resistance at this time was the Earl of Moray. Not strong enough to face the enemy in direct attack, he limited his actions to small scale operations in the rear of the main English army, attacking supply columns amongst other things. The opportunity for more decisive action came about the time the two wings of the enemy army met at Glasgow. Guy of Namur, cousin to Queen Philipa, had arrived at Berwick with his retinue to late to join the invasion. With his company reinforced by a party of English archers, he set out from Berwick intent on catching up with the King in central Scotland. But he only made it as far as the Boroughmuir near Edinburgh, where on 30 July he was intercepted by a combined force led by the earls of Moray and Dunbar assisted by Sir Alexander Ramsay and Lawrence Preston. In the ensuing fight the Scots were reinforced by a company under the command of Sir William Douglas, who descended from the nearby Pentland Hills. Namur was beaten back to Edinburgh, then an open town. The count and his men made for the ruins of the castle, where they killed their horses to build a barricade of flesh; all to no avail, because thirst compelled them to surrender the following day.

Namur was treated well by Moray. After agreeing to ransom terms, and swearing never again to take up arms against the supporters of David Bruce, he was escorted back to the border with his surviving followers and set at liberty. Moray paid dearly for this act of chivalry. On his way back he was ambushed by an English force from Jedburgh Castle under William Pressen. James Douglas, brother to Sir William, was killed, and Moray was taken prisoner. He was to spend the next five years in English gaols. Namur returned to Berwick, and sailed with Queen Philipa to join Edward at Perth. He was well received by the King, although his recent discomfiture must have been the occasion for some political embarrassment. Because of his pact with Moray the count was of no military value to Edward, and he soon left Scotland never to return. With his reputation compromised the unfortunate Namur was to be severely reprimanded by the English chroniclers for daring to enter enemy territory with such a modest force.

Edward and Balliol entered Perth in early August, and the great offensive came to a premature conclusion. Rather than continue into the north, as his grandfather surely would have done, Edward seemed content to sit and await events, while his troops raided the surrounding countryside, capturing Cupar Castle from the Earl of Fife on 7 August, apparently without a fight. He may have felt that his presence alone at the head of so grand an army would be enough to intimidate and demoralise the Scots into surrender. The problem with this was that the Scots at this time were so fragmented and disorganised that there was no agreed authority with which Edward would be able to deal. There were those like Andrew Murray who would continue to resist regardless; while there were others like Strathbogie who had taken no part in the struggle, and simply waited for a convenient opportunity to surrender. But there was no Guardian, no representative of the community or government, who would come, as the Red Comyn had to Strathord in 1304, to agree a general capitulation. However, Edward was deluded into believing that the Red Comyn's grandson, David de Strathbogie, could be cast in this role when he entered into negotiations with him on the same day that Cupar Castle fell.

Strathbogie had put himself at the head of a group of former Balliol loyalists, including Alexander and Geoffrey Mowbray, Godfrey Ross and William Bullock, who all wished to make peace. But he also brought with him a powerful fraction of the Scottish nobility, most notably Robert Stewart and the earls of Mentieth and Fife, which helped convince Edward that this was a surrender of the whole national community. A peace was concluded with Strathbogie and his allies, with the exception for the moment of the Stewart, at Perth on 18 August. As far as Edward was concerned this was the final capitulation he had set out to achieve. He certainly viewed Strathbogie as some kind of plenipotentiary, and dignified his personal submission by promising to maintain the liberty of the Scottish church and agreeing that the laws of Alexander III should be adhered to in that part of Scotland ruled by Edward Balliol, an echo of the Ordinances of 1305. Edward was content enough with this illusory peace that he firmly rejected French and papal attempts at arbitration, believing that matters in Scotland were settled. Yet to the north, south, east and west there were still castles held for David Bruce. An attempt to dislodge Alan de Vipont from Loch Leven Castle, only a few miles south of Perth, was foiled by a skilful defence. Edward felt secure enough to ignore these awkward pockets of resistance and allowed the bulk of his army to disband in September. From Perth he returned south to attend to the security of his Scottish domains.

Edward arrived in Edinburgh with the recent Namur fiasco in the front of his mind. He immediately gave orders for the repair of the ruined castle. When the work was completed in November command of the fortress was given to Sir John Stirling, a Scottish knight in Edward's service. Whilst at Edinburgh Edward had the satisfaction of at last receiving the submission of the Stewart and a party of his followers, confirming his confidence in the Pacification of Perth. Some effort was also made to persuade the captive Earl of Moray to agree to the peace, but he refused, despite the harsh conditions of his imprisonment.

With the completion of the repairs to Edinburgh Castle Edward moved the fulcrum of English power north to the Forth, reducing as a consequence the garrisons of Berwick and Roxburgh. The defence of the new territories was entrusted to three marcher lordships: Henry Percy at Jedburgh controlled the east; William Montagu at Peebles controlled the central counties, including the forests of Ettrick and Selkirk; and Edward Bohun dominated the west march and eastern Galloway from the fortress of Lochmaben. The grant of Jedburgh to Percy was especially contentious, and began the great cross border feud with the house of Douglas.

From the end of 1335 Edward's main concern was to maintain his hold on southern Scotland. Further assistance to Balliol was of a limited nature and contingent on this primary purpose. His great army of 1335 was gone, not to be equalled again until the Crecy campaign of 1346. The whole policy was ill-judged and short sighted. He took from Balliol the only parts of Scotland, especially Galloway, where he might be expected to attract sufficient support to consolidate his rule. The extreme weakness of Balliol in what remained of his kingdom seriously undermined the security of Edward's own territories. Moreover, the repair of Edinburgh Castle notwithstanding, Edward still had insufficient strongpoints to be confident of his hold on southern Scotland, and those that he did have were seriously undermanned. Beyond the illusory Pacification of Perth the expensive campaign of 1335 had achieved virtually nothing: the Scots had not been destroyed in battle; the Bruce party continued to hold castles in lands nominally under the control of both Edward and Balliol; and the new English stronghold at Edinburgh had been created at the expense of the border fortresses. This was a house of cards, soon to collapse in the wind.

When Balliol returned from his abortive campaign 'beyond the mountains' he appears not to have shared Edward's confidence in the completeness of the 'victory'. After appointing Strathbogie as his lieutenant in northern Scotland he left Perth, hurrying south to join his master at Berwick. He may have intended to return before winter. He was, however, prevented from doing so by an important change in circumstances: the Scottish victory at the Battle of Culblean on St. Andrews day, 30 November 1335, showed to all that the gains of the summer had been built, once again, on the constantly shifting sands of the northern war.

At the end of September those who remained loyal to David Bruce gathered at Dumbarton Castle. The situation was grim the English and their allies controlled almost all of central and southern Scotland. In this area it was said that only children at play admitted to being King Davy's men. The defection of Strathbogie, Robert Stewart and the earls of Fife and Mentieth had severely weakened the nationalist cause, as had the capture of the Earl of Moray. National government had virtually ceased to exist. In this atmosphere of crisis Andrew Murray was chosen, for the second time in his career, as Guardian of Scotland. Within a short period he was to become one of the country's greatest leaders, and a skilled student of the kind of guerrilla warfare practised by Robert Bruce. Murray's credentials were impeccable: he was constant in his defence of the national cause, never at any time submitting to Edward lll or Balliol. The men who gathered round him at Dumbarton formed the nucleus of the national revival—the earls of March and Ross, Sir William Douglas, Maurice Moray and William Keith.

Murray recognised that the country was close to exhaustion and agreed to enter into truce negotiations with the English. Talks were held at Bathgate in West Lothian. Edward probably hoped that these discussions would lead to a general peace on the basis of the Perth declaration; if so, he was to be disappointed. Balliol was not party to the talks and his chief representative in Scotland, David de Strathbogie, continued to pursue a war of attrition in the north.

After he was appointed Balliol's lieutenant Strathbogie showed greater determination in his attacks on the supporters of Bruce than he had ever demonstrated in the defence of the national cause. He began his operations north of the Forth by attempting to eradicate all freeholders, who from the time of William Wallace had been the backbone of Scottish resistance. Strathbogie's actions mirrored the policy of King Edward in southern Scotland, where over one hundred freeholders were forfeited in the period from 1335 to 1337. The Scottish chronicler John of Fordun reports the situation thus:

> But the great tyranny and cruelty this earl (Strathbogie) practised among the people words cannot bring within the mind's grasp: some he disinherited, others he murdered; and in the end, he cast in his mind how he might wipe out the freeholders from the face of the earth.

Strathbogie crowned his campaign by laying siege to Kildrummy

Castle in the Don valley. Kildrummy had for some time been held for King David by his aunt, the Lady Christian Bruce, the wife of Andrew Murray. When Murray learned of Strathbogie's actions he broke off the talks at Bathgate and hurried to her assistance. With the help of the Earl of March, William Douglas, Alexander Ramsay and Lawrence Preston he gathered a small force of some eight hundred men and rode north. Strathbogie's army, according to the historian Lord Hailes, amounted to some three thousand men. Murray's tactics were risky: he was marching into battle, which all Scots leaders had carefully avoided since Halidon Hill. But the situation was critical; the fall of Kildrummy would have been a serious setback for the national cause in the north. From the south the English were well aware of what was going on, and would have been gratified that the Scots were being forced into battle at last. If Lord Hailes is correct, Strathbogie's army was greater than that which Balliol and Beaumont brought to Scotland in 1332, and he could therefore be expected to give a good account of himself against the Guardian's much more modest force.

Strathbogie was warned of Murray's approach. He raised the siege of Kildrummy, moving south to face his enemy in the forest of Culblean. Murray was joined a few miles north of the River Dee, to the east of Strathbogie's position near Culblean Hill, by a party of three hundred men from Kildrummy led by John of the Craig. John's knowledge of the local countryside was invaluable. On the night of 29–30 of November he guided Murray's force on a wide sweeping movement to the south and west, designed to take Strathbogie in the rear. As Murray approached at dawn the element of surprise was lost when he was spotted by Strathbogie's scouts. The camp was warned and Strathbogie made ready. But his troops were largely recruited from the local area, probably by impressment, and he appears to have had no archers.

Murray's force was divided in two, the forward unit being commanded by William Douglas. When he saw Strathbogie arrayed for battle Douglas halted as if hesitating in the face of the enemy's preparedness. This had the desired effect and Strathbogie led his men in a downhill charge; but their ranks began to break on reaching a burn, and Douglas ordered a counter charge. Sir Andrew Murray with the rearguard immediately launched an assault on the enemy's exposed flank. Murray's charge was so fierce that the bushes in his path were born down. Pinned down in front and attacked from the side, Strathbogie's army broke. Unable to escape, and refusing the humiliation of a second surrender, Strathbogie stood with his back to an oak tree and was killed in a last stand with a small group of followers, including Sir Robert Brady and two brothers, Walter and Thomas Comyn. Some of the survivors from the battle took refuge in the nearby island castle of Loch Kinnord, but were forced to surrender the following day.

Compared with the other great battles of the Wars of Independence, Culblean was a relatively small affair. Nevertheless, its size was greatly outweighed by its importance on the road to national recovery. Dr Douglas Simpson passed the final verdict on the battle when he wrote: 'Culblean was the turning point in the second war of Scottish Independence, and therefore an event of great historical importance.' Small as it was, it nullified the effects of Edward's great summer parade, ending forever Balliol's hope of standing as an independent king. Its effects were immediately felt. Balliol spent the winter of 1335–6, so says *Lanercost*, 'with his people at Elande, in England, because he does not yet possess in Scotland any castle or town where he could dwell in safety.'

When the English Parliament met at Westminster in early March 1336, it was now completely clear that Edward's confidence in the Perth settlement had been misplaced, and that the northern war was no where near an end. Edward recognised this himself when he complained that there were Scots breaking the truce on the border because 'they held of the Lion and none other', an echo of William Oliphant's defiance of 1304.

CHAPTER 13

Scotland and the Start of the Hundred Years War, 1336–1338

The year 1336 opened with the prospect of a diplomatic settlement. Mediators sent by Pope Benedict XII, John XXII's successor, worked out a draft agreement which seemed to be acceptable to King Edward, who lifted the threat of immediate military action against the Scots in January, prolonging the current truce until mid April. The draft agreement was a facesaver for Edward and a lifeline for Balliol. It was proposed that Balliol, who was middle aged and unmarried, would be allowed to retain the crown of Scotland during his lifetime, while David Bruce would be recognised as his heir. There was a precedent for this kind of arrangement in 1154, when Henry II had succeeded King Stephen to the throne of England. The question of Balliol's territorial concessions to Edward was, however, passed over in silence.

Clearly, an agreement of this kind required the assent of David II, still in French exile. A party of Scots crossed the Channel to meet him, and were expected to return in time for the Parliament summoned to meet at Westminster on 11 March 1336. They failed to appear. Instead, King David sent messengers announcing his rejection both of the proposed treaty and any further truces. Parliament had no choice but to grant the King further subsidies to continue the war.

It was suspected in England that David's resolve had been strengthened by King Philip. Throughout the previous year the French king had been taking an increasingly close interest in the Scottish question. It was known that he had been sending supplies to the patriots at least as early as February 1335, when a ship was seen unloading arms and wine at Dumbarton Castle. Even more serious, from the spring of the same year Scottish privateers had been permitted the use of the French Channel ports, and soon became a serious threat to the undefended towns of the English south coast, for whom hitherto the war in Scotland had been very remote. In April 1335, as the first sign of the new danger, the Scottish privateer, John of St. Agatha, captured and sank an English ship, the *Little Lechevard* from Southampton.

Most serious of all, it was widely believed that Philip himself was getting ready to intervene directly in the war. In July 1335, as Edward was about to embark on his great summer offensive in the north, Philip's council decided to send a large seaborne armada to Scotland. These plans were discussed quite openly. The Archbishop of Rouen announced the decision to a large gathering at the royal palace in Paris. His audience were reminded of the treaties of 1295 and 1326, and Edward's conduct in supporting Balliol and disinheriting his brother-in-law was denounced. When King Philip was at Lyon during the Easter celebrations of 1336, he was met by a Scots delegation, which reminded him that the current truce was due to expire on 5 May, and asking for help. Philip promised to send a large army, in excess of 20,000 men, to the east coast of Scotland as soon as he had sufficient ships. In England the invasion scare was heightened when a force of eight ships entered the Solent in August 1335, landing some soldiers who proceeded to set fire to several villages. All of this obliged Edward to direct men and resources away from the north. Finally, a new critical direction in the affairs of France and England was signalled in the summer of 1336 when Philip abandoned his long cherished plans for a crusade, and ordered the French fleet to move from the Mediterranean to the Channel. Time was clearly running out for Edward in Scotland.

Murray's victory at the Battle of Culblean secured his position as leader of the Scottish national resistance. He was confirmed in the post of Guardian in the spring of 1336 by a council at Dunfermline, in time to face the last great challenge of his life.

The war of 1336 was to be of a more limited character than that of the preceding three years. For one thing Edward could no longer turn his back on France for any length of time; for another he was beginning to realise that Balliol was a hopeless cause, and no amount of effort would secure his shaky throne. It was also abundantly clear that the endless war in Scotland was simply no longer worth the expense.

Edward III was one of history's great freebooters: for him war and profit were the two sides of the same coin. Always pragmatic, he possessed none of his grandfather's obsessive determination, or his father's pointless intransigence. He started the Scottish war with high hopes of easy pickings and new riches. In the period just before the outbreak of the Hundred Years War in 1337, it was increasingly obvious that the promise had been far greater than the results. His campaigns up to Christmas 1334 had cost over £12,000 in soldiers' wages alone. His coming campaign, a very modest affair compared with that of 1335, was to cost a staggering £16,000. By 1337 the cost of maintaining garrisons and carrying out repairs at Edinburgh, Roxburgh, Perth and Stirling were together costing about £10,000 a year. All of this far outweighed the revenue Edward was able to gather from his war torn conquests. There were also clear signs of a general war weariness in England: few of the great magnates had made any gains from their investment, and the Meaux chronicler complains of the heavy burden of taxation imposed by the campaign of 1335. Edward now determined to secure maximum results from minimum investment.

After Culblean Balliol's kingdom virtually disappeared. Perth was taken. Only Cupar Castle in Fife and remote Lochindorb kept his cause alive. In Lochindorb the widow of Strathbogie, Katherine de Beaumont, daughter of Henry Beaumont, had been under siege by Andrew Murray since late 1335. The rescue of Katherine de Beaumont was to allow Edward to drape a cloak of high chivalry over one of his most destructive military adventures. English action took the form of a large scale punitive raid, intended to knock out Scots resistance and, at the same time, forestall a possible French landing in the north east. The resources devoted to the campaign were very modest. As if to confirm the reduced importance of the Scottish theatre, Edward gave command to Henry of Lancaster, Henry Beaumont's son-in-law. Lancaster came north in May with a force of 500 men-at-arms and 1,000 mounted archers. Beaumont came with him, as did Edward Balliol, surely a more persistent student of spiders than Robert Bruce had ever been.

Balliol had spent an unhappy winter near the border. Although Edward's sheriff in Dumfries, Eustace Maxwell, continued to exercise some control in Galloway, Balliol seems not to have been able to collect any rents, owing, it must be assumed, to the dislocations of war. He was unable to pay the expenses he incurred while living on Holy Island, and suffered the indignity of having his goods and horses seized on the orders of King Edward to pay his outstanding bills. Thereafter he became a pensioner of the English crown.

Lancaster, Beaumont and Balliol reached Perth in early June 1336. The defences were restored, and Balliol set up his headquarters in the town for the third time. When Lancaster arrived the Scots were engage in the siege of Lochindorb in the north and Cupar Castle in Fife, commanded by William Bullock, Balliol's chancellor. Cupar was under attack by three Scottish earls—March, Sutherland

and Fife, who had now abandoned his allegiance to Edward III. To coincide with Lancaster's occupation of Perth, John de Stirling, the keeper of Edinburgh Castle, led a raiding party across the Forth from Leith, launched a surprise attack on the earls, and forced them to abandon the siege. Balliol's hold on the area was strengthened by Henry Beaumont and Henry Ferrers, who rebuilt and garrisoned the castles at St. Andrews and Leuchars. The capture of Fife was only the first stage of Lancaster's operation; the ultimate objective was to be Aberdeen. Not only was Aberdeen the major seaport in the north east, and as such a vital supply point for Murray's army, it was also the only place in all of eastern Scotland that the anticipated French expeditionary force could land safely.

The danger that the French might send military assistance to the Scots was becoming increasingly real for Edward, who received intelligence in early June that a French force was set to land somewhere in the north east. For the French this would be an extremely risky enterprise. It would be vital for its success that they had a secure port, and a friendly hinterland with an adequate source of fresh supplies. The English intended to deny them these things. Sir Thomas Rosselin, one of Lancaster's retainers, was given the task of establishing a forward base just south of Aberdeen. Rosselin sailed from King's Lynn with a small force of eight ships, landing near the ruined castle of Dunnotar with one hundred and sixty men and horses, together with a body of masons and carpenters to repair the castle. His landing met with some local opposition, and Rosselin was killed. However, his men were able to drive off the Scots and take possession of the castle, which was promptly repaired.

Before Lancaster was able to set out for the north himself, King Edward arrived at Perth in person, to the astonishment of the garrison, with a small force, scratched together from the royal household and the retinue of his friend, William Montagu. He came through territory in which guerrilla bands led by Sir William Douglas were active. Considering the experience of Guy of Namur, Edward's actions verged on the imprudent. But his adventure is described with admiration by the chroniclers, earning none of the reproofs heaped on the ill favoured Count. Once in Perth Edward wasted no time: on 12 July, with his force augmented by part of Lancaster's army, he set out into northern Scotland, for the first and only time in his career. He had three tasks before him: the relief of the beleaguered Katherine de Beaumont, the defeat of Andrew

Murray's army, and the destruction of the north east as a possible base for French operations.

Edward advanced rapidly towards Lochindorb, hoping to trap Murray, who had based himself in the wood of Stronkalter, near the Countess's castle. He arrived within four days of leaving Perth, having travelled a hundred miles. The Guardian allowed the English to come close enough to engage in some skirmishing, and then used his superior knowledge of the countryside to withdraw to safety. Edward arrived just in time, for Countess Katherine and her garrison were close to starvation. As Katherine was reunited with her father, Edward set out from Lochindorb on his destructive progress through the north east, in an action which mirrored the Rape of Buchan in 1308. His troops rounded up all the cattle they could find and slaughtered them, over 1,000 on the first day alone. By 17 July Edward had reached the Moray Firth. The food stores at Kinloss Abbey were taken, and Forres and Elgin were both razed. The surrounding countryside was harried and the crops burned in the fields. Only the cathedral at Elgin was spared from the whirlwind of violence.

Edward turned south east from Elgin towards Aberdeen, which he reached on the night of 21 July. At his approach ten foreign ships put out to sea, not pausing to pay customs duties. Over a period of three days the old town of Aberdeen was destroyed with systematic thoroughness. That which could not be burned was demolished. Edward only withdrew when he was satisfied that nothing remained standing above ground. The King's punitive action in the north east was matched in the south west by his brother, John of Eltham, Earl of Cornwall, who crossed the border on 1 August with several thousand men. Eltham's force ravaged Carrick and the Clyde valley, burning people in the churches where they fled for refuge, so it was later claimed by the Scots. Douglas shadowed Eltham, attacking outlying columns when he could.

Edward and Eltham's actions, destructive as they were, showed that the Scots could not be forced into battle. It was finally clear that the only way of holding down the hostile countryside was by a chain of fortresses. Edward spent the remainder of July and August in Angus and the Mearns supervising the repair of fortifications. Dunnotar Castle was joined by strongpoints at Lauriston and Kinneff, all intended to hold down the area between Aberdeen and the Tay, and to act as the final disincentive to a French landing. These three castles matched the newly repaired fortresses in Fife.

Edward then returned to Perth, where he was met by Eltham. The repairs to the defences of the town carried out in June by Lancaster were augmented by new walls and towers financed by a levy on the local monasteries. Perth was now as strong as it had been in 1313, when it was taken by King Robert. John of Eltham was left in charge at Perth while Edward set out for the south. When he reached the ruined castle of Stirling he ordered the building of a new tower. From there he turned south westwards towards Bothwell, where he began the reconstruction of the old fortress partially demolished after Bannockburn, intending to use it as a base against William Douglas, whose guerrilla army was becoming increasingly troublesome. While he was at Bothwell he received news from England which forced a temporary postponement of his plans.

While Edward had been active in the north east of Scotland England's relations with France had approached a critical point. In August King Philip informed an English embassy led by the bishops of Durham and Winchester that he intended to assist Scotland with all the power at his disposal. He had assembled a fleet and army, the ambassadors were informed, with which he intended to invade England and Scotland immediately. The bishops sent a clerk, William Tickhill, to warn the Royal Council of this threat. Tickhill gave his news to the Council at Northampton on 24 August. Philip's promise of aggressive intervention seemed about to begin when French ships began raiding the south coast of England in late August. John Stratford, the Archbishop of Canterbury, immediately arranged for another Great Council to meet at Nottingham on 23 September. Tickhill was then sent north to find the King and ask him to return to England. In Scotland Douglas's bands made travel through the lowlands very dangerous, and Tickhill's bodyguard refused to take him further than Fife. With some difficulty he finally managed to reach the King at Bothwell in the second week in September. Edward promptly set out for the south, arriving at Nottingham on 24 September, where the Great Council had already assembled. Here Edward received news of the French embassy and of the raids on Suffolk and the Isle of Wight. The Council authorised the gathering of a new army for the defence of England. War with France was now accepted as inevitable.

From Nottingham Edward returned to Bothwell to finish his work in Scotland. The repair of the castle was completed with some difficulty, as supply columns were continually attacked by Douglas. When the work was at last complete Edward took up residence in the castle, where he remained until just before Christmas 1336. While at Bothwell he issued a number of important decrees, including orders for the defence of southern England and a summons for Parliament to meet in London to prepare for the coming war with France. Walter de Selby was appointed governor of the castle, and the barony of Bothwell was granted to Robert de Ufford, the Earl of Suffolk, notwithstanding the fact that both castle and barony were part of the nominal kingdom of his ally, Edward Balliol.

It is difficult to determine Balliol's exact status at this time. It seems that he was little more than a rather awkward figurehead. Both his political value and his credibility appear to have been exhausted, and Edward seems to have had little trust or confidence in him. When the King left Perth command of the English forces was left with the Earl of Cornwall rather than with Balliol. When Cornwall died in October command of the town was soon to pass on Edward's insistence to Sir Thomas Ughtred. Balliol spent his time trying to widen his dangerously narrow base of support in Scotland. He tempted the neutral John of the Isles, chief of the MacDonalds, to join the war on his behalf in September 1336 by granting him additional lands in Kintyre, Knapdale and the Isle of Skye. John was happy to take the lands but made no effort to assist his beleaguered benefactor. Balliol spent a gloomy winter in Perth, according to *Lanercost*, 'with an extremely modest following'. This presumably refers to his personal entourage rather than to the garrison of what was now the key to the English occupation in Scotland.

It was in this season that Henry Beaumont embarked on his last actions in Scotland, by seeking vengeance against those whom he held responsible for the death of his son-in-law, David de Strathbogie. Pluscarden describes his conduct thus: 'Henry Beaumont, to avenge his son-in-law, the Earl of Atholl, who was slain at Culblean, either cast into prison or put to cruel death all who had taken part in the engagement in which he was slain; whereby much innocent blood was shed.' He must have achieved little, for Andrew Murray soon came out of his northern hiding place to conduct a brilliant hit and run offensive against Edward's 'Maginot Line'.

Edward's fortresses ran in a line from Bothwell to Dunnotar, with Perth holding the centre. But the castles were simply too far apart to offer effective mutual support. Even while the King was still at Bothwell, on the western extreme of his defensive chain, his new strategy was already beginning to unravel. No sooner had he left the north east than Murray took the offensive. Before the end of the year he captured and destroyed the outposts at Dunnotar, Lauriston and Kinneff. He continued his ruthless guerrilla war throughout the winter of 1336–7. The attacks and counter attacks were so savage that the whole of Gowrie, Angus and the Mearns was reduced to a virtual desert, so the chroniclers report.

In February 1337 Murray carried his war almost to the gates of Perth when he captured Kinclaven Castle, just to the north of the town. Leaving a force to cover the Perth garrison he then joined William Douglas and the earls of Fife and March in an attack on the English strongholds in Fife. The garrisons were isolated and without hope of reinforcement, for Edward, who had now returned to England, was too preoccupied with the French threat to come to their assistance; and the English forces elsewhere in Scotland were of little use, for the King had stretched his power too thinly. Even the English chronicler, Sir Thomas Gray, who had first-hand experience of the Scottish war, ventured a criticism of the King when he wrote: 'King Edward lost . . . all the castles and towns, that he had forfeited for lack of diligent pursuing of his victory.'

Murray's campaign in Fife brought quick success. Falkland Tower and Leuchars soon fell. St Andrews Castle held out for three weeks before being captured on 28 February 1337 with the aid of a wooden tower called 'Boustour', which appears to have been the kind of siege engine known at the time as a malvoisin—'bad neighbour'—which enabled the besiegers to attack the battlements from above, while undermining the walls from below. Only Cupar Castle, defended by William Bullock, continued to hold out. Murray then turned west, taking Boustour to the walls of his own castle at Bothwell, which was captured in March after a short siege, in mockery of all of Edward's effort only a few months before. It was destroyed for the second time in its history. What remained stood as a symbol of Edward's failure in Scotland.

So, even before the usual campaigning season began, the English lost almost all of Scotland north of the Tay. Balliol's holdings now amounted to little more than Perth and the garrisons of Stirling and Cupar. Clearly, it was becoming too uncomfortable for him in Scotland, as he left for England in May to make yet another appeal for help. As he did so Murray began a further onslaught on Galloway and, the *Lanercost Chronicle* laments, 'once more destroyed the wretched Galwegians . . . like beasts, because they adhered so firmly to their lord, King Edward de Balliol.' As Murray was taking Bothwell

Castle, the Parliament Edward summoned while he was there the previous autumn met at Westminster. The most important matter under discussion was the coming war with France. The struggle in the north, and the defence of King Balliol's empty crown, now acquired a very low priority.

The Anglo-French crisis finally came to a head on 24 May 1337, when Philip VI formally confiscated Edward III's Duchy of Aquitaine. It was claimed that Edward had broken the conditions of vassalage, which English kings had owed to the French crown since the Treaty of Paris of 1259, by harbouring Robert of Artois, Philip's brother-in-law and mortal enemy, and for 'certain other reasons', which were not specified. Edward was now faced with exactly the same situation as his grandfather in 1294, when the Duchy was confiscated by Philip IV. Then the matter had been resolved, after some limited warfare, by a diplomatic compromise. This time Edward decided to give the perennial Anglo-French conflict an entirely new dimension by throwing off the subordinate status bestowed upon him by the Treaty of Paris, and laying claim to the throne of France in right of his mother Isabella, daughter of King Philip IV. He had first made a formal claim to be considered for the throne in 1328, after the death of his uncle, Charles IV, the last Capetian King of France. It was decided at the time that the so called Salic Law precluded succession in the female line, and the throne passed to Charles's nearest male relative, Philip of Valois. Now, with a whole series of quarrels coming to a head in Scotland, Gascony and the Low Countries, Edward considered the time right to renew his claim.

Edward's bid was a poor one: even if the Salic Law had been set aside he had cousins, descendants in the female line from Philip IV, through his sons Louis X and Philip V, who had a far stronger claim to the throne of France. If the matter had been put to a feudal court as the Scottish succession had in 1292, Edward's bid would have been no stronger than that of John Hastings of Abergavenny, who came a definite third to John Balliol and Bruce the Competitor. But none of this made any difference; for Edward was prepared to back his claim with all the power of England. His official declaration of war was addressed to 'Philip of Valois who calls himself King of France'; and in January 1340 Edward finally took the title for himself. The Hundred Years War had begun. France's agony was to be Scotland's salvation.

To defend his interests in Scotland Edward appointed Thomas Beauchamp, Earl of Warwick, as 'captain and leader to represent the person of the lord King' in March 1337. But the small field army that Warwick was allowed was simply not equal to the task of defending all of southern Scotland. Castle garrisons, moreover, were all seriously under strength, even a fortress as important as Edinburgh, where John de Stirling continued to plead for more men. To the east the Earl of March's castle at Dunbar continued to be held for the Bruce cause, in defiance of English claims to control Lothian. Warwick seems to have been able to do little to stop Murray, who after his success at Bothwell laid siege to Stirling Castle in May. Edward came north with Balliol for a brief period in June, in an abortive attempt to trap the Guardian in battle. The siege of Stirling was raised, and Murray retired in good order, having avoided Edward's embrace for a second time. The King remained at Stirling for a few days before retiring south in frustration. Edward Balliol remained in Perth, staying there on and off until the summer of 1338 in a largely decorative role.

In May 1337 Balliol lost his only base of support in Scotland when Eustace Maxwell and the men of Galloway, clearly aware of the decline of English power in the north, decided to change their allegiance. From this date English administration in Dumfriesshire largely ceased to exist. In retaliation Edward awarded Maxwell's lands and his castle of Caerlaverock to Rafe de Dacre, Lord of Gilsland. Dacre led a raid over the border and harried Maxwell's lands. But this did nothing to improve the English position in Scotland. Warwick's impotence was plain to all when Murray began a series of retaliatory raids across the English border in August. Raids and counter raids now became the dominant form of warfare on the border; and the embers of this kind of limited conflict continued to burn as late as the sixteenth century.

Murray's raids in Cumberland and Northumberland were an embarrassment to Edward, who was busy preparing for his first continental expedition. Warwick and the isolated garrisons in Scotland were obviously providing no effective deterrent to Murray's guerrilla tactics, and the communities of northern England were now faced with precisely the same dangers that they had after Bannockburn. Thomas Gray, himself a northern knight, was later to condemn Edward for wasting resources on building up an expensive anti- French alliance on the continent without first securing his northern border, and completing the conquest of Scotland.

The strength of Gray's criticism was confirmed when Murray,

returning from a large scale raid into England, laid siege to Edinburgh Castle, now an exposed and vulnerable outpost. Warwick was
apparently powerless to stop him. A force under Dacre and the
Bishop of Carlisle was hastily assembled, to be joined by Edward
Balliol at Roxburgh, and hurried to the assistance of John de
Stirling. Murray broke off the siege and turned to meet the English
in battle just south of Edinburgh at Crichton Castle. The engagement was fierce but indecisive, although losses were greater on the
English side. The battle was eventually broken off, although fighting
in the area continued intermittently until the end of the year, visiting
upon the people of Lothian the same kind of destruction experienced
in the previous year by the communities of north east Scotland.

Faced with the anxieties of the people of northern England, and
the general failure of his containment strategy in Scotland, Edward
replaced the unsuccessful Warwick by his close associate, William
Montagu, recently named Earl of Salisbury. Salisbury was joined in
command by Richard Fitzalen, Earl of Arundel. Edward had been
busy gathering an army for an invasion of the Low Countries.
However, it was now late in the season and he was forced to abandon
his plans. He looked to Salisbury and Arundel to bring him at least
some limited success in the north.

The appointment of Salisbury and Arundel saw a new departure
in English strategy in Scotland. Rather than waste time and resources in the fruitless pursuit of Andrew Murray and his 'grey
wolves', the two commanders began a long overdue policy of reducing Bruce strongholds, beginning with the troublesome castle at
Dunbar, which for some years had been left unmolested as the
centre of anti-English resistance in the south east, and an entry
point for French supplies into Scotland. In the absence of the Earl
of March, who was with the Scottish field army, the defence of the
castle had been entrusted to his wife, Agnes Dunbar, daughter of
the great Thomas Randolph and sister of the imprisoned Earl of
Moray. Because of her swarthy complexion she is known to history
as Black Agnes.

With a reasonably sized army of some 4,000 men, as well as a
corps of military engineers, the two earls began the siege of Dunbar
on 13 January 1338. Engines had been shipped from Berwick and
London to bombard the castle. As the artillery started to hurl
boulders down on the battlements the sappers and engineers, the
competent and experienced John Crabb foremost among them,
went to work. Agnes and her garrison of some forty men were

155

For the Lion

bombarded from land and blockaded by sea; still they did not surrender. The siege continued week after week until June, longer than the siege of Stirling Castle in 1304, but all attempts to dislodge the formidable Agnes failed. With great courage and much coolness she mocked the best efforts of Salisbury's siege engines. In the words of Pluscarden: 'She indeed laughed at the English and would, in the sight of all, wipe with a most beautiful cloth the spot where the stone from the engine hit the castle wall.' Her brother, John Randolph, was brought from his English prison and threatened with execution if she did not surrender. Agnes called the bluff, saying that the earldom of Moray would then be hers, and Randolph was sent back to jail unharmed.

Edward, fully preoccupied with plans for another continental expedition, came north in person to nearby Whitekirk to find out what was going wrong. He could not afford further delays. Salisbury and Arundel increased their efforts to no avail. Agnes was assisted in her defence by one of Murray's guerrilla chiefs, Sir Alexander Ramsay of Dalhousie, who led a series of attacks from his hideout at Hawthornden near Roslin Castle. Ramsay conducted his operations in a wide area around Dunbar, surprising English supply columns. At Pressen near Wark-on-Tweed he defeated an enemy force, taking the leader, Robert de Manners, prisoner. After conducting an effective defence for some months Agnes was beginning to run dangerously short of supplies. The English blockade was broken by Ramsay, who managed to get fresh victuals through the castle's sea gate. Salisbury and Arundel were themselves running short of provisions, so Agnes sent them a mocking gift of bread and wine. Edward waiting impatiently at the port of Orwell on the south coast could no longer afford the time and manpower devoted to the capture of Dunbar, and the siege was lifted on 13 June. Salisbury took the bulk of the troops south to join the King at Orwell, while Arundel remained in the north to organise the defence of the border as best he could. The Scots were granted a truce to last until Michaelmas 1339. The siege of Dunbar, which cost almost £6,000, had been an expensive fiasco. It is best summarised by the words put into the mouth of Salisbury by the chronicler: 'Came I early, Came I late, I found Black Agnes at the gate.'

The chief architect of the remarkable Scottish recovery since the dark summer of 1335 was undoubtedly Andrew Murray, who died at his castle of Avoch in the spring of 1338. Fordun summarises his actions thus: 'He did a good deal for his country's freedom; and assaulted and destroyed all of the castles and strongholds held by the English above the water of Forth, except Cupar and Perth.' The struggle had not been easy, and the scorched earth policy which brought success against the English also caused much misery to the ordinary people. The roads to freedom have seldom provided a comfortable passage.

Shortly after Edward left for Flanders Balliol re-entered Scotland with a small following and returned to Perth. The high expectations of the summer of 1332 were long gone. Most of the companions he had brought with him were either dead or dispersed. Some, like Gilbert de Umfraville, the pretender Earl of Angus, had been financially ruined by the failure to establish the hapless Balliol on the throne of Scotland. Even the most determined of the disinherited clearly had had enough. Henry Beaumont, recently named Justiciar of Scotland, had grown weary of his empty titles. Rather than return to Scotland with Balliol the old warrior accompanied the King to the Low Countries, from whence he had come to England with Edward I in 1298, where he died in March 1340, his long struggle incomplete. His son John never claimed the earldom of Buchan. When Beaumont's wife, Alice, died in 1342 the Comyn line of Buchan, which stretched back to the early 13th century, finally came to an end. Edward Balliol was left alone like King Canute to try to stop the tide of Scottish national resurgence.

CHAPTER 14
The Road to Neville's Cross,
1339–1346

On the death of Andrew Murray the Guardianship passed to Robert Stewart, who had long since abandoned his allegiance to Edward III. The Stewart, grandson of King Robert by his daughter Marjory, also had the distinction of being heir presumptive to the Scottish throne after his young uncle, King David. When he assumed the post of Guardian the initiative in the war was firmly with the Scots. Edward's outposts were in exactly the same position as his father's in 1309: isolated from one another, and without any foreseeable prospect of assistance from the south, they looked out apprehensively over hostile countryside. The most vulnerable were those which comprised Balliol's little 'kingdom'—Perth, and the castles of Cupar and Stirling. However, they all enjoyed a temporary respite, for the Stewart continued to observe the truce concluded at the end of the siege of Dunbar.

William Douglas, now one of Scotland's most experienced commanders, took the opportunity offered by the truce to visit King David at Chateau Galliard. The substance of their discussions is unknown. At the very least they presumably considered a strategy for the further prosecution of the war. Douglas certainly received some financial assistance from David and the French government, for he was able to return to Scotland in the early summer of 1339 with a small force of French galleys, commanded by a privateer named Hugh Hautpool. With him came several exiled Scots and a number of French knights with their retinues. These were to be the first French troops to fight in Scotland, a shadow of the great expeditionary force promised in 1336, but living proof nevertheless of the value of the Auld Alliance.

The Scots renounced the truce in April 1339 and began action at once. In May the Stewart began the siege of Perth. He was joined in July by Douglas's newly arrived French flotilla, which closed the ring around the English commander, Sir Thomas Ughtred, and his besieged garrison by blockading the Tay, thus severing their last link with the outside world. On his way overland to join the Scottish

158

army before Perth, Douglas paused at Cupar Castle and managed to persuade William Bullock to surrender, in return for a bribe. Bullock finally abandoned Balliol and swore allegiance to King David. From Cupar Douglas marched on Perth with the Earl of March and the French mercenaries. The situation in the town was critical. Access had always been dangerous, but it was not impossible so long as the sea route remained open. Ughtred was running short of supplies and could not be expected to hold out without immediate assistance. This task was given to Edward Balliol.

The existing records make it difficult to give a precise account of Balliol's movements between the end of the siege of Dunbar and the beginning of the siege of Perth. He appears to have been in the town in August 1338, when he was instructed by Edward to place the command of the garrison, for a second time, in the hands of Sir Thomas Ughtred. Some time after this he left, never to return. With the siege approaching the point of crisis, he was put in command of a force of 1200 hobelars and 64 men-at-arms recruited in northern England, and rode north to the town's relief, accompanied by Gilbert de Umfraville, Henry Percy, Ralph Neville, Anthony de Lucy and Richard Talbot. But it was already too late. Inside the town the defenders were starving. The Scots had drained the moat and started to undermine the walls. With no sign of Balliol's relief force Ughtred surrendered on terms on 17 August 1339. The English soldiers were allowed to withdraw unmolested. According to John of Fordun, 'They left Scotland with all haste—some by sea voyage, others by land journey—amid much jeering.' Balliol's army, perhaps not strong enough for the task, hovered ineffectually on the fringes of the siege, achieved nothing and soon returned to England. Thomas Ughtred was later to be tried before Parliament for his conduct in surrendering the town. He defended himself vigorously, and was acquitted with honour. The walls of the town were destroyed, and it was never again to fall into English hands.

The victory had been a hard one for the local peasantry. The countryside was so wasted that many died of hunger in the fields. There is even some suggestion in the sources that cannibalism was practised. Andrew Wyntoun tells the terrible tale of one such practitioner in his rhyming chronicle:

> Thay said als that a carll harby
> Wuld mak netts and set quayantly
> Childer and women for to ta,

and cum them on thaim and tham sla,
And eit tham all, that he might get mycht.
Criste Cleke to name he hecht.

English power in Scotland was now confined to the castles of
Stirling and Edinburgh, and to a chain of border fortresses, running
from Lochmaben in the west through Jedburgh and Roxburgh to
Berwick in the east. Balliol, once more an exile, had one small
consolation in 1339 when the men of Galloway, for reasons un-
known, returned to their traditional loyalties. Now leader of
Edward's forces in the north, he was confident enough to return to
Galloway to establish a base in his ancestral lands. For a time after
King David's return to Scotland, and again after the Battle of
Neville's Cross, Edward Balliol, king in name only, was to exercise
an uneasy rule as the English Lord of Galloway. A manor house was
built for him on Hestan Island at the entrance to Auchencairn Bay.
It was completed in 1342, command being then given to Duncan
MacDouall.

After the capture of Perth the war in Scotland entered a temporary
stalemate. Unable to make headway against the enemy strongpoints
the Scots recommenced their destructive onslaught on northern
England. In one large scale raid in 1340 Scottish forces utterly
destroyed twenty four villages in Northumberland. These incursions
had a serious impact on the economic well being of the border
counties, weakening any contribution they were able to make to the
French war. The forces at Balliol's disposal were either too weak or
too ill-led to mount an effective counter-action against the invaders.
Serious financial problems also hampered the defence of northern
England: desertions caused by arrears of wages owing to men-at-
arms and archers forced Balliol to withdraw from the border in
1342. Prior to this the position was so bad that he was empowered
to pardon all who had taken asylum in the various ecclesiastical
foundations in the north, on condition that they agree to serve in
Scotland.

In France Scotland's young King had grown to manhood. It was
suspected in England that his 'government in exile' was responsible
for the seaborne raids on the south coast, which became increasingly troublesome in 1339. In 1340 the sixteen year old David took
part in his first military operation, when he joined King Philip and
his allies, the kings of Navarre and Bohemia, in a campaign against
Edward and his Flemish supporters. The earls of Salisbury and

Suffolk were captured in an engagement near Lille. King Philip arranged for them to be exchanged for the Earl of Moray, who returned to Scotland in the autumn of 1340. He soon rejoined the war by leading an attack on the English in Annandale.

From 1340 onwards Scottish offensive action was concentrated on that part of the country annexed by England in 1335. On 16 April 1341 William Douglas, assisted by William Bullock, captured Edinburgh Castle by a daring piece of effrontery. Bullock and his men disguised themselves as English merchants. When the gates were opened to admit them they used their carts to jam the portcullis. Douglas and his men emerged from their nearby hide-outs, as the people of Edinburgh rushed to their assistance. The garrison commander, Sir Thomas Rokeby surrendered. Apart from Stirling, standing alone in the Forth valley, English holdings in Scotland had been pushed back close to the border. In recognition of this a new Scottish command was established on the march: John Randolph was given charge of operations in the west, John Douglas in the centre and Alexander Ramsay in the east.

With most of the interior of Scotland free from the English the economy began to recover and the harvests were good. Conditions were judged to be settled enough to allow King David to return from France. He left Chateau Gaillard in May, the same season he arrived, and on 2 June 1341 landed with Queen Joan at Inverberie near Montrose. The King was now seventeen years old, the same age as King Edward when he had seized power from Roger Mortimer, and ready to take the government of Scotland into his own hands from his 'dearest nephew', Robert Stewart.

Edward could do virtually nothing to stop these alarming developments in the north. His fruitless two year campaign in the low countries had been ruinously expensive, bringing him close to bankruptcy. His financial problems and disappointments in the French war brought increasing political difficulties at home, culminating in a serious political crisis in 1340–1. With Edward fully engaged in domestic and continental difficulties, David continued to put pressure on the border, while arranging to put the nation's finances and government in order.

Scotland was settled enough to allow national Parliaments to meet at Dundee and Scone. New taxes were raised and royal finances put on a sound basis, thanks to the efforts of William Bullock, who now served King David in the office of Chamberlain, a post he had held under Balliol but probably never carried out owing to the unsettled conditions of the country. A number of outstanding political problems were also settled. John of the Isles, who had long stood on the sidelines in the national struggle, was received into the peace of King David, although he was not allowed to keep the additional lands with which Balliol had tried to bribe him. In 1342 David successfully petitioned Pope Benedict to appoint William Landallis to the long vacant see of St. Andrews. David also busied himself rewarding his oldest allies. Malcolm Fleming, who had given him refuge in Dumbarton Castle, was created Earl of Wigtoun, and William Douglas was named Earl of Atholl.

As if to remind David that the threat from the south was not completely dormant, Edward III came north to Melrose in November 1341, where he spent a melancholy Christmas. After some aimless raiding in the Ettrick Forest he returned to England, after granting yet another short truce. Sir Thomas Gray was of the opinion that Edward was now bored with Scotland; bored with a war he had started but was now unsure how to finish. His appearance and early withdrawal only served to underline the decline of English power. Henry of Lancaster was put in charge of security on the border; but when his troops disbanded in February 1342, David raided Northumberland as far as the Tyne, his first experience of border war. Greater success followed. On 30 March 1342 Alexander Ramsay captured Roxburgh Castle using much the same techniques employed by Sir James Douglas almost thirty years before; and on the 10th of April Stirling Castle capitulated after a six month siege. In England, where Edward was busy preparing for the invasion of Brittany, the fall of Stirling, whose defence had cost the nation so much in 1314, went virtually unnoticed. The Scots were now so confident of their own strength, and the decline of English interest in Scotland, that they no longer bothered to destroy the castles that fell into their hands, an oversight that was to have serious future consequences, in the border area at least. The fall of Stirling Castle was the high noon of Scotland's recovery. Soon, a dark shadow passed over this triumph.

In the years since the death of Andrew Murray, William Douglas and Alexander Ramsay had proved themselves to be the country's most skilled commanders. Unfortunately, they had also become bitter rivals. Both had power bases in the borders, which they were keen to extend. William Douglas was warden of Liddesdale in the west march, which he held for his underage godson, also called William, the future first Earl of Douglas. Although he had recently

162

been created Earl of Atholl, Douglas's ambitions were firmly rooted in the borders, and he persuaded the Royal Council to allow him to surrender this title to Robert Stewart in return for the Lordship of Liddesdale. Douglas's request was granted, even though it meant the disinheritance of his own godson. Henceforth he was to be known as the 'Knight of Liddesdale'; he was also called by some unconscious irony 'The Flower of Chivalry', but the fragrance of the bloom was soon to acquire a particularly repellent stench.

Douglas's jealousy of Ramsay was intensified by the capture of Roxburgh, a fortress he himself had tried to take without success. David rewarded Ramsay's triumph by appointing him sheriff of Teviotdale in Roxburghshire. Douglas believed he had a stronger claim to this honour, and his resentment of Ramsay intensified. On 20 June 1342 he came in force to Hawick, where Ramsay was holding a court, kidnapped the sheriff and carried him to his castle of Hermitage in Liddesdale. Ramsay was cast into a dungeon and allowed to starve to death; a tragic end for the hero of Dunbar and Roxburgh. David had seriously misjudged the complexity of border politics and now seemed incapable of avenging the crime. He was finally persuaded to pardon Douglas by the intervention of the Stewart. However, the barbarous murder of Alexander Ramsay cast a long shadow into the future. According to the historian John of Fordun, it also marked the end of the run of good fortune the Scots had enjoyed since the Battle of Culblean.

Over the next four years there was a tense peace on the borders, broken from time to time by brief flurries of military activity. The general situation, though, was quite different from the mid 1330s, when the initiative lay with the English. With Edward so heavily committed to his war with France, the Scots waited to profit from any opportunity that might arise. The English were well aware of the danger. At Westminster in June 1344, the Chancellor warned the assembled Parliament that 'In Scotland they are saying quite openly that they will break the truce as soon as our adversary [France] desires, and will march against England doing all the damage in their power.'

The following August Edward Balliol was appointed once again as Edward's captain in the north, but he was able to do virtually nothing to shore up his meagre holdings in Scotland. In 1345 he lost his last toehold when Dougal MacDouall and the clans of Galloway made their peace with King David. This invited a retaliatory strike by the English, who took Hestan by surprise and sent

Dougall into captivity in the Tower of London. David himself came over the border in October 1345 to carry out a six day raid in search of plunder, free from any apparent interference from Balliol. The following year this limited manoeuvring on the border ended: the 'real' war was coming back to life, with fateful consequences for both Scotland and France.

Throughout the spring of 1346 Edward prepared for a great expedition to France. All along the south coast of England troops gathered and ships assembled. As summer approached there was panic in government circles in Paris. The exact purpose and direction of Edward's armada was unknown; by early July it looked as if the hammer was going to fall on Normandy. King Philip turned to his ally King David for help. David's actions on the border had so far failed to draw off sufficient English forces. Something more decisive than a raid was required. Philip was desperate: 'I beg you', he wrote to David, 'I implore you with all the force I can, to remember the bonds of blood and friendship between us. Do for me what I would do for you in such a crisis and do it quickly and thoroughly as with God's help you are able.'

King Edward sailed from Portsmouth on 28 June and anchored his fleet off the coast off Normandy on 12 July. Far to the north John Randolph invaded England about the same time, raiding deep into Cumberland and Westmoreland, setting fire to the town of Penrith. King David placed himself under Murray's command in what appears to have been a 'reconnaissance in strength'. He was not yet ready, however, for a major offensive. Although Percy and Neville responded to Moray and David's raid by a counter attack into the Scottish lowlands, the situation in the north was far from good. There were too few troops on the border and morale was low. Suffering from neglect by central government many threatened to desert, including the garrison of Berwick.

David was presumably aware of some of these facts, which would have encouraged him to return to England with a much larger army. Philip was certainly anxious for him to do so. He wrote to David again, advising him of the English landing in Normandy, and urging offensive action. Edward had most of his army with him, Philip reasoned, so England was a 'defenceless void.' A major Scots invasion would surely draw the English away from France, and Philip promised to follow this withdrawal by his own invasion of England. David began to gather a national army, as Archibald Douglas had in 1333, and waited for further news from France.

When it came it was very bad indeed: Edward had taken Caen and defeated King Philip at a great battle at Crecy on 26 August 1346. The arrow storm had now fallen on France as it had on Scotland in 1332 and 1333. From the field of Crecy Edward moved northwards to begin the long siege of Calais.

If the news of the Battle of Crecy caused David to reconsider the wisdom of his planned invasion, he soon brushed caution aside, because he believed himself bound in honour to open a 'second front', and repay all the assistance France had given to Scotland since 1334. With the examples of Donald of Mar and Archibald Douglas before him he should have been wary about the risks posed by a pitched battle. But with Edward at Calais with the bulk of his forces it was reasonable to assume, as Philip had, that England would be extremely vulnerable. Above all, David now appeared to have the chance of ending the stalemate on the border. He would have been mindful that his father's struggle had not been finished at Bannockburn, but by the repeated humiliation of England in a series of large scale raids. The force he now gathered was far greater than those that had prevailed at Myton, Old Byland and Stanhope Park; it was the greatest army that Scotland had seen since that which marched with Douglas to disaster at Halidon Hill.

The Scottish army which assembled at Perth on 6 October 1346 came from all corners of the realm. All the magnates were present, with the exception of the Earl of Caithness and John of the Isles. There was also a small French contingent, no doubt keen to avenge the humiliation of Crecy. Official English sources estimated the army's strength at some 12,000 men, a reasonable figure, considerably more modest than the usual tens of thousands given by the chroniclers. The soldiers were better equipped than usual, some being supplied with the latest French weapons and armour. But with so many men gathered discipline was hard to maintain, and some old rivalries quickly came to the surface. A dispute between Ranald MacRuaridh, who brought a contingent from the 'Outer Isles', and the Earl of Ross resulted in the murder of MacRuaridh. This was followed, according to Andrew Wyntoun, by wholesale desertions from the assembled host, a bad omen for the start of the campaign. None of this deflected David from his purpose.

David entered England by the west march, just north of Carlisle, having announced, in the *Lanercost* account, that he 'would soon see London'; a prediction that came true, although not in the manner he would have wished.

From the outset he showed himself to be an indifferent commander, with none of the military genius of his great father. Several days were wasted laying siege to the Peel of Liddel, a powerful but unimportant border fortress, giving the marcher lords time to organise their defences. The peel was taken and its commander, Sir Walter Selby, was butchered. Carlisle was in a poor state of defence, and so agreed to pay a great indemnity to be left unmolested. David thus passed up the opportunity of taking a prize that had eluded various Scots commanders, his own father included, since 1296. From the vicinity of Carlisle the Scots turned in a south easterly direction, advancing on a wide front and destroying everything in their path, in emulation of the English armies in Scotland in 1335 and 1336. A further three days were wasted looting the Priory of Hexham. In the meantime a large English force was deploying near Durham. On 16 October the Scots arrived in the neighbourhood of the town, camping at Beaurepaire, the country residence of the monks of the cathedral monastery. To avoid the usual desecration the clerics offered to pay David £1,000 in protection money, payable on 18 October. David settled down to wait for the promised bounty.

Despite David and Philip's optimism about the poor state of England's defences things had improved since the summer. As early as August English spies had kept the authorities informed of David's preparations. Money was more readily available; troops had been armed and were ready to assemble as soon as the Scots had crossed the border. David's leisurely progress from Liddel to Durham deprived him of all the advantages he may have gained by speed and mobility. By the time he arrived at the cathedral city the English commanders were ready.

The English force at Durham was under the command of the marcher lords Henry Percy and Ralph Neville. They were joined by the Archbishop of York, William de la Zouche, who was also the warden of the eastern march. A far more worldly man than William Melton, he came fully armed, ready to avenge the Chapter of Myton. The Archbishop had overseen the muster of the English army at Richmond in north Yorkshire. The troops—some 3,000 to 4,000 in all—had been collected from Cumberland, Northumberland and Lancashire. A further 3,000 Yorkshiremen set out to join the Archbishop at Richmond, but he decided to take to the field before they arrived. The march towards Durham began on 14 October.

At Beaurepaire David was confident in his delusion that there were no significant English forces in the area. He sent out no scouts and only learned of the approach of the Archbishop by accident. On the morning of 17 October William Douglas of Liddesdale was out pillaging just south of Durham, when he came across the rearguard of the English army emerging from the morning mist. In the ensuing fight Douglas and his men were driven off with heavy losses. The news was carried back to King David and the alert soon spread through the sleeping camp. The men were quickly organised in their battle divisions. David then advanced towards the English, taking up position at a place called Neville's Cross, so named from an old Anglo-Saxon stone cross.

The Scots were arranged in three battalions, matching the nearby enemy. For once they heavily outnumbered the English, but David lost any advantage this may have given by a poor choice of ground. His army looked out over land intersected by walls and ditches, which severely restricted its freedom to manoeuvre. The terrain suited an army fighting in a defensive position, but the Scots would not be allowed to dig in. David commanded the centre, the Earl of Moray and the Knight of Liddesdale were on the right, while the Stewart and the Earl of March commanded the left. The three English battalions under the Archbishop, Neville and Percy took up the usual defensive position, with the archers on the flanks, all too familiar to the Scots, and now the French. Both armies were in position by mid-day, but nothing happened for some time. Past experience with the power and accuracy of the longbow made the Scots unwilling to attack. The English broke the deadlock by abandoning their initial position and moving forward to bring the Scots within arrow range, a move later emulated by Henry V at Agincourt. This was, perhaps, David's lost opportunity: a rapid advance at this point might conceivably caught the enemy off balance. Sir John Graham did in fact suggest an immediate cavalry charge, but none was ordered. In any case, the badly chosen ground probably prevented any rapid reaction on David's part.

Once the Scots had been brought within range the English army took up position and the archers began their rapid fire into the Scottish ranks, forcing them to abandon their exposed location in a forward charge. Moray's men were the first to attack, keeping their heads down in a vain attempt to break the enemies arrows on their helmets and shoulder pieces. All momentum Moray's charge had was soon lost amongst the walls and ditches, which forced his schiltron to break ranks. Most of his men never reached the English; those that did were soon cut down by the men-at-arms and dismounted knights. The disorganised survivors fell back on King David in the centre. With the collapse of the right the full force of the arrow fire was now concentrated on the King's battalion, now completely exposed on the flank. Observing the rout of the Earl of Moray, Robert Stewart and Patrick de Dunbar, placed on a slightly less exposed position on the left, decided to make off, without troubling themselves about the fate of the King. David was never to forgive his nephew for this desertion. The chroniclers on both sides of the national divide show rare unanimity in condemning the actions of the two magnates. The English were gleeful: 'if one was worth little, the other was good for nothing . . . these two turning tail, fought with success, for with their battalion, without any hurt, they returned to Scotland and thus led off the dance, leaving David to caper as he wished.' The later Scottish historian Lord Hailes is a little kinder in his assessment: 'That the Stewart fought, and that he did not retire without loss, is evident from the number of barons of the name of Stewart who were either killed or made prisoner. For, it must be presumed, that some of them, if not all, fought under the banner of the chief of their family.' All that can really be said is that Robert Stewart had a remarkable talent for survival, and he made good his escape from Neville's Cross as he had from Halidon Hill thirteen years before, possibly the only man to have done so on both occasions.

After the flight of the left David was left to face the onslaught of the English army alone. He tried to make up for his poor generalship by showing great personal courage in a desperate battle. It availed him little. Towards the end of the afternoon the King, badly wounded by two arrows, one in the face, was forced to flee as best he could with the other survivors from his decimated schiltron. Even after he was overtaken and surrounded, he refused to surrender, although he was now alone and unarmed. John Coupland, a gentleman of Northumberland, managed to overpower him in a hand to hand struggle, losing two teeth in the process. The rump of David's fleeing army was pursued twenty miles across County Durham in the fading autumn light.

In his essay *Edward III and David II* Balfour Melville has written that Neville's Cross was 'one of the most disastrous battles in Scottish history, for whose outcome the disposition of the troops "in til a ful noyous place" was as much to blame as David's delusion that in England none were left but monks, cannons, friars and priests.' England now had its second great victory in a remarkable year. For Scotland the Battle of Neville's Cross was, if anything, a worse defeat than Crecy had been for France, bearing comparison with the later French catastrophe at Poitiers. The country was now back almost in the same position that it had been after Halidon. The list of the dead was grievous: John Randolph, Earl of Moray, and Maurice Moray, Earl of Strathearn; David de la Haye, the Constable, Robert Keith, the Marshall, and Thomas Charteris, the Chancellor of Scotland, together with 'other innumerable barons, knights, esquires and persons of worth.' As usual, the number of common people slain is not recorded. Total casualties, though, may not have been as high as Halidon because of the timely withdrawal of Robert Stewart.

King David was joined in captivity by the Knight of Liddesdale—'not so much valiant as malevolent', so said the monks of Durham—as well as the earls of Fife, Mentieth, Sutherland and Wigtoun, together with many others of lesser note. Two of the captives, Duncan MacDuff of Fife and John Graham of Mentieth, were now to pay for their submission to Edward at Perth in 1335. Both were tried for treason. Mentieth was drawn, hanged and quartered. Fife was only spared by reason of his kinship to Edward III. From his camp at Calais Edward gave orders that none of the remaining prisoners were to be ransomed at any price. All were to be conveyed at the earliest opportunity to the Tower of London. This was the cause of much resentment by those who wished to make a quick profit from their individual captives. Some were hidden from the King's officers and released by private treaty, but most were duly taken to London. One of the prisoners, a man with the improbable name of 'Makebeth de Scotia', was released by his captor, Roger de Wyderyngton, after promising to 'stay in the King's peace' in the company of Edward Balliol.

After the battle David himself, the most valuable captive in the whole of the Anglo-Scottish war, was taken to Bamburgh Castle, where he lay for some weeks, too ill to move. Great care was taken to ensure his recovery, and he was well attended by surgeons brought from York. By January 1347 he had recovered sufficiently to be taken to London under heavy guard, where he was paraded round the streets on a tall black horse, before being housed in the Tower, an exile for the second time in his life. Here he remained, a state prisoner, for the next eleven years

CHAPTER 15
The Return of the King, 1347–1357

The capture of David Bruce was by far the most damaging result of the Battle of Neville's Cross. He was the first Scottish monarch to fall into English hands since William the Lion in 1174. On that occasion the English King, Henry II, had used his prisoner to extract major political concessions from Scotland. Edward III now had the chance of ending once and for all the long Bruce and Balliol struggle in favour of his neglected protégé. Two things acted in Scotland's favour: first, Edward was too heavily committed to the capture of Calais to permit any immediate intervention in Scotland; and second, the King, always quick to see the chance of profit, was soon to realise that David was a greater political and financial asset than the hopeless Edward Balliol, who on past experience was not acceptable to the Scots on any terms whatsoever. The irony of Neville's Cross was that, in the long run, England came to recognise the legitimacy of the Bruce dynasty, however grudgingly, while allowing the claims of the Balliol pretender to wither and die.

There is some evidence that Edward Balliol was present at Neville's Cross, but it is not conclusive. If he was it must have been in a subordinate role, for he exercised no significant command as he had at Halidon Hill. He was, however, keen to take advantage of the new situation in Scotland to breathe new life into his moribund claim to the throne. Soon after the battle he entered Galloway and took up residence at Caerlaverock Castle, in preparation for more decisive action. In the same season Gilbert de Umfraville and Ralph Neville entered Scotland and took Roxburgh Castle, apparently without any kind of contest. Hermitage Castle was also captured, and English control of the border was secure once more. But beyond this there was no further action for the time being, and the Scots were allowed to put their affairs in order.

After his return from Neville's Cross, Robert the Stewart was appointed to lead the country by his fellow magnates in the absence of the King. He was named Locum Tenens—Lieutenant—and not Guardian, as if to imply his subordinate status to the captive King, with whom nominal authority continued to lie. The Stewart's luck in war was not matched by any skill in politics. He was a weak governor, and many took advantage of the absence of strong central authority to increase their own power at the expense of the national government; most notably, the independent minded John of the Isles, who by 1350 was widely acknowledged as 'Lord of the Isles'. To his Gaelic speaking kinsmen he was *Ri Innse Gall*—the 'King of the Hebrides'. His descendants were to cause much trouble to successive Scottish monarchs, until the Lordship of the Isles was finally abolished during the reign of James IV.

If the Stewart was a weak ruler the Scottish Church, under the leadership of William Landallis, recovered some of the spirit it had shown in the days of Robert Bruce. Landallis was to be closely involved in the negotiations for the release of King David, and proved to Edward that he was as bold a champion of the liberty of the Scottish church as his predecessor, William Lamberton.

The main task facing the Stewart was the defence of Scotland against the after-shock of Neville's Cross. The nation's guard was down, judging by the ease with which the English were able to take the border fortresses; and the Stewart's skill as a soldier was surely not great enough to prevent the enemy taking much more if they had made a determined push. But it's fairly obvious that Edward's interest in Scotland from his camp at Calais in 1347 was limited to recovering the lands ceded to him by Balliol, rather than restoring the latter to the Scottish throne. So, when the expected invasion finally came in the spring of 1347, it was a modest affair; and despite being launched under the banner of Edward Balliol, its aims were of a limited nature.

Balliol had been allowed to recruit troops in northern England, presumably at Edward's expense, for what was to be his last Scottish campaign. In January 1347 Henry Percy and John de Neville contracted to serve under him for one year. They were joined by Gilbert de Umfraville, the titular Earl of Angus and one of the last of the disinherited. Umfraville is likely to have been motivated by personal gain, for he seems to have long lost interest in his elusive earldom. Balliol's total force amounted to almost a thousand men, made up equally of men-at-arms and archers, considerably less than the fantastic figure of 320,000 claimed by Henry Knighton. He entered Scotland on 13 May 1347 on the final military adventure of his life. The Stewart withdrew before the invaders, who were allowed to occupy southern Scotland unopposed, advancing as far as Falkirk. The Lothians were wasted, but Edinburgh Castle was not taken. There was some suggestion of an advance on Perth, but the

English are said to have been bought off for the sum of £9,000. Having gone so far it doesn't seem very likely that Balliol would have been prepared to sell his 'right' so readily. It is, perhaps, more probable that Percy and Neville would not have been willing to go much further north with so modest a force, leaving Stirling and Edinburgh untaken in their rear. Most likely of all, having overrun the English-speaking lowlands, the prize most valued by their King, and gained some booty, the two commanders were quite happy to return south and abandon King Balliol, well short of the period they had contracted to serve him for. The English returned to Galloway by the south-west, ravaging Cunningham and Nithsdale on the way. Balliol was then deposited in his parental lands. His final bid for the crown of Scotland had now come to a premature end.

For Balliol the invasion of 1347 was a disappointment. Edward, on the other hand, had the satisfaction of knowing that the march is now said to have run from Cockburnspath on the Berwickshire coast, along the line of the Lammermuir and Pentland Hills, through Biggar in Lanarkshire, and on to the Ayrshire coast. While the border was still south of the Firth of Forth, almost all that had been gained by the Scots since the death of Andrew Murray had been lost again. The one consolation for the patriots was that Edward had learned nothing from the past, for this was not an occupation in any real depth. English forces on the ground were not numerous, and all of the great castles were to the south on or near the old march. Once again, through lack of commitment and resources, no serious attempt was made to consolidate these illusory gains.

Balliol had not been able to make good his royal title, but he was at least able to take up residence once more in his manor house at Hestan, and with the support of Herbert Maxwell and Duncan MacDouall, who returned to his cause in August 1347, he was able for a time to exercise some real power as the Lord of Galloway. His security was increased with the re-establishment of the English sheriffdom of Dumfriesshire in October, when Amyer de Atholl was appointed to the post and established a base the following year at the newly repaired castle of Dalswinton, a stronghold that had once belonged to the Red Comyn. The patriots were not totally inactive, however, and from his base in Carrick John Kennedy of Dunure waged a steady guerrilla war against the Balliol faction.

On 3 August 1347 Calais surrendered to Edward III, thus ending one of the greatest sieges of the middle ages. In September a truce was agreed between England and France, extended to include Scotland, to last until the summer of 1348. The King returned to England in October to enjoy the fruits of his victories and reflect on his future course of action. At the front of his mind was the problem of what to do with David Bruce. In March 1348 a Parliament, attended by Edward Balliol, tried to limit his freedom of action by making it a condition of a new grant of taxation that 'David Bruce, William Douglas, and the other chief men of Scotland, are in no manner to be set free, either for ransom or upon their word of honour.' Balliol, who as early as 1335 had pointed out the dangers of ransoming leading Scots, is likely to have been closely involved in this stipulation. The release of David on any terms whatsoever would clearly put and end to his own pretence of kingship. But Balliol's fears and Parliament's assertiveness did nothing to stop Edward from considering how to gain maximum advantage from his illustrious captive.

Balliol was now little more than an awkward obstacle in the way of the King's schemes. In 1349 he wrote to Ralph Neville informing him that his affairs were being hindered 'because Sir Edward de Balliol would not agree to good ways of establishing peace such as would seem reasonable to one side or the other.' Balliol was now quite clearly 'yesterday's man', while the ransom of David Bruce offered a way of recouping some of the losses of the Scottish war. Edward would keep as much of the border land as he could, gain a large money prize, and might even find a way to claim the Scottish crown, either for himself or a member of his family, by some backdoor negotiations. The objections of Edward Balliol would simply be ignored.

Preliminary discussions began not long after Edward's return. By 1350 David was being referred to as 'King of Scots' in official records. In August 1350 safe conducts were issued for a Scots embassy coming to York to discuss the question of 'our brother David Bruce'. The English negotiator was Ralph de Stafford, ironically one of those who fought with Balliol at Dupplin. Increasingly concerned for his own status, Balliol sent three Galloway knights—Patrick MacUlach, William de Aldeburgh and John de Wiggintoun—to appear before Edward and protest at this infringement of their master's rights as King of Scotland. But Balliol was soon fobbed off, and either Ralph de Stafford or Ralph Neville—the records do not make it clear which—was appointed by Edward to persuade him to drop his objections to the negotiations. Balliol in gloomy isolation in Galloway, perhaps in the company of Makebeth the Scot, was not allowed to stand in the way of national policy.

Edward's initial demands were high. In return for his freedom David had to recognise English overlordship, accept King Edward as his heir if he should die childless, restore the survivors amongst the disinherited, serve England in its war with France and attend English Parliaments. To guarantee that he would abide by these terms, Edward was to be given custody of all of the major Scottish castles. If these conditions had been accepted David would have been little more than a royal 'tenant', holding his throne under circumstances worse than those enjoyed by John Balliol.

The terms of this provisional treaty were outlined by David in a letter to Pope Clement VI in 1350. He gives no indication that they were acceptable to him; and he must have been perfectly well aware that there were no circumstances in which they would have been acceptable to the magnates and prelates of Scotland. There is also no clarification on the rather interesting question of who would now be considered as the 'disinherited': at the very least it would have to include, one assumes, Edward Balliol as the Lord of Galloway, although Edward probably assumed that this lordship would remain within the English domain.

By December 1350 Edward appears to have thought the better of these sweeping demands. The Knight of Liddesdale was allowed to return to Scotland on a temporary parole to advise the Scots that their King might be released on a ransom of £40,000, provided that they agreed to recognise one of Edward's younger sons as heir to the throne should David die childless. English troops would occupy the castles until the first instalment of the ransom was paid. This package is likely to have been much more acceptable to David himself, for it did not compromise the issue of national independence for which his father had fought. Moreover, he was still only twenty six years old, and while his marriage to Joan had so far been fruitless, he would fully expect to conceive his own heirs. The only loser was Robert Stewart, for whom David had formed an intense suspicion and dislike. David came north himself on parole in February 1352 to press these terms on a reluctant community. The proposal was considered by Parliament at Scone in February and March. One assumes that the Stewart would have been busy defending the liberty of the realm and, by happy coincidence, his own inheritance, for Edward's terms were rejected 'with one consent, in one voice'. The Scots showed their determination to adhere to the Declaration of Arbroath and, while willing to pay a heavy ransom for David's release, refused to consider an English heir. This rejection seems to have caused Edward to consider using David in much the same way that he had used Balliol in 1332. David and the Knight of Liddesdale were given permission to remain at Newcastle or Berwick to progress matters 'in another way.' But David was not willing to be a catspaw for Edward, and duly returned to the Tower.

Edward's scheming did manage to secure one small success. The Knight of Liddesdale, no doubt anxious about the possible decline of his border power base in his absence, was keen to secure his freedom at any price. He therefore concluded a private agreement with Edward on 17 July 1352, which allowed him to go free and occupy Hermitage Castle as Edward's liegeman. In return for his services he was awarded lands in Annandale and Moffatdale to add to those he already held in Liddesdale. One of Scotland's greatest guerrilla leaders had entered into a treasonable pact with England, ruining a reputation already darkened by the murder of Alexander Ramsay. His nefarious career was not destined to last much longer.

Despite the periodic truces warfare was never far below the surface on the borders. Scots forces had already penetrated far into the territory won by the English after Neville's Cross by the time Douglas was released in the summer of 1352. Balliol's territory in Galloway appears to have been particularly hard pressed, for the sheriff of Dumfriesshire, Amyer de Atholl, was engaged in continuous defensive action by the close of the year. Scots resistance was inspired by a new champion—William, Lord of Douglas, the godson of the Knight of Liddesdale and the son of Archibald Douglas, the former Guardian killed at Halidon. Like King David he had spent his youth in French exile, coming back to Scotland soon after Neville's Cross to claim his inheritance in the difficult circumstances of the time. He was Lord of Douglas, and rightfully Lord of Liddesdale, but he had been deprived of this title by the machinations of his godfather in 1342. He now took a leading part in the border conflict which, with the return of the Knight, ranged Douglas against Douglas. In August 1353 the Lord of Douglas ambushed and killed the Knight of Liddesdale in Ettrick Forest, avenging both the personal injustice that had been done to him and the death of Alexander Ramsay. Thus ended any remaining hope Edward had of using the Knight to further his schemes. He granted Hermitage

Castle to the Dacre family, who managed to hold it for England until the 1360s.

So far Edward had achieved nothing either from his previous support of Edward Balliol or his capture of David Bruce. In 1354 he reduced his demands considerably, in an attempt to find a way through the political deadlock. This time the negotiations went as far as a draft treaty, drawn up at Berwick in July. All the political demands had been dropped, and Edward now simply asked for money. In return for David's release the Scots agreed to pay a ransom of 90,000 merks (£60,000), payable in nine annual instalments, during which time a truce would be observed. To guarantee compliance the Scots would hand over twenty nine noble hostages. But this treaty was never executed because the war in France, which had been dormant for some years, was about to come back to life.

The Anglo-French truce was due to expire in 1355 and Edward prepared once more for war. The French King, John II, who succeeded to the throne on the death of his father Philip in 1350, appealed to Scotland for help. To encourage them to break the truce with England he sent a small military force, commanded by the Sire de Garencieres, to Scotland in March 1355, together with a rich bribe of 40,000 *moutons d'or*, to be paid to the leading men of the realm on condition that the war was renewed. The Scots may have hoped that trouble on the border would have caused Edward, heavily involved in France, to reduce the price for the release of King David.

The Scots began the new war, in the accustomed fashion, by a cross border raid in August 1355. The raiders were led by William Ramsay of Dalhousie, the son of Alexander Ramsay, and the Earl of March. On their return they were intercepted by the warden of Norham Castle, Sir Thomas Gray, who was defeated and taken prisoner; a sad blow for him, but a stroke of good fortune for future students of the Wars of Independence. Gray was sent into captivity in Edinburgh Castle, where he used his forced leisure to study and compose his history, *The Scalacronica*. An English counter raid was defeated by the Lord of Douglas at Nesbit Muir in Berwickshire. But a worse blow for England came later in the year. In November Garancieres and Thomas Stewart, the Earl of Angus, approached Berwick from the sea, climbed the walls and took the town in a surprise night attack. The castle held out and was besieged.

This was too great a blow to English prestige for Edward to ignore. He broke off his operations in France, returned to England and advanced quickly to the relief of Berwick Castle. When he reached the town the French had already gone home and the Scots force was too weak to hold out against him. No relief was mounted because if disputes amongst the Scots magnates, no doubt anxious to avoid a repeat of Halidon Hill. The town was retaken in January 1356. Edward then moved to Roxburgh, where he decided, once and for all, to end the long running tragedy of Edward Balliol.

For some years Balliol had continued to exercise some nominal authority as Lord of Galloway, while stubbornly clinging to his claim to be the rightful King of Scotland. By 1351 it must have been perfectly clear to him, though, that he could expect little further help from his mentor King Edward, who was busy trying to make the best deal he could out of David Bruce. Balliol was forced to stand unhappily on the sidelines while negotiations for the release of David, his principal enemy, continued. His frustration with the uncertainty of his position may have caused him to turn briefly to France, with a view to giving up his hopeless cause in Scotland and returning to his home in Picardy, which he hadn't seen for twenty years. Some overtures appear to have been made, for in 1351 John II promised to restore Balliol's French estates if he abandoned his allegiance to Edward. But it was probably too late for initiatives of this kind, and nothing more is heard of John's promise.

Amazingly, Balliol also opened up negotiations with the Scots on his own initiative, causing Edward some annoyance; for in March 1351, it is noted in *Rymer's Foedera* that 'King Edward accepts the protestations of Edward de Balliol, King of Scots, that his negotiations with the Scots shall not prejudice his treaty with the King of England.' In return, Edward was obliged in March 1352 to reassure his protégé that the proposed treaty with the Scots would not prejudice his own 'rights.' Just what 'rights' he had in mind at this time is not at all clear. However, the tentative discussions between Balliol and the Stewart, both in their own ways worried about the outcome of Edward's negotiations with David, came to nothing.

By the middle of the 1350s Balliol's best hope was to hang on to what was left of Galloway. In the abortive agreement prepared at Berwick in July 1354 the proposed nine year truce between the two nations was extended to include Edward Balliol. By this time the unfortunate Balliol was in desperate need of some kind of respite. He had received little in the way of financial or military assistance from Edward. In August 1355 William, Lord of Douglas, invaded Galloway and compelled Balliol's chief supporter, Duncan

MacDouall, to submit. Much of Galloway seems to have been overrun, and Balliol's holdings shrunk to the coastal strip around Hestan, and Caerlaverock and Buittle castles. The English managed to maintain an equally precarious hold on Dalswinton Castle. Most of what was left was lost when the Scots under Roger Kirkpatrick recaptured Nithsdale in 1355 and 1356. Balliol now well into his sixties and unmarried had had enough. By prior arrangement he agreed to meet Edward at Roxburgh to put an end to his pointless struggle.

On 20 January 1356 Balliol met Edward and began the process of abdication. In a dramatic and symbolic gesture he handed his crown and a handful of Scottish earth to Edward III, thus making him his heir, declaring to all 'Most excellent prince, . . . I do here before all your chivalry . . . resign, yield and relinquish to you all my right which I have, claim, or may hereafter have to the throne of Scotland, to the end that you may avenge me of mine enemies, the infamous Scots, who ruthlessly cast me off that I should not reign over them.' He also surrendered his ancestral lands in Galloway and Picardy, from which he had derived little profit. 'He himself gave nothing,' wrote John of Fordun, 'because from the beginning he had no right to anything.' Lord Hailes summarises his career thus:

> The fate of Edward Balliol was singular. In his invasion of Scotland . . . he displayed a bold spirit of enterprise, and a courage superior to all difficulties. By the victory of Dupplin he won a crown; some weeks after, he was surprised at Annan and lost it. The overthrow of the Scots at Halidon, to which he signally contributed, availed not to his re-establishment. Year after year he saw his partisans fall away, and range themselves under the banner of his competitor. He became the pensioner of Edward III and the tool of his policy, assumed and laid aside at his pleasure.

The reasons he gave for his abdication were the approach of old age and the rebelliousness of the Scots. Quite simply, he was worn out. If as Fordun says Balliol gave nothing, he certainly received much in return. Edward agreed to an immediate gift of 5,000 merks to pay off his debts, and to an annual pension of £2,000. There is some historical irony in the latter figure; for it was Balliol's promise at Roxburgh in 1332 to give Edward £2,000 worth of Scottish land that eventually ruined all prospect he had of establishing himself as the uncontested King of Scotland. Edward was to gain practically nothing from Balliol's abdication, while his protégé was at least to have the satisfaction of drawing his considerable pension for the next eight years. Balliol retired to obscurity near Knaresborough in Yorkshire, where he spent his time poaching on the King's estates. He died in January 1364, the last of the Anglo-Scots. Long forgotten in Scotland, he was remembered for some time after his death by the monks of Beauvale in Nottinghamshire, who received a grant to pray for the soul of Edward Balliol 'chevaler' in perpetuity.

Soon after Balliol's abdication Edward, now styling himself King of Scotland, as well as England and France, issued a proclamation promising to maintain the country's ancient laws. If he expected any submissions as a result, he was disappointed. The King then set out to make good his title by leading his last invasion of Scotland in February 1356. His passage was destructive, but no more successful than his father's last campaign in 1322. Crossing the Lammermuir Hills, he descended on Haddington, where the Franciscan friary and its church, known as the 'Lamp of Lothian', was set alight. A further act of desecration was carried out by English sailors, who pillaged the shrine of the Virgin Mary at Whitekirk. Shortly after this the English fleet, carrying supplies for the army, was dispersed by unfavourable winds, and some ships were sunk, by the intervention of the Virgin herself, so said the Scots. This was a serious setback, and the King was soon dangerously short of supplies. Robert of Avesbury wrote:

> They (the army) had very little food, and many ships coming from England to the King were so horribly tossed by the tempests of the sea, that some of them were lost, others were driven by winds to various English ports, and some were borne to foreign ports. So, as food failed them, our King returned to England, being for the time frustrated in his purpose.'

The invasion achieved nothing, but was remembered for its destructiveness as the 'Burnt Candelmas.'

Edward arrived back in London in March. He made up his mind that further efforts in Scotland were futile and appointed commissioners to treat with the Scots on the border for a temporary cessation of hostilities. On 18 April the Lord of Douglas concluded a six months truce with the Earl of Northampton at Roxburgh, and an uneasy quite settled down on the border.

With the borders enjoying a temporary peace, Scots hopes at this time rested on the efforts of their French ally. A small expeditionary force commanded by the Lord of Douglas was sent to France to assist king John, only to share in the defeat of the French army by Edward, Prince of Wales, at the Battle of Poitiers on 19 September 1356. King John was taken captive, soon to join David in the Tower. France now fell into the most chaotic period of her medieval history, and it was to be some time before Scotland received any further succour from this quarter. There was no alternative but to reopen negotiations for the release of David.

In January 1357 the national council at Perth agreed to send an embassy under William Landallis to London to agree the final terms for David's release. Edward, now close to his goal in France, was eager to dispose of the Scottish question. David was sent north to Berwick and made ready for release. The Treaty of Berwick was sealed on 3 October 1357. Its terms were basically the same as the draft treaty of 1354, except that the price had gone up. The ransom demanded was now 100,000 merks or almost £67,000. This was to be paid in ten annual instalments, payment to continue even if David died. This was no 'final peace', but a truce would be maintained over the period the ransom was being paid, and trade links between the two countries would be re-established. The twenty-nine hostages of 1354 were to be supplemented by an additional group drawn from magnates of the first rank. The terms agreed, David returned to Scotland, a free man, on 7 October 1357. The Wars of Independence were over.

CHAPTER 16
The Aftermath

The Treaty of Berwick, it is rightly said, settled no issue but that of David's release. Although he was given the title 'King of Scotland' in the Treaty this did not imply recognition of the Bruce claim, and later English documents avoid referring to David as King. Berwick was in no sense a treaty of peace like Northampton. Many important issues were left unresolved, most notably the English King's claim to be the Lord Paramount of Scotland. It also left a significant part of Scotland still under occupation: on the west march the English continued to control Annandale from Lochmaben Castle; and, in the east, they held a large swath of territory in the vicinity of Jedburgh, Roxburgh and Berwick. All of this was unfinished business, and the cause of future warfare. Nevertheless, viewed in retrospect, the Treaty of Berwick is a significant milestone, marking the end of the Wars of Independence in a way that the Treaty of Northampton failed to do. Never again was their to be any serious attempt to replace a Scottish King, or to end the country's political independence. For the remainder of Edward III's life the two countries were at peace. Future military action was of a limited nature, and warfare settled down to a long and often semi-official struggle on and around the borders.

David II came back to Scotland in the flower of his manhood, sobered by his long years in captivity. If he had been a bad general he was to prove himself a competent administrator; a lesser man than his father, but considerably greater than the Stewart. He took steps to bring order to the country in general and to royal finances in particular, both of which his Lieutenant had allowed to slip into chaos. He was still childless, and the issue of the succession was uppermost in his mind, along with that of the royal ransom. These issues interacted to become the dominant theme for the remainder of David's reign.

The King was deeply suspicious of his constitutionally designated successor, Robert Stewart, the man who had abandoned him at Neville's Cross. Although the Stewart was honoured in 1357 with the earldom of Strathearn, he soon lost all of his political influence. When Queen Joan died in 1362 the King proposed to marry

Margaret Logie, the widow of Sir John Logie and daughter of Sir Malcolm Drummond. Dame Margaret was known to be fertile, and the marriage threatened to end any prospect of a Stewart succession. This was too much for Robert, who promptly allied himself with William, now Earl of Douglas, and the Earl of March, both worried about their declining influence in royal government. All three rose in rebellion against the King in January 1363. David reacted quickly to the crisis and dispersed the force gathered by the Earl of Douglas at Lanark. Robert Stewart proved no more steadfast in rebellion than he had in battle, and abandoned his noble allies, who were forced to submit to the King. David married Margaret in April 1363 and turned his attention to achieving a more final settlement with England than that which had been concluded at Berwick.

Soon after he returned to Scotland David was keen to turn Berwick into a permanent settlement. Queen John had been involved in this, and had gone to London before the end of 1357 'to speak to her brother the King and start negotiations for a greater treaty.' David himself had returned to England in February 1359 to speak with Edward. His failure to make any progress led to renewed contacts with France. David proposed to renew the war in the north if the Dauphin Charles, who headed the government in the absence of the imprisoned King John, would have paid his ransom. But the war of 1356 had severely weakened the French economy, and the most Charles was able to offer was 50,000 marks. However, the prospect of even receiving this sum ended when Edward undertook a fresh invasion of France, and forced the government to conclude peace in May 1360. In the Treaty of Bretigny Edward agreed to give up his claim to the throne of France in return for full sovereignty over a greatly enhanced Duchy of Aquitaine. The French also agreed to pay a huge ransom for King John and to abandon the Scottish alliance. Bretigny was to be one of the most unstable of all medieval peace treaties; but for the time being David had to accept that any definitive Anglo-Scottish peace would have to be concluded on terms acceptable to Edward III.

When David and Edward met in November 1363 the ransom payments agreed at Berwick were considerably in arrears. Edward had been preoccupied with French affairs, and had not been able to give the matter his full attention: now his demands for money—or political concessions—and David's desire for a firm peace, meant that the issue could be delayed no longer. The two kings reached an agreement whereby the remainder of the ransom would be dropped, the hostages freed, and Berwick and the other occupied lands restored to Scotland in return for the formal recognition of Edward as David's heir should he die childless. If Edward succeeded to the throne of Scotland he promised to respect the country's liberty. The union would be purely personal: the King of England would undergo a second coronation at Scone as King of Scotland. The Stone of Destiny would be restored for this purpose. This agreement was supplemented by a second, less sweeping proposal, which would allow one of the King's younger sons, possibly Lionel of Clarence, to be recognised as David's heir in return for fewer concessions on England's part. As agreements of this kind could not be undertaken by a private person David was formally recognised by Edward as King of Scotland.

These draft treaties were more favourable than that concluded at Birgham over seventy years before, when a union of the two crowns was agreed in the person of Queen Margaret and Edward of Caernarvon; but much blood had been spilt in the intervening years, and the Scots were understandably suspicious of English motives. When Parliament assembled at Scone in March 1364 both proposals were rejected. The magnates and prelates, now supplemented by representatives from the burghs, gave an unequivocal answer: 'It was expressly answered by the three estates . . . that they in no wise wished to grant, nor in any wise assent to, those things that were sought by the King of England and his council.' David's reaction to this rejection is unrecorded. Edward was clearly annoyed and continued to refuse any more permanent settlement, or to lengthen the truce. The best that could be obtained by the Scots was a new ransom agreement concluded on 20 May 1365. The 20,000 merks already paid under the Treaty of Berwick was set aside. The Scots now agreed to pay £100,000 in instalments of £4,000 a year, payable from 2 February 1366. Edward only extended the truce until February 1370, reserving the right to renew the war with six months' notice. In that event the balance of the £100,000 need not be paid, but Scotland would still have to pay the 80,000 merks still owing from the 1357 treaty. This was extortion on a grand scale.

David continued in his attempts to persuade Edward to adopt a less intransigent position, with no success. However, with the renewal of the French war in 1369 the situation improved. The fundamental weakness of the Treaty of Berwick was now exposed: for in concluding a purely financial agreement, and resisting all attempts to arrive at a comprehensive solution of the Anglo-Scottish question, the English had left it open for the Scots to renew the alliance with France. While neither Scotland nor France represented any danger to Edward in 1357, by 1369 the circumstances were entirely different. King John II had died in captivity in 1364 and was succeeded by his son Charles V. Charles was a far more skilful politician and tactician than his father or grandfather, and quickly undermined English power in France. Faced with this new threat from the south the ageing Edward was forced to direct resources away from the northern march. He also attempted to pacify Scotland by some minor territorial concessions and a new ransom treaty.

David assisted this process by playing a clever double game: he himself came to meet Edward in London, while at the same time sending Sir Archibald Douglas, 'The Grim', on a mission to the court of King Charles V. The new ransom treaty was agreed in June 1369, using the 1357 treaty as a basis. The 1365 treaty was set aside, and the sums already paid deducted from the balance outstanding under the Berwick agreement, leaving 56,000 merks still to be paid. The truce would be extended for a further fourteen years, up to February 1384. During this period the Scots would pay the ransom in yearly instalments of 4,000 merks.

David was now well into middle age, and his marriage to Margaret Logie had been no more fertile than his marriage to Joan. Still reluctant to concede a Stewart succession he divorced Margaret and considered marriage to Agnes Dunbar. Before he could complete his plans he died suddenly at Edinburgh Castle on 22 February 1371. He was succeeded by his despised nephew, who was crowned and anointed at Scone on 26 March as King Robert II, the first in the long line of Stewart monarchs.

One of the first acts of the new King's reign was the renewal of the Franco-Scottish alliance. For Edward, now in his twilight years, and with his fortunes in France in sharp decline, the new treaty served to underline the failures of his reign; but there was at least no renewal of the war in the north. King Robert II was also well advanced in years, and had learnt enough of English prowess to desire security rather than seek adventure. For as long as Edward lived the peace on the border was maintained, and Scotland continued to pay the dead King's ransom. Payment was only interrupted by the death of Edward III on 21 June 1377. A balance of 24,000 merks remained which was never settled.

With the death of King Edward, and despite the truce, Scots pressure on the march began to increase. From 1378 a new form of warfare began to take shape. Scottish central government under Robert II and his successor Robert III was too feeble to pursue any co-ordinated strategy. The initiative was taken up by the Scottish marcher lords, led by the house of Douglas, who conducted an ongoing private border war with their English counterparts, the Percys of Northumberland and the Nevilles of Westmoreland. The border lords were motivated less by national pride and much more by the prospect of booty and self aggrandisement. The age of the 'rievers' had begun.

John of Gaunt, Duke of Lancaster, and guardian of Edward's young grandson and successor, King Richard II, came north in October 1380 with a large retinue to one of the periodic truce conferences on the border to try to intimidate the Scots into accepting the existing demarcations on the border. There was still, however, no permanent peace; and when the truce finally expired in February 1384 both sides prepared for a renewal of the 'official' war. In the previous August King Robert had arranged for French military and financial assistance. Soon after the truce ended a party of French troops landed at Montrose. This was followed up a year later by a larger force of over a thousand knights, bannerets and men-at-arms under Jean de Vienne, admiral of France. These gentlemen were to experience a form of warfare with which they were entirely unaccustomed.

The Scots were quick off the mark. On 4 February 1384 Archibald the Grim, Lord of Galloway, and George Dunbar, Earl of March, captured and destroyed Lochmaben Castle, ending the last traces of half a century of English domination in Annandale and the west march. When John of Gaunt came north in retaliation he advanced with his army to the gates of Edinburgh, but retired after receiving a ransom. He came north again in 1385, this time with his nephew, King Richard II. Archibald the Grim, having achieved his own objectives, and in complete disregard of the weak Robert II, concluded his own private truce with England in March 1385. Leaving Archibald unmolested, Richard and Lancaster advanced up the eastern route towards Edinburgh, destroying on the way the great religious houses at Melrose, Dryburgh and Newbattle. Edinburgh and the church of St. Giles were also set alight. Holyrood Abbey in the adjacent burgh of Cannongate was only saved by the intervention of Lancaster, who had been given refuge there during the

Peasants Revolt in England. This was a time when England and Scotland followed rival popes at Rome and Avignon, lending a superficial sanction to the destruction of rival religious centres; but the desecration of sacred sites was usually just a matter of course. In retaliation for the English invasion a body of French and Scottish troops raided extensively in the north of England. Richard's progress through the lowlands was even more destructive than his grandfather's had been during the Burnt Candelmas. The outcome, however, was just the same: faced with rigorous scorched earth tactics the English soon ran short of victuals and were forced to retreat. Richard had, at least, been able to reduce the pressure on the border, and a series of truces were concluded up to 1388. For the knights of France the northern war was too plain a fare: the hardships and lack of glory were not much to their liking, and the allies soon parted on very poor terms.

Once again, the Scots were ready to take the offensive as soon as the truce expired. With Richard now heavily involved in serious domestic difficulties James, Earl of Douglas, and his allies Archibald the Grim and Robert, Earl of Fife, led a large cross border raid in the early summer of 1388. A further raid followed later in the year, with the Scots dividing their forces in the east and west march. The smaller of these two parties was commanded by the Earl of Douglas and the earls of Moray and March. At Otterburn in Redesdale they met an English force under the command of Harry Percy or 'Hotspur', son of the Earl of Northumberland. The Battle of Otterburn was fought on 5 August 1388 in the dying summer light and on into the moonlight. The Earl of Douglas was mortally wounded, but his men continued to fight until victory was won. Hotspur was taken prisoner, only to be freed after a large ransom was paid. The honours of the battle were awarded in history and romance to the dead Earl of Douglas.

In 1400 Henry IV, great grandson on his mother's side of Henry Beaumont, was the last English King to lead an invasion of Scotland in person. He had written to Robert III, who succeeded his father to the throne in 1390, reminding him that the Kings of England were the Lords Superior of Scotland. Prior to this he had rejected a proposal to conclude a final peace on the basis of the 1328 treaty. His demand for submission was backed up by an advance on Edinburgh. He arrived at Leith on 21 August, achieved nothing and soon retired. Peace talks were subsequently held at Yetholm in October 1401, only to flounder on the English insistence on feudal superiority. The English negotiators suggested that King Robert consent to having the issue of homage put to arbitration, to which Matthew Glendonwyn, the Bishop of Glasgow, replied that Henry IV, who had usurped the throne of England from his cousin Richard II, might submit his own right to the crown to a similar process of arbitration. No further discussions were held, and the border war continued on its usual intermittent course.

In 1402 the archers of England won two notable victories at the Battle of Nesbit Muir in June, and again at the Battle of Homildon Hill in September, where Harry Hotspur was more than avenged for Otterburn, taking Archibald, Earl of Douglas, prisoner along with the earls of Moray and Angus as well Murdoch Stewart, son of the premier Scottish nobleman, the Duke of Albany. But the English won their greatest prize since the capture of David II in March 1406, when the heir to the Scottish throne, James Stewart, was seized by English pirates off Flambourgh Head on his way to France. He was to remain a prisoner of the English crown until 1424. His father, King Robert III, died in April 1406, shortly after the Prince's capture, reputedly of a broken heart. Arguably the most feeble ruler to have occupied the throne of Scotland since the days of John Balliol, he is reputed on the point of his death to have suggested the following epitaph—'Here lies the worst of kings and the most wretched of men.'

In spite of these reverses the Scots continued to seize any advantage that presented itself. In May 1409 Jedburgh Castle was captured, according to the records, by 'mediocre persons of Teviotdale.' It was immediately destroyed on the orders of the Regent, the Duke of Albany, governing Scotland in the absence of James I. When England descended into the anarchy of the Wars of the Roses the Scots used the occasion to recover the remaining lands on the border still under occupation. In 1460 King James II laid siege to Roxburgh Castle, which had been in English hands for well over a hundred years. James was killed when a cannon he was inspecting accidentally exploded; but the siege continued and the castle was taken a few days later and demolished, thus ending the English occupation of Teviotdale. Finally, in an attempt to buy Scottish support against the Yorkists in the English dynastic war, Margaret of Anjou, wife of the Lancastrian King Henry VI, surrendered the castle and town of Berwick on 25 April 1461. This was the last English outpost in Scotland, and the borders were finally restored to those of 1296 and 1328. But this final prize, so cheaply won, was soon to be lost again. England achieved stability once more under King Edward IV, and was quick to exploit the serious differences that had grown up between King James III and his own magnates. An army led by Richard, Duke of Gloucester, the future King Richard III, retook Berwick and its hinterland in November 1482. This time it passed out of Scottish hands forever, and stands today as the last reminder of the Wars of Independence.

In 1707 the Scots Parliament agreed to dissolve itself and merge with its English counterpart in a new Parliament for Great Britain. The independence for which the men and women of the thirteenth and fourteenth centuries had struggled so hard was given away, and Scotland, one of Europe's oldest nations, was soon to 'disappear' in a new imperial state. This had been a lengthy process. During the Reformation in the mid-sixteenth century the Scots had cut the last ties with their old Catholic ally France, and grew closer to the Protestant England of Queen Elizabeth I. As if to wipe out the memories of the past a mob destroyed Dunfermline Abbey on 28 March 1560, the final resting place of many Scottish kings and heroes, most notably Robert Bruce, Thomas Randolph and Andrew Murray. The tombs were lost in this act of desecration. The remains of what are thought to be Robert Bruce were found in 1819 and reinterred in the new abbey church. But while the English can visit the tombs of the first three Edwards, no Scot can with any certainty visit the graves of their own lost kings.

When James VI of Scotland moved to London to become King James I of England the process that ended with the Act of Union in 1707 was firmly underway. Between 1603 and 1707, despite periodic bouts of assertiveness, Scotland enjoyed at best a shadowy independence. In 1649 the English Parliament was arrogant enough to order the illegal execution of a head of state, King Charles I, without any reference to its Scottish counterpart. This encouraged the enraged Scots to reassert their ancient right of self determination, and Charles II was duly proclaimed King a few days after his father's death, while England declared itself to be a republic. Charles was crowned at Scone in January 1651, the last monarch to receive this honour. But Scotland was defeated by Oliver Cromwell in battle at Dunbar, ironically under circumstances not dissimilar to those of 1296, and again at Worcester. Charles fled abroad and Scotland was forcibly incorporated into the English Commonwealth.

In 1707 a section of the Scottish oligarchy voluntarily agreed to a new incorporation. The fact that the country kept its own laws and religious institutions is surely no greater compensation for the loss of national self determination than it had been centuries before when these things were promised by Edward III. The ghosts of those ancient warriors who gather in the ruins of Arbroath Abbey and on the battlefields of Stirling, Bannockburn and Culblean will surely haunt the Scottish people until they free themselves from the shackles of a union that has long since served its purpose and once again take their place amongst the independent nations of Europe.

Select Bibliography

Primary Sources

Anglo-Scottish Relations, 1174–1328. Selected Documents, edited and translated by E.L.G Stones, 1965.
Anonimalle Chronicle, 1333–81, edited by V.H. Galbraith, 1927.
Barbour, John, *The Bruce*, translated by A.A.H. Douglas, 1964.
Boece, Hector, *The Chronicles of Scotland*, edited by E. Batho and W. Husbands, 1941.
Bower, Walter, *Scotichronicon*, edited by D.E.R. Watt, 1987–1993.
Brut or the Chronicles of England, edited by F.W.D. Brie, 1906.
Capgrave, John, *The Book of the Illustrious Henries*, edited by F Hingeston, 1858.
Capgrave, John, *Chronicle of England*, edited by F. Hingeston, 1858.
Calendar of Close Rolls 1892–1954.
Calender of Documents Relating to Scotland, edited by J. Bain, 1887.
Calendar of Patent Rolls 1891–1982.
Documents Illustrative of the History of Scotland, translated and arranged by Joseph Stevenson, 1870.
Edward III and his Wars: Extracts from the Chroniclers, edited and translated by W.J. Ashley, 1887.
Fordun, John of, *Chronicles of the Scottish Nation*, edited by W.F. Skene, 1872.
Froissart, Jean, *Chronicle of Froissart*, translated by Sir John Bourchier, 1901 edition.
Gray, Thomas, *Scalacronica*, edited and translated by H. Maxwell, 1913.
Holinshead, Raphael, *Scottish Chronicle*, 1806.
The Lanercost Chronicle, edited and translated by H. Maxwell, 1913.
Matthew of Westminster, *The Flowers of History*, edited and translated by C.D. Yonge, 1853.
Minot, Laurence, *Poems*, edited by J. Rilson, 1825.
Pluscarden, the Book of, edited by F.J.H. Skene, 1880.
The Song of Lewes, edited and translated by C.L. Kingsford, 1890.
A Source Book of Scottish History, edited and translated by W. Croft Dickinson, G. Donaldson and I. Milne, 1952.
Syllabus of Rymer's Foedera, vol. 1, edited by T.D. Hardy, 1869.
Vita Edwardi Secundi, edited by N. Denholm Young, 1957.
Wyntoun, Andrew, *The Original Chronicle of Scotland*, edited by F.J. Amours, 1907.

Secondary Works.

Anderson, W., *The Scottish Nation etc*, biographical history, 3 vols, 1863.

Cumming-Bruce, M.E., *Family Records of the Bruces and Comyns*, 1870.

Balfour-Melville, E.W.M., *Edward III and David II*, Historical Association Pamphlet G. 27, 1954.

Balfour-Melville, E.W.M., The Death of Edward Balliol, in *The Scottish Historical Review*, vol. 35, pp 82–3, 1955–6.

Balfour-Melville, E.W.M., David II's Appeal to the Pope, *The Scottish Historical Review*, vol. 41, p 86, 1962.

Bain, J., *The Edwards in Scotland, 1296–1377*, 1961.

Barnes, J., *The History of Edward III*, 1688.

Barrow, G.W.S., 'The Wood of Stronkalter: a Note on the Relief of Lochindorb Castle by Edward III in 1336', *The Scottish Historical Review*, vol. 46, pp 77–9, 1967.

Barrow, G.W.S., 'The Wars of Independence', in *The Scottish Nation*, edited by G. Menzies, 1972.

Barrow, G.W.S., *The Kingdom of the Scots*, 1973

Barrow, G.W.S., 'Lothian in the First War of Independence, 1296–1328', *The Scottish Historical Review*, vol. 55, pp 151–71, 1976.

Barrow, G.W.S., *Robert Bruce and the Community of the Realm of Scotland*, 2nd edn., 1976.

Barrow, G.W.S., *Kingship and Unity: Scotland, 1000–1306*, 1981.

Barrow, G.W.S., *Scotland and its Neighbours in the Middle Ages*, 1992

Barron, E.M., *The Scottish War of Independence*, 2nd edition, 1934.

Burns, W., *The Scottish War of Independence*, 2 vol., 1874

Bingham, C., *The Life and Times of Edward II*, 1973.

Bingham, C., *Beyond the Highland Line: Highland History and Culture*, 1991.

Campbell, T., 'England, Scotland and the Hundred Years War', in *Europe in the Late Midddle Ages*, edited by John Hale, Roger Highfield and Beryl Smalley, 1970.

Chambers, R. (ed), *Scottish Biographical Dictionary*, 1832.

Conway-Davies, J., *The Baronial Opposition to Edward II*, 1918.

Croft-Dickinson, W., *Scotland from the Earliest Times to 1603*, 3rd edn, revised and edited by A.A.M. Duncan, 1977.

Douglas-Simpson, W., 'Campaign and Battle of Culblean' *Proceedings of the Society of Antiquarians of Scotland*, vol 64, pp 201–11, 1929–30.

Douglas-Simpson, W., *Dundarg Castle: A History of the Site and Record of the Excavations in 1950 and 1951*, 1954.

Duncan, A.A.M., 'The Community of the Realm of Scotland and Robert Bruce: a Review', *Scottish Historical Review*, vol. 46, pp 184–201, 1966.

Duncan, A.A.M., 'Honi soit qui mal y pense: David II and Edward III' *Scottish Historical Review, vol 67, pp 113–41, 1988*.

Fergusson, W., *Scotland's Relations with England: a Survey to 1707*, 1977

Select Bibliography

Ferguson, J., *William Wallace: Guardian of Scotland*, 1948.

Fisher, A., *William Wallace*, 1986.

Fisher, A., 'Wallace and Bruce: Scotland's Uneasy Heroes', *History Today*, pp 18–23, Feb. 1989.

Gibbs, V., (ed) *The Complete Peerage*, vols 1–12, 1910–1959.

Goronway Edwards, J., 'Edward I's Castle Building in Wales', *Proceedings of the British Academy*, vol. 32, pp 15–81, 1946.

Grant, A., *Independence and Nationhood: Scotland, 1306–1469*, 1984.

Hailes, Lord (David Dalrymple), *The Annals of Scotland*, vols 1, 2, 1776.

Hodgson, J.C., 'The Barony of Balliol', in *A History of Northumberland*, vol 6, 1893.

Hutchison, H.F., *Edward II: The Pliant King*, 1971.

Johnson, C., 'Negotiations for the Release of David Bruce in 1349', *English Historical Review*, vol. 36, pp 57–8, 1921.

Keen, M.H., *England in the Later Middle Ages*, 1973.

Lingard, J., *History of England*, vol. 3, 1819.

Lydon, J., 'Edward I, Ireland and the War in Scotland, 1303–4', in *England and Ireland in the Later Middle Ages*, edited by J. Lydon, 1981.

Lynch, M., *A New History of Scotland*, 1991.

March, Agnes, Countess of, *Black Agnes and the Defence of Dunbar*, 1804.

Mackie, J.D., *A History of Scotland*, 1964.

Maxwell, H., *A History of Dumfries and Galloway*, 1896.

Maxwell, H., *Robert Bruce and the Struggle for Scottish Independence*, 1901

Maxwell, H., *History of the House of Douglas*, 2 vols, 1902.

Maxwell, H., *The Making of Scotland*, 1911.

McKisack, M., *The Fourteenth Century, 1307–1399*, 1959.

McNair Scott, R., *Robert Bruce, King of Scots*, 1982.

McNeil, P. and Nicholson, R., *Historical Atlas of Scotland, c400–c1600*, 1975.

Meldrum, E., 'Bruce's Buchan Campaign', *Deeside Field*, vol 5, 1966.

Miller, E., *War in the North*, 1960.

Morris, J.E., 'The Archers at Crecy', *English Historical Review*, vol 12, pp 427–36, 1897.

Morris, J.E., *The Welsh Wars of Edward I*, reprint 1994.

Mure Mackenzie, A., *The Rise of The Stewarts*, 1935.

Neilson, G., 'The Battle of Dornock', *Transactions of the Dumfriesshire and Galloway Natural History and Antiquarian Society*, pp 154–8, 1895–6.

Nicholson, R., 'The Siege of Berwick, 1333', *Scottish Historical Review*, vol 40, pp 19–42, 1961.

Nicholson, R., *Edward III and the Scots*, 1965.

Nicholson, R., 'David II and the Historians', *The Scottish Historical Review*, vol. 45, pp 59–78, 1966.

Nicholson, R., *Scotland: the Later Middle Ages*, 1974.

Oman, C., *The Art of War in the Middle Ages*, 2nd edn, 2 vols., 1898.

Ormond, W.M., *The Reign of Edward III*, 1990

For the Lion

Otway-Ruthven, A.J., *A History of Medieval Ireland*, 1968.

Paul, J.B., (ed) *The Scots Peerage*, vols 1–9, 1904–14.

Prebble, J., *The Lion in the North*, 1971.

Prestwich, M., *The Three Edwards: War and State in England, 1272–1377*, 1980.

Prestwich, M., *Edward I*, 1988.

Prestwich, M., *War, Politics and Finance Under Edward I*, 1991.

Powicke, M., The English Commons in Scotland and the Deposition of Edward II, *Speculum*, vol. 35, pp 556–562, 1960.

Prince, A.E., 'The Strength of English Armies in the Reign of Edward III', *English Historical Review*, vol. 46, pp 353–71, 1931.

Prince, A.E., 'The Importance of the Campaign of 1327', *English Historical Review*, vol 40, pp 299–302, 1935.

Ralegh Radford, C.A., 'Balliol's Manor on Hestan Island', *Transactions of the Dumfriesshire and Galloway Natural History and Antiquarian Society*, 3rd series, vol 35, pp 33–37, 1965–7.

Ramsay, J.H., 'Edward Balliol's Scottish Expedition in 1347', *English Historical Review*, vol. 25, p 707, 1910.

Ramsay, J.H., *The Genesis of Lancaster, 1307–99*, 1913.

Reid, N., 'Crown and Community under Robert I', in *Medieval Scotland: Crown, Lordship and Community*, edited by A, Grant and K.J. Stringer, 1993.

Reid, N., 'The Kingless Kingdom; the Scottish Guardianship of 1286–1306', *Scottish Historical Review*, vol. 61, pp 105–129, 1982.

Reid, R. C., 'Edward de Balliol', *Transactions of the Dumfriesshire and Galloway Antiquarian and Natural History Society*, 3rd series, vol. 35, pp 38–63, 1956–7.

Ridpath, G., *The Border History of England and Scotland*, 1810.

Salzman, L. F., *Edward I*, 1968.

Scammel, J., 'Robert I and the North of England', *English Historical Review*, vol 73, pp 385–403, 1958.

Scott, J., *Berwick-Upon-Tweed: A History of the Town and Guild*, 1888.

Simpson, G.G., 'Why was John Balliol called Toom Tabard?', *Scottish Historical Review*, vol 47, pp 196–99, 1968

Stevenson, L., (ed) *Dictionary of National Biography*, vols 1–63, 1885–1900.

Stones, E.L.G., 'The English Mission to Edinburgh in 1328', *Scottish Historical Review*, vol 28, pp 121–32, 1949.

Stones, E.L.G., 'The Anglo Scottish Negotiations of 1327', *Scottish Historical Review*, vol 30, pp 49–54, 1951.

Stones, E.L.G., 'The Submission of Robert Bruce to Edward I in 1301–2', *Scottish Historical Review*, vol 34, pp 122–34, 1955.

Stones, E.L.G., *Edward I*, 1968.

Sumpton, J., *The Hundred Years War: Trial by Battle*, 1990

Tout, T.F., *The History of England from the Accession of Henry III to the Death of Edward III*, 1920.

Select Bibliography

Tuck, A., *Crown and Nobility: Political Conflict in Late Medieval England*, 1985.

Webster, B., 'The English Occupation of Dumfriesshire in the Fourteenth Century', *Transactions of the Dumfriesshire and Galloway Natural History and Antiquarian Society*, 3rd series, 35, pp 64–80, 1956–7.

Webster, B., 'Scotland Without a King: 1329–1341', in *Medieval Scotland: Crown, Lordship and Community*, edited by A Grant and K.J. Stringer, 1993.

Index

196

Index

Index

Index

Index

Index

207